THE PHILIPPINES
PEOPLE, POVERTY AND POLITICS

The Philippines People, Poverty and Politics

Leonard Davis
Principal Lecturer, Department of Social Administration
City Polytechnic, Hong Kong

St. Martin's Press   New York

First published in the United States of America in 1987

Printed in Hong Kong

ISBN 0–312–00412–5

Library of Congress Cataloging-in-Publication Data
Davis, Leonard.
The Philippines.
Bibliography: p.
Includes index.
1. Philippines—Politics and government.
2. Philippines—Description and travel—1975— .
3. Poor—Philippines.   I. Title.
DS686.5.D383   1987   959.9′046   86–27990
ISBN 0–312–00412–5

To the late Sister Nanette Berentsen, CJP

Contents

List of Plates

ix

Preface

It is no easy task to move into another country, another culture, and to make sense of the attitudes, values and experiences of the people that are the result of traditions, origins, history and opportunity. The experience of the individual faced with this mountain of new material – reading, discussion, observation and participation – is unique. It is also selective, relies heavily on the perceptions of others, weighs up opposing views, and emerges as a reflection of the author's own beliefs, values and aspirations. 'Truth' is impossible to establish. The Philippine presidential elections in 1986 made that quite clear. Facts – in the form of statistics, direct observation and personal accounts – remain open to question but are more difficult to refute. In this book – describing poverty, brutality and the determination of the United States – the reader is asked to focus on the implications for the individual citizen and his family, on the quality of their lives, and on the uncertainty of their very existence. The people I have spoken to, the people I have lived with, deserve better than this. Is it possible that Corazon Aquino can introduce sufficient change to prevent a real revolution?

I have received considerable support and encouragement on my travels in the Philippines and, above all, friendship. Many people crossed my path just once; others throughout a six-year period. Sometimes, the circumstances have been difficult; always the welcome has been complete.

As case illustrations, I have used – as far as possible – those associated with people I have known, people I have met, people I have admired. Some have died but are well known – Nanette Berensten, Cesar Climaco and Tullio Favali – and their memories and achievements live on; others have died almost anonymously, many children among them.

In writing this book I have drawn on a number of unmarked documents and unreferenced photocopied articles, circulated in haste to groups of church workers and others. A list of formal references is given in the Bibliography. I am, however, especially grateful to Sophie Dick of Kapatiran-Kaunlaran Foundation Inc., Manila, for permission to use in Chapter 4 some of her information on prostitution, especially in relation to Samar, Leyte and Pagsanjan; to the *Komite ng Sambayanang Pilipino* (Filipino People's

Committee), Utrecht, Holland, for allowing me to make use of their publication, *Health – The Fruit of Struggle*; and to the publishers of IBON Databank Philippines, Inc., Manila, for permission to extract material from one of their fortnightly issues of *IBON Facts and Figures*, no. 160, 15 April 1985.

All the photographs in the plate section were taken by me except plate XV(a); I do not know who that photographer was.

This book would never have been written without the help of two groups of people: the Rural Missionaries of the Philippines; and the Columban Fathers, a missionary group working in the country.

With the cooperation of colleagues at the City Polytechnic of Hong Kong I was able to arrange my work schedule in a way which allowed me to complete the book: Tina Leung of the Department of Social Administration led the team – Mandy Chiu, Agnes Choi, Carmen Chung, Kitty Kwok – who worked hard to type and re-type numerous drafts of the text. Rhodalyn Morató kindly assisted with the index. My thanks to them all.

LEONARD DAVIS
Hong Kong

List of Abbreviations

ACTS	Active Counter Terrorist Sector
AI	Amnesty International
AFP	Armed Forces of the Philippines
AMRSP	Association of Major Religious Superiors of the Philippines
ASEAN	Association of South-east Asian Nations
ASSO	Arrest, Search and Seizure Order
BALAI	Building Asian Links Against Imperialism
BCC	Basic Christian Community/Communities
BEPZ	Bataan Export Processing Zone
BMA	Bangsa Moro Army
CDC	Commonwealth Development Corporation
CIA	Central Intelligence Agency
COMELEC	Commission on Elections
CNL	Christians for Liberation
CPP	Communist Party of the Philippines
ECP	Experimental Cinema of the Philippines
Huk	*Hukbó ng Bayan Laban sa Hapón*
IB	Infantry Battalion
ICHDF	Integrated Civilian Home Defence Force
IMF	International Monetary Fund
INP	Integrated National Police
IRRI	International Rice Research Institute
4Ks or 4KKs	*Kalihokan sa mga Kabos Alang sa Kagawasan ng Kalingkawasan*
KAGUMA	*Katipunan ng mga Gurong Makabayan*
KAPATID	*Kapisanan para sa Pagpapalaya at Amnestiya ng mga Detenido sa Pilipinas*
KBL	*Kilusang Bagong Lipunan*
KKK	*Kilusang Kabuhayan sa Kaunlaran*
KM	*Kabatang Makabayan*
LIKADA	*Liga sa Kabataan sa Davao*
MASAPA	*Makabayang Samahan Pankalusugan*
MBA	Military Bases Agreement
MMC	Metro Manila Commission
MNLF	Moro National Liberation Front
NAMFREL	National Citizens' Movement

NASUTRA	National Sugar Trading Agency
NDF	National Democratic Front
NISA	National Intelligence Security Agency
NPA	New People's Army
NSL	National Service Law
PANAMIN	Presidential Assistance to Tribal Minorities
PC	Philippine Constabulary
PCO	Presidential Commitment Order
PD	Presidential Decree
PDA	Preventive Detention Order
PHILSUCOM	Philippine Sugar Company
PIME	Pontifical Institute for Foreign Missions
PMBA	Philippines Missionary Benevolent Association
PSC	Presidential Security Command
RUC	Regional Unified Command
SEALS	Sea, Air and Land Services
SOF	Special Operations Force
SPI	Summary Preliminary Investigations
SPRA	Sasa-Panakan Residents' Alliance
STOP	Stop Trafficking of Pilipinas
SVD	Society of the Divine Word
UNESCO	United Nations Educational, Scientific and Cultural Organisation
WB	World Bank

Glossary

Alpha Omega	Beginning and End
anitos	spirits
anting-anting	amulets
apparatchik	political agent (Russian)
armado	armed men
Bagong Alyansang Makabayan	New Alliance Party
Bagong Jerusalem	New Jerusalem
bakla	homosexual(s)
barangay	small community, smaller than a *barrio*
barkada	gang/group of friends
barrio	village
Batasang Pambansa	National Assembly
Bathalang Maykapál	The Creator
bodong	peace pact
bolo	large knife
bugaw	pimp(s)
Caballeros de Rizal	Friends of Rizal
camote	sweet potato
carabao	water buffalo
carinderia	eating places
cogon	type of dried grass
communides ecclesial de base	Basic Christian Communities
conquistadores	conquerors
diwatas	fairies
Doce Pares	Twelve Pairs
Dos por Dos	Two by Two
encomiendas	grants of land made by Spanish kings
ermitano	hermit
fiesta	feast day
funeraria	funeral parlour
Gamay nga Kristianong Katilingban	Basic Christian Community
ginamos	dried salted fish
hacienda	sugar plantation
haciendero	sugar plantation owner

Hukbalaháp	shortened form of *Hukbó ng Bayan Laban sa Hapón*
Hukbó ng Bayan Laban sa Hapón	People's Anti-Japanese Army
hulbot	military practice of forcefully taking detainees for interrogation or to act as guides
Ilaga	Rats
Ka	brother
kaaway	enemy
kababayan	townmate(s)
Kabataang Makabayan	Patriotic Youth
kaingin	clearing
Kalihokan sa mga Kabos Alang sa Kagawasan ng Kalingkawasan	Philippine Democratic Missionary Church
Kapisanan para sa Pagpapalaya at Amnestiya ng mga Detenido sa Pilipinas	Group for Freedom and Amnesty for Filipino Detainees
Kataastaasang Katipunan nang manga Anak nang Bayan	Highest and Most Respectable Society of the Sons of the People
Katipunan ng mga Gurong Makabayan	Federation of Patriotic Teachers
Katoliko Largo	Catholic League
Kilusang Bagong Lipunan	New Society Movement
Kilusang Kabuhayan sa Kaunlaran	Movement for a Better Life
Komite ng Sambayanang Pilipino	Filipino People's Committee
kumbento	priests' house
Kumunoy ng Kahirapan	Whirlpool of Poverty
lana	oil
libretas	little books
Liga sa Kabataan sa Davao	Davao Youth Alliance
Makabayang Samahan Pankalusugan	Patriotic Association of Health Workers
mestizos	those of mixed blood
ninang	godmother
ninong	godfather
nipa	type of grass used in making huts

Oplan Katatagan	Operation Plan Stability
pakyaw system	piecework system
pamatdan	preparing cane sticks for planting
pangat	leader
Patay-Buhi	Die and Live
PC'ing Yapak	Barefoot Philippine Constabulary
Piniling Nasud	Chosen People
rebelde	rebels
Samahan ng Demokratikong Kabataan	Association of Democratic Youth
sari-sari store	small general store
sekreta	intelligence men
sitio	housing site
Tadtad	Chop-chop
tambay	street urchin
tong	bribe (for protection)
tuba	drink obtained by tapping the top of a coconut tree
wagwag	type of rice
welgang bayan	people's strike
welgistas	strikers

When I give food to the poor, they call me a saint. When I ask why the poor have no food, they call me a communist.

Dom Helder Camara

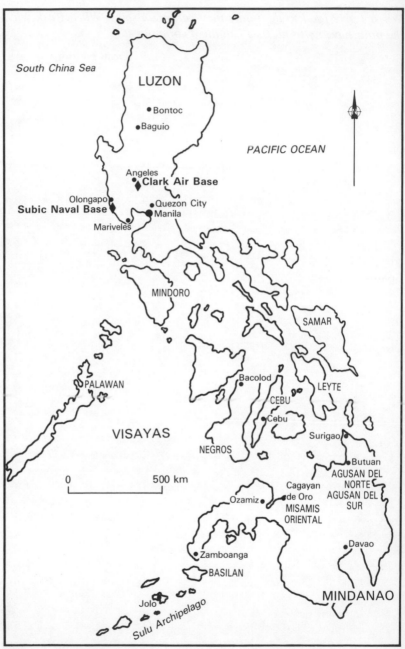

Map of the Philippines

1 Custom, Practice and Impression

The Republic of the Philippines is made up of 7107 islands with a total land area of 115 739 square miles, although the Philippines archipelago embraces some 520 700 square miles of land and sea. It stretches 1143 miles from north to south. Eleven islands occupy 96 per cent of the land area and more than half the 55 million population live on the two largest islands, Luzon and Mindanao. Less than one-tenth of the islands are inhabited, and more than 2000 have yet to be named.

Filipinos are basically of Malayo-Polynesian origin, though in the traditional trading areas there is evidence of Chinese, Indian, Arab, Spanish and North American influences. There are 111 cultural and linguistic groups and the national language is Tagalog, the tongue of the people of Southern Luzon and Mindoro. English, the second official language, is widely understood and spoken.

The tropical climate is governed by the south-west and north-east monsoons, with three main seasons: the wet or typhoon season from June to October; the cool, dry season from November to February; and the hot, dry season from March to May. In the mountains, for example, in Baguio city situated at 5000 feet and four hours' drive to the north of Manila, the weather can become quite cold.

The Philippines is a fertile country rich in natural resources, and with extensive mountain ranges. Flora and fauna abound – although some species are disappearing at an alarming rate – and the widest possible varieties of fruits and vegetables are to be found. There are, for example, 24 types of banana, a fact of considerable importance to people living on low incomes seeking an enriched diet. Fish abound although exploitation and over-fishing by the Japanese and others reduce the stocks year by year, destroying the traditional lifestyle of thousands of families. For instance, in Lake Laguna, not far from Manila, 23 species of fish could be found ten years ago. Now there are only six.

Before considering, in Chapter 2, the historical and religious background of the Philippines together with the political and economic pressures facing both government and people, a few impressions of everyday life in the islands make the book relevant

1

for today, and for understanding the changes that will occur before the end of the decade as the new administration under President Corazon Aquino either responds to the needs of the people, or moves the country towards revolution.

Basically Filipinos are a caring, hospitable people, living in large families in tight community networks. The extended family has special significance. The majority of the people are poor. Most of these are very poor and in all areas of the country – urban and rural – large groups live in conditions of abject poverty. Filipinos are a religious people, 84 per cent Roman Catholic, and the priests and sisters, Filipino and expatriate, have a very special place in the hearts and minds of the people, and a particular influence. It is this battle for the 'hearts and minds' of the people that the Marcos government and the army failed to win. For several years the preference has increasingly been for the New People's Army (NPA), the freedom fighters, whose public image has been high among the people in the small village communities. Islam has a strong following in the south, with three million Muslims living in Mindanao and the adjacent islands forming the Sulu Archipelago. This area is also the centre of the activities of the Moro National Liberation Front (MNLF). The recessionist Muslim rebels, whose leaders are based abroad, have been waging a political and armed offensive against the government since 1972.

THE IMPORTANCE OF RELIGION

Filipinos – and I am here referring to the Roman Catholic section of the community – have an ease of relationship with their God and with their Church. Large numbers attend mass regularly, and the church or chapel is the centre of community life with the formality found in the West largely unknown. In Bacolod city on the island of Negros, for example, girls on their way to work as shop assistants will often spend half an hour sitting in the cathedral, touching or kissing the feet of a statue as they make their way to or from the pews. During Holy Week, churches are crowded. On Good Friday, places of worship become a sea of people, tightly packed and intent on their devotion, reciting the 14 Stations of the Cross, often as family groups, or just standing silently in prayer. Quiapo Church and Malate Church, in the heart of Manila, have a particular attraction for the crowds. Men carrying heavy, black crosses – symbolically scourged and offered water on their journey – can be seen in the neighbouring streets as they re-enact Christ's climb to Calvary.

For Filipinos, Holy Week is the culmination of a further 12 months of struggle, near starvation and political unrest. Unlike countries in the West, where Easter Sunday is the most important feast day, Good Friday in the Philippines has greater significance. Parallels with the agony of Christ on the Cross and the people's daily suffering are vividly portrayed each year, in verse, song and drama. Such identification has enabled many to cross thresholds of fear in their determination to be liberated from oppression.

Extremism, however, has crept into the observance of this day in the Christian calendar, with hundreds of devout Filipinos engaging in rituals involving flagellation. The bishops, of course, frown on these activities but can do little to prevent them or to stop the thousands who turn out to watch; 1985 was no exception in this frenzy of religious fervour.

Three women were nailed aloft in Malolos, 30 kilometres north of Manila, while a reprieved murderer hung from a cross for 15 minutes in the courtyard of a maximum security jail south of the city. Twenty prisoners in Manila city jail beat their tattooed backs bloody with bamboo whips, and 24-year-old faith healer Rudolfo Virano, his forehead bleeding from a crown of thorns, was 'crucified' outside a church in a slum area of the capital.

At Muntinlupa Prison, south of Manila, murderer Gerardo Calubag was hammered to a cross with four-inch nails while two thieves were tied to crosses beside him. Fellow inmates then hauled him into the chapel to prise the nails from his hands and feet with a crowbar and remove the crown of barbed wire from his head. Heavily tattooed, in the style of many long-term prisoners, Calubag pledged to repeat his action in 1986, saying: 'I want to atone for the sins of the dregs of society. I want to set an example for others to lead a new life.'

In Malolos, also, 26-year-old Luciana Reyes, a pig dealer and faith healer, was nailed to a cross for the ninth time 'to cleanse the sins of the people'. She was joined by Ingracia Jumaquio, 17 years old, and Efinania Enriquez, a mother of nine children who had a nail driven through her left hand. The other arm was bound by rope.

A BASIC CHRISTIAN COMMUNITY

On the other hand, however, the concept of community, the place of religion and the full meaning of the *Gamay nga Kristianong Katilingban*, Basic Christian Community (BCC) – in the best tradition – are illustrated by personal experience, a 24-hour event which remains among the most memorable of my life. The event happened in Mantoganoy in 1983 in the municipality of San Luis in the diocese of Butuan in Mindanao. This unique occasion was the wedding of 15 couples and the baptism of a large group of people, including some of those about to be married.

Mantoganoy is a remote and beautiful area, an uphill climb nearly four kilometres from the Agusan River. The heat was intense: nearly 40°C. To reach the rough pathway leading to the community – a dried-up creek bounded on both sides by dense undergrowth – the journey downstream from San Luis took about 45 minutes, passing massive logs waiting to be towed to Butuan city.

The crocodiles have long since gone from the area, but other wildlife is still abundant. A man was killing a pig beside the river, people were washing their clothes and their bodies, children swam naked and water buffaloes soaked themselves at the water's edge. The river is both friend and enemy: each year there are deaths by drowning. Flooding is to be expected.

The village of Mantoganoy, the name originally given to the creek by the tribal Filipinos, appeared quite suddenly at the end of the climb, nestling in a hollow in a ridge of hills with about 35 wooden houses forming the BCC that was being developed. Because of the military situation in the area at that time, there was undoubtedly tension and fear, but the community spirit was something to be experienced. There was a committee for everything: for water, for visitors and for the half-finished church. The affairs of the community were indeed managed collectively.

The president of the community was Hubert 'Itjong' Pelegro, a farmer and a widower with three children, who worked hard on behalf of the community as well as caring for his children single-handed. His 12-year-old son was recognised as brave and loyal. Many church workers had for a long while been suspected and accused by the military of being subversives. On one occasion, in the face of the interrogation of his father by the military, the boy worked out how best to use his catapult should his father be manhandled.

Some people hoped that Itjong would marry the schoolteacher. She was on the point of leaving the area – there were only two grades in the small school – and it was thought a good idea to encourage her to stay and to help Itjong with his family at the same time. Filipinos are great matchmakers. This time they were unsuccessful. The teacher did not want to marry a widower.

We were first welcomed by our hosts – Alfredo 'Bido' Lontoco and Dioscota 'Doling', his wife – with very sweet locally grown coffee, and bananas. On the night before the mass, five visitors to Mantoganoy joined Bido, his wife and two children, the children's grandmother and Doling's brother in their three-roomed house, all sleeping on mats on the floor.

The priest, Father Alfons Meyers, was supported by Sister Mary Teresa Cordero, Sister Annie and Dorrie, a student on exposure in the parish. Others in the community invited the group to drink from instantly cut coconuts, to scrape the cream from inside and to drink *tuba*, obtained by tapping the top of the coconut palm. *Tuba* is sweet when fresh, becoming bitter if left standing.

Most of the settlers in Mantoganoy came originally from the smaller island of Bohol some ten years previously; others a few years later. These were pioneers, first building their houses and subsequently earning a meagre livelihood as farmers growing coffee and corn. Coconuts and bananas were plentiful. Pigs, chickens, dogs and cats were everywhere. Monkeys were kept as pets.

A number of tribal Filipinos, Manobos, had been integrated into the community. In the even more remote mountain areas, the Manobos are among the most disadvantaged groups, often existing only on *camote* (sweet potato) and bananas, and with whole communities affected by malaria and schistosomiasis. The latter – as described in Chapter 3 – is a water-borne disease attacking the intestines and the brain of both children and adults, most frequently resulting in a painful death.

Real marriages did take place on 10 May: one young couple who had walked four kilometres before the early morning mass were married in the traditional way – the bride in white – because they had not been living together; and 14 couples because they had never had a Catholic wedding, having previously only been married 'on the mat'. Most had never before been able to afford a wedding; others had in the past been unsatisfactorily united in ceremonies within small sects under whose influence they had temporarily fallen.

The idea of marriage – for one couple after 23 years, for others after five years – came from the people themselves. As preparation all had joined in seminars: first for men and women separately, and later in a mixed group. Ricardo was 63 years of age and living with his second wife. He could not remember the number of grandchildren he had, nor the number who had died, but was keen to participate in the ceremony.

First there was baptism for six adults from among the couples – in the open air under a tree. Then all moved into the church, or rather, as many as could be accommodated. Young children of the couples grouped themselves around the altar table beside the priest. The young couple received special attention on their own, the bridegroom being a tribal Filipino, and then followed the ceremony involving the other 28 people. Three other couples were also natives.

The traditions of the people were evident in the informal approach to the mass. A cord was draped around the young couple as a symbol of binding together, and a very long cord covered with white tape encircled all the other men and women; this was the idea of those being married. Token gifts were presented to the wives by their husbands: money, corn and coffee beans.

The men promised to provide for their wives and not to spend money on drinking or on friends. In return, the women promised to spend the money wisely. In rural Filipino culture men and women have defined roles: the man works and the woman keeps the money. (In fact, she also works extremely hard.) The couples exchanged rings. Most had had to borrow them from friends.

The ceremony over, it was time for lunch. Everybody in the community had contributed to the meal, fish, chicken and corn in large cooking pots appearing swiftly on tables set up outside the church. Children and adults ate contentedly, and with obvious appetite. The marriage ceremonies and the visit of the priest were rare occasions for celebration.

There was, however, a sad note. A young man, suffering from severe anaemia, sat silently in the shade. Determined to attend the mass, he remained weak and very sick. There was no medical attention at hand, and without money he had little hope of treatment.

There is, however, an even sadder footnote to this personal experience. Militarization increased during the following year, and every family was forced to post a list of all people living in each house so that the soldiers could check that no members of the NPA were being sheltered. Anxiety and fear later gave way to terror and the villagers abandoned their community, seeking 'security' in a nearby town. Their hope – in 1985 – was eventually to return to Mantoganoy.

THE REALITY OF LIFE

There are huge slums throughout the country where – most often without electricity, with inadequate sanitation and lacking safe drinking water – families eke out a living. In the cities this is by buying and selling. In the rural communities subsistence farming means unending toil and brings few rewards, but usually prevents starvation. Peasant farmers and their families still make up 70 per cent of the population. Apart from some Muslims and the tribal groups living in the mountains, the sugar workers on the island of Negros are among the most deprived, trapped in the feudalism of the past.

Government health care in the Philippines is minimal, few can afford the cost of private treatment, infant mortality is high and there are noticeable numbers of people with untreated physical conditions: goitres, deformities and hare-lips. Many Filipinos are blind, and all have to compete in the fight for survival. Cigarette consumption appears extraordinarily high, indicating a future increase in the incidence of cancer and bronchial-type illnesses, the latter already one of the most common causes of death.

NATURAL DISASTERS

Depending on the season and the part of the country, people have to live with natural disasters: drought, floods, typhoons and volcanic eruptions. In 1983 there was prolonged drought in many areas. The effects were especially severe in Mindanao where the ecological balance – already disrupted by the systematic exploitation of the land by foreign investors – was further upset. From the air the whole terrain appeared brown. On the ground the earth was hard, dry and cracked. Mighty rivers were reduced to streams or dried up completely, a whole rice crop was lost and coffee bushes withered on the hillsides. People, already accustomed to carrying water some distance, had even longer treks to make. This scene, from my experience along the Agusan River particularly, was in contrast to the flooding of the same river in 1981. Overnight, houses were washed away. Whole communities disappeared while other villagers returned later to the mud of the river banks to rebuild their dwellings and start anew. In a country where life must be designed around natural sources of water – for washing clothes, bathing and animal needs, especially the needs of water buffaloes – there is no other place to set up home despite the regular periods of danger. Forty-three people died on 21 January 1985 when a giant waterspout made a river overflow in the central part of the country. The floods affected eight villages in Tanjay, Negros Oriental province.

Another disaster year was 1984. Typhoon Ike which struck many provinces in early September with winds up to 115 m.p.h. left more than 1200 people dead. No accurate count could be made of the number of homeless people. In Surigao city, Mindanao, the death toll was at least 700. The city ran out of coffins and embalming fluid and had to bury its dead in mass graves in order to prevent an epidemic. Typhoon Ike struck the southern Philippines and carved a path of destruction through the Visayas region before dying out over the South China Sea. It was the second major storm to hit the country within a week and one of the worst since Typhoon Lois struck Mindanao in 1964, killing more than 700 people.

Within a few days of Typhoon Ike in 1984, Mount Mayon, an 8125 feet volcano 250 miles south-east of Manila, erupted necessitating the evacuation of more than 30 000 residents from 45 villages. One Legaspi resident described the sight on the night the south-west lip of the near-perfect cone-shaped crater ripped away as 'a spectacular fireworks display of red hot lava, rocks and incandescent smoke'. Legaspi is about seven miles from Mount Mayon which as recently as 1978 spewed lava, smoke and ash for eight weeks, making 27 000 people leave the area. Several deaths were reported in the 1984 explosion and the disruption to farming and the destruction of vegetation were ruinous for those forced to flee from the mountain as the hot ash rolled towards them. Mount Mayon's most devastating eruption was in 1814 when 1200 people were killed. Those living in the vicinity of one of the dozen or more active volcanoes in the Philippines are always ready: to run for their lives. Among the most unpredictable are Mount Bulusan which is about 50 miles south of Mount Mayon and had moderate eruptions in 1978 and 1983; Mount Taal, on an island in a lake some 50 miles south of Manila; Mount Hibok-Hibok on Camiguin island in the Mindanao Sea; and Mount Kanla-on on the island of Negros, 325 miles south-east of Manila. Kanla-on, with its purple hues, is a source of legend and symbolism. An old story in the Philippines describes how one day a stranger came to the slopes of volcanic Kanla-on in search of gold. He set up markers here and there around the mountain. Out of the crater of the volcano rushed a huge black horse with a rider as tall as a giant, and the horse ate all the markers. Then the rider, the king of the mountain himself, said: 'I will not barter this mountain with you, even if you give me two countries like yours in exchange.' Because of the continuing exploitation of the sugar workers the mountain has come to represent an aspect of life today: the social volcano ready to erupt at any time.

FIRE

Fire is perhaps a more common hazard for the millions of people who live in small wooden houses in closely-packed communities. It is not unusual for 300 or more houses to be destroyed by fire in one night, often with loss of life. On 28 February 1985, fire raged through two blocks of a populous slum district in Tondo, Manila, leaving at least 2000 families homeless. Flames lit up the night sky in the area blacked out by a power cut after the fire broke out. Squatter families hauled away their belongings – even pots and plates filled with their uneaten supper. Salvaged possessions were dumped at safe distances and guarded by family members, while other residents braved the fire to retrieve more things from their houses. The blaze was the largest in Manila since 1978.

The speed with which people rebuild their communities, using any materials that come to hand, is a further mark of Filipino determination. At times of slum clearance when there has been resistance to resettlement – 'relocation' as it is called – fires have been started deliberately by the local government, anticipating the work of the bulldozers and speeding up the process.

Families may be decimated, crops destroyed, animals lost, livelihoods taken away as a result of fire, flood, tempest or drought, but communities always reform. They have to. There is nowhere else to go.

This spirit of determination is well illustrated by the events which followed a fire in a squatter area in Davao city on 7 October 1983.[1] On that date a despondent resident of the community, known locally as Immaculada Conception/Kilometre 12, committed suicide.

It is generally believed that he was overwhelmed by the bills resulting from his recent stay in hospital and the prospect of further medical expenses. After what most thought was a 'welcome home' lunch with his family, he went to the sleeping quarters of the small house while others cleared up after the meal. Here he doused himself with petrol and struck a match. The fire and explosion killed him and destroyed the homes of 57 neighbouring families. An infant died when the metal ring on the top of a propane gas container flew more than 30 yards through the air and embedded itself in the baby's skull.

Without delay the residents put into practice the lessons learned from three years of community organising. Their first priority was to re-occupy the land for fear that government officials would cordon it off and prevent them from entering. This had happened in several other areas of the city after a fire. On the very morning after the tragedy the members of the community met and, following a lengthy discussion, decided that:

(a) the area would be divided into 30 equal plots each 23 feet by 25 feet;

(b) one lot would be given to each of the 24 house-owners who were burned out;

(c) one lot would be given to each of the six largest 'renters';

(d) two or three absentee house-owners with property elsewhere in the city would be disqualified (when a small delegation went to each of the absentee owners to talk about the community's decision the absentees agreed to the plan once it was explained to them);

(e) the other 27 'renters' families who were burned out would be assigned temporary quarters, with the option of returning later when their former lodging places had been rebuilt;

(f) all sources of water – wells and pumps – would become 'community property' for common use;

(g) one lane would be set aside for a straight access from the national highway to the shores for the benefit of the fishermen and the convenience of the jeeps going to pick up their daily catch;

(h) smaller walkways would be designated between the houses with a view to making proper arrangements for drainage and sanitation;

(i) a committee would be set up for the distribution of food and medicines, with other groups assigned to the tasks of salvaging burnt materials and trying to obtain essential items for reconstruction.

With the help of the Sasa-Panakan Residents' Alliance (SPRA) each of the 30 lot owners was given a loan of 1000 pesos to be used for the immediate reconstruction of their houses. SPRA is a grouping of small communities in the area – from Kilometre 11 to Kilometre 13 – centred around their respective chapels and which had been organised to face up to the reality of possible demolition and relocation.

So poor are the people in the community that the scale of repayment of the interest-free loan was figured not only in monthly instalments but also in 15-day intervals and even at a daily rate since many of the people involved receive a daily wage in their predominantly service-type work.

The people worked feverishly to rebuild their community, despite the warnings of government officials who visited the site and told them that the Southern Philippines Development Authority had 'plans for this area' – presumably for industrial and manufacturing plants. The threat of being turned out added to their efforts. The area was literally barricaded against a demolition team with the people prepared to fight physically in order to preserve their community. At the entrance to the group of houses – at the top of the line heading from the main road – is now printed 'Igsama Village' and 'People's Property'. Flowers, shrubs and climbing plants begin to grow again. By June 1984 the village had an air of normality, although there was yet work to be done. One or two families had still not been able to rebuild reasonable dwellings and continued to live – without windows and adequate ventilation – behind large sheets of tinplate nailed to a wooden framework; and the community hall which also served as the chapel had yet to be rebuilt. In most parts of the village, however, the reminders were still visible: charred posts sticking out of the ground and partially burnt planks of wood reused in the new buildings.

In matters of building I had already come across this spirit of determination in the face of difficulty and the use of small short-term interest free loans: in Butuan city and Cagayan de Oro city. One family in Butuan city described to me how, 20 years previously, they were part of a whole community that fled from the mountains and found themselves urban dwellers with nowhere to live. As a group they decided on a plot of land to occupy – at that time of year a swamp under three or four feet of water – and by working throughout the night waist-deep in water were able to put up sufficient poles and planks to provide the framework for their future houses on stilts. The people used the hours of darkness to avoid conflict with government officials. By daylight they were sufficiently established to resist attempts to move them and have been there ever since. For a visitor unused to the dwellings, they feel somewhat strange: the buildings sway all the time, caused by the movements of the inhabitants.

At Piaping Puti in Cagayan de Oro, a mysterious fire destroyed a huge section of the *barrio*. A privileged occasion for me was the time I spent with the treasurer of the Piaping Puti United Neighbours' Organisation and two workers from the *barrio*. The loyalty of the workers, their efficiency, the spirit in the *barrio*, the determination to fight and the understanding shown towards those falling behind in their repayments to the loan fund set up after the fire, left me with a feeling of great humility.

Very many everyday activities bring tragedy to the unprotected population. For example, on 23 September 1984 at least 18 people digging for gold nuggets were buried alive, and several others injured, when four tunnels collapsed in Davao del Norte province. Only three bodies were recovered. The miners were using crowbars to break a giant boulder inside a tunnel in Monkayo town when it caved in, causing the other tunnels to collapse. During the previous year thousands of people flocked to Monkayo to prospect for gold in an abandoned mine site on Mount Diwata. In two previous cave-ins in the area, about 40 miners were killed. Mining claimed more lives in 1985. On 12 January, seven people in search of gold were buried when a tunnel collapsed in Davao del Norte province, about 570 miles south of Manila. Mount Diwata was the scene of a further tragedy on 20 October 1985, when a landslide crashed on to a gold mine and a shanty town, killing more than 100 people. Mount Diwata is about 100 kilometres from Davao city.

DAILY LIVING

There are high levels of pollution in some cities. People in the streets and on public transport cover their mouths with paper tissues or handkerchiefs in an attempt to filter out the worst of the fumes.

In country areas, especially, people have to contend with mosquitoes (and the associated outbreaks of malaria), flies, ants, flying ants, rats, huge cockroaches and in some districts snakes. Domestic animals – pigs, chickens and dogs – form a natural part of most households, wandering about in search of food, young children playing with them and beside them, often in a sea of mud.

Dogs are eaten and black dogs are favoured in some regions. Seaweed, large frogs (called American frogs), dried fish and squid are often part of the diet, and rice is served at every meal. Some families can afford to eat rice only once a day, others scarcely at all. When the supply of rice dries up, and in communities where it is too expensive or difficult to grow, corn is used as a substitute. It is natural for many Filipinos to eat with their fingers. Banana catsup, tomato catsup and soy sauce are used generously. Coca-cola is a universal drink, found in even the most remote areas, and sometimes kept chilled in home-made 'ice-boxes'. Filipinos like their coffee sweet, and there seems to be an increase in the amount of alcohol being purchased. By Western standards, however, the people are not heavy drinkers. The nutritional value of the diet of most Filipinos is generally inadequate and malnutrition, especially among children, is widespread.

Filipinos love to talk, to attend rallies and to participate in *fiestas*. Theirs is an outdoor life: the climate encourages this and the tiny houses of the majority of the people provide little more than bedspace for the large numbers who live in each dwelling. Privacy is rarely sought. Even given the temporary opportunity to sleep in separate rooms, three Filipinos would most frequently choose to share the same room, and probably the same bed. Most people sleep on mats on the floor. Sometimes a wooden block serves as a pillow. Even those using beds raised from the ground rarely sleep on Western style mattresses, but merely on a thin mat.

Houses are usually built on stilts to stand several feet above the ground. This is for many reasons. The animals find shelter beneath; it provides a storage space; in many areas flooding is to be expected in the rainy season; and, in dry weather – when the soil is baked hard – it is essential to keep the surroundings of the house very carefully swept in order to reduce the number of crawling insects that can enter the house, and even to discourage snakes and scorpions.

The streets are social centres, and people stand around for hours, chatting earnestly or idly. Unemployment is high. In some towns and cities, street vendors are so numerous that they can hardly find space to display their wares – bananas, mangoes, cigarettes, newspapers, peanuts or sweets – and in the afternoon sun they often fall asleep over their merchandise. The midday heat is, of course, sometimes scarcely bearable for Filipinos and foreigners alike. Strength is easily sapped, and a siesta fits easily into the pattern of daily life. Some newsvendors not only sell newspapers and comics but allow comics to be read *in situ* on tiny benches for, say, 50 sentimos each. Many adults can be seen reading comics and picture stories despite official literacy figures of nearly 80 per cent.

In the towns and cities, dodging between the vehicles, adults and children sell cigarettes, usually just one at a time, to passing taxi drivers, motorists or jeepney passengers held up in traffic jams or stopped briefly at traffic lights. The air heavy with smoke from exhausts, congested and noisy, Manila – and most other large towns and cities to a lesser degree – displays the unacceptable face of tourism: exploitation. In any society where the rich live beside the poor, one group exploits the other. With a severely declining tourist trade, and many hotels in Manila finding it difficult to remain open, exploitation has an even sharper edge. An unaccompanied male is frequently accosted, especially at night: a girl of 14 or 15 years with a tiny baby in her arms emerges from the shadows of Roxas Boulevard asking for money; a man offers 'a very beautiful girl, only 17 years' (his daughter, he says) for 200 pesos; and a 16-year-old youth – with an opening 'Do you like boys?' – tries to convince a stranger that he does. Some infants learn to say 'One peso, sir' as their first words.

Education is generally of a low standard, especially in the rural areas. Teachers are poorly paid, premises are dilapidated, and equipment is scarce. I spoke to the principal of a large elementary school in Mindanao. He had ten classes of 40 pupils in his school, with a 50 per cent drop-out rate by 12 years of age. In April 1985 only four children actually took up a high school place in the neighbouring town. He had no school nurse; many children fell asleep at their desks through lack of food; and, at best, he had ten books for every 40 pupils.

The loudest cry throughout the country is for 'dollars', more than ever apparent since the 1986 election. Everywhere Westerners are approached: outside post offices, in tourist spots or simply walking along the road. There is a thriving exchange on the black market, accelerated by the devaluation of the peso in 1983 and 1984.

Provided the youth who endeavours to exchange money does not run off with the dollars before the transaction is completed, or it is possible to outwit him as he tries to make folded-back peso notes count twice, payment at five or six pesos above the official exchange rate is made.

ROAD TRAVEL

Many aspects of Filipino life leave strong impressions in the mind of a Westerner: buildings are dilapidated; paint is rarely used, the sun burning it within a few weeks; most towns and cities appear crowded and chaotic; and the majority of vehicles are extremely old. Taxi drivers in Manila are notorious for their attempts to 'fix' their meters or to 'forget' to use them. Many are keen, too, to drive their male customers to the homes of prostitutes. They often ask: 'Would you like a nice girl for the night, sir?' If the reply is in the negative, some will make a further suggestion: 'Or perhaps a little boy?' Their attitude to the abuse of taxi regulations is perhaps understandable. Many drivers hire their vehicles for 24 hours for 300 pesos, or more, and have to recoup that sum before starting to pay for the petrol they are using or to make a profit. They are in competition with the jeepneys found in every town and city, with the cheapest ride less than two pesos. There are more than 40 000 jeepneys in Manila, originally made from jeeps left by United States military forces after the Second World War. Motorised tricycles are an additional form of transport in most towns and cities. On the island of Jolo, in the Sulu Archipelago, as elsewhere, tricycle drivers still ply for hire with nothing but muscle power at their disposal, a punishing occupation in the heat of the sun. In the small town of Lamitan, on the nearby island of Basilan, the horse and buggy is a common form of public transport.

With exceptions, road travel between towns and cities is slow, exhausting and sometimes unpredictable. Concrete and tarmac roads are often in poor condition – crumbling and not repaired – pitted by the consequences of drought, flooding and pounding by heavy lorries, with many secondary roads merely dirt tracks. In the rainy season they become lakes of mud. In the remote areas – for example, on the roads leading from Buenavista near Butuan city to the villages nestling in the foothills – vehicles have to be driven through numerous streams and waterways, the journey becoming impossible when rivers are in spate. On the mountain tracks, landslides are common and drivers can be faced with huge boulders or a mound of earth on turning a corner. The drop into the gorge below may be 2000 feet or more.

Filipinos are expert drivers, they travel fast, drive on their brakes and horns, and disregard most conventions of the road at will. Vehicles are customarily overloaded. Long-distance buses are usually filled with all manner of objects and packages: sacks of rice, supplies for village stores, bundles of firewood or bamboo canes, cases of beer and soft drinks, chickens and crates of vegetables, fruit and fish. Passengers sit on the roof when necessary. They may shout at the driver to encourage him to slow down. On occasions he may 'race' a fellow driver, perhaps one from a rival company. The fare collector doubles as mechanic, and it is possible to have several punctures during a single journey on the stony roads. Brakes may fail. Delays are thus inevitable. Sometimes, because of the speed of vehicles, elderly people are scared to go further, and get off to await a slower vehicle. 'I don't want to die yet,' an elderly woman said, 'I want to eat more rice.' People stop the bus to urinate at the side of the road, women discreetly endeavouring to find the protection of trees, shrubs or tall grass while the men rarely move more than a few yards from the bus.

Military checkpoints have been frequent, but many were usually unmanned: to be used principally in 'zoning' operations, that is, when there were house-to-house searches by the military or paramilitary groups looking for 'subversives'. The extent to which the military and the NPA will be as active under the new administration has yet to be tested and experienced. Vehicles must, however, slow down at all times at checkpoints. Logs and boulders are placed halfway across the road in the path of oncoming traffic and the obstacles have to be driven around. These checkpoints are especially dangerous at night on the unlit roads.

During recent years soldiers have often ridden on buses. Other passengers then appeared particularly quiet. At no time – even following the election – does it pay to have a conversation of any depth when travelling on public transport. Intelligence men and informers – sometimes feeding into a tight but widespread Central Intelligence Agency (CIA) network – are everywhere. Many of these men, underpaid and not very skilled at their job, are recognised without difficulty. Sometimes their revolvers give them away, bulging beneath their jackets. Others, however, and often those least suspected, are shrewd and determined. Ordinary people, suspected of being sympathetic to the 'subversives', have for years been summarily shot every day. Life has been – and still is – cheap in the Philippines. Many people, even those only mildly sympathetic to the 'movement', have always preferred not to be seen in the company of strangers even, for instance, while shopping in the market. A tradition has grown up that it is better not to be noticed.

In the rural areas people ride even more frequently on the roofs and mudguards of jeepneys, the 14-seater vehicles carrying as many as 30 additional passengers. Most jeepneys do not start on their journeys until they have a full complement. On the other hand, an inter-city bus may well depart half an hour before its scheduled time if all the seats are taken. Increasingly there are improved services by new, air-conditioned buses between the major cities when road conditions permit. For the mass of the people, however, the cost of a ticket would be out of all proportion to their daily income so they continue to ride on the slower, overcrowded, uncomfortable vehicles.

Buses and jeepneys are usually decorated with all sorts of signs and religious mottoes and biblical texts. 'God Bless our Trip' is a common sign. Even greater comfort can perhaps be drawn from reading the notice painted above the head of a driver of a 50-seater bus as he snakes it along the winding road between Cagayan de Oro city and Butuan city: 'God is my Co-driver'.

Filipinos are ingenious. They will fix, mend and weld all types of gadgets and machinery, blending intuition, imagination and natural materials to make things 'work', especially motor vehicles. I had one dramatic experience of both the expert driving of Filipinos and their ingenuity. Travelling downhill in a jeepney full of passengers, quite fast, near the town of Lamitan on the island of Basilan, the brakes failed. The vehicle 'jumped' over a huge boulder being used by the military to slow traffic at a checkpoint, but with expert steering by the driver he was able to keep control of the vehicle. Eventually it came to a halt some considerable distance along the road. The temptation to leap out after the impact was strong but fellow passengers shouted, 'No', and each restrained the other. Some had had similar experiences before. The jeepney was swiftly made 'roadworthy' again by the mere twisting of a wire and the reconnection of a spring near the driver's foot pedal. Later it was discovered that one of the main bars making up the chassis had been snapped off on hitting the boulder. That, too, was quickly drilled and bolted by a local garage.

In rural areas the beast of burden for everyday local journeys to the ricefields, for ploughing, for hauling carts – and ultimately a source of food – is an animal previously referred to: the water buffalo, or *Carabao*. There are nearly three million of them, each weighing about 300 kilos. Not too long ago they were much heavier, nearly 350 kilos each, but farmers often castrate the finest bulls, thus over time weakening the strain.

GENUS CARABAO

Sturdy of patience, in the sun industrious.
Bearing with us what burdens bow our breed
Undaunted. Hail the common as illustrious.
Even as the sweat that gives the soil our seed.

Nick Jaojuin

AIR TRAVEL

Internal travel by air is generally reliable and safe. Yet there is an austerity associated with the need to cut costs. Even on the longest flights, for instance, from Zamboanga to Manila, no refreshments are served, although small glasses of water are available. Many airport lounges, basically equipped and once of reasonable standard, have fallen into decay. Toilets always seem dirty or blocked. The planes themselves now appear old. Particularly on landing I have heard noises from the structure of the aircraft experienced nowhere else in the world. There are many tales of the skill of pilots in handling planes in frightening incidents. Without considerable capital investment it is difficult to see where the funds for new aircraft will come from. And the fleet must be replaced soon.

RAIL TRAVEL

Apart from 'sugar trains' on the island of Negros, rail links are limited, one running from north to south on the island of Panay, and the other – much longer – from the north-west of Luzon to the south-east tip. That is all. Mindanao, with a population of ten million, has no rail network of any sort.

The Philippines' first modern mass transit system was introduced in May 1985. Nicknamed Metrorail, the 14-kilometre light railway bisects Metropolitan Manila, cutting travelling time from Caloocan city in the north to Pasay city in the south from two hours to 30 minutes. The beige and orange rail cars, whose trim design seems prudish compared to the flamboyant rainbow colours and chrome trimmings of the jeepneys, glide over Manila's dreary scenery, offering views of the brownish rust of tenement roofs and grimy factory smokestacks. The elevated railway, built over five years at a cost of US$183 million with Belgian government loans has been the subject of criticism. The Meralco Transit Organisation, which operates the railway, does not give out figures on operating costs, but observers say that it will take years before the investment is recovered and the loans paid back. It is estimated that the government will need nearly US$30 million a year for six years before it can raise enough revenue to cover its operations and start to pay its debts.

SEA TRAVEL

Sea travel is altogether another question. For many people inter-island journeys are an everyday occurrence, because of the number of islands in the archipelago. On some of the larger islands, coastal towns are only easily accessible by sea. Huge sections of the population depend on fishing for their livelihood and their daily supply of protein. They spend hours and hours at sea in their tiny craft. Whirlpools can be a navigational hazard. On the ferry crossing from Zamboanga city to Basilan island, for example, the surface of the sea is pitted with treacherous moving circles of various sizes ready to suck small craft beneath the surface. Safe for larger ferries to traverse, they are dangerous for ten-foot vessels.

I spoke to one girl whose home is on a small island not far from Surigao city. In 1985 two members of her family were among 13 passengers in a 'pump boat' that failed to arrive after what was supposed to have been a two-hour journey. No trace was ever found of the vessel or its passengers.

Most goods, of course, have to be carried across the water and only a very small percentage of people travel by plane. Many coastal and inter-island ferries sail through the night. Row upon row of stretcher beds are placed on the decks. A special eye has to be kept on the weather. Gales, typhoons and tidal waves are an ever-present threat. Many ships are old and rusty, totally unseaworthy by Western standards. Tragedies do occur, far more frequently than are ever considered worth reporting in the Western press.

The loss of the MV *Dona Cassandra* is a sad example. On 21 November 1983, the ship sank off Camiguin island in the Surigao Strait with the loss of more than 200 lives. The *Dona Cassandra*, like so many other passenger vessels in the Philippines, was purchased from Japan in a run-down condition. The shipping company Carlos A. Gothong Lines, however, still considered it good enough to operate in Philippine waters.

The ship was unable to leave Nasipit, Agusan del Norte, during the evening of 20 November, because of Typhoon Warling but, despite continuing bad weather, lifted anchor at 6.15 the following morning. As usual, many people were issued with tickets on board and were not, therefore, listed on the manifest. As often happens, the *Dona Cassandra* was overcrowded. The shipping company aims to maximise profits; members of the crew will allow their friends aboard 'as a favour'.

Survivors of the subsequent disaster reported disturbing details about the deplorable circumstances surrounding the loss of the *Dona Cassandra*. According to witnesses, the ship made water through a hole in the side shortly after departure, and the cargo began to shift. The passengers panicked but received no instructions about the use of lifejackets. In fact, when people made efforts to put them on, members of the crew told them to take them off. When the ship finally turned on its side many had to jump into the churning shark-infested waters without lifejackets. Several were cut to pieces by the propellers of the ship, their blood turning the sea red. Others were trapped inside the hull, and went down with the ship. By several accounts, the captain and the crew were among the first to jump overboard. Only those who could get hold of a liferaft had a chance of survival, and many who were thus fortunate floated around aimlessly for more than 30 hours before they reached neighbouring islands. Only then, two days after the shipwreck, did the shipping company start rescue operations. Less than 200 passengers were rescued.

Among the victims were several nuns, a priest and a number of lay church workers, including Sister Nanette Berentsen. Sister Nanette and her companions were on their way to Cebu city, some to attend a retreat, others a meeting concerning their apostolate in the service of the poor. In the face of death they continued to serve: several were seen distributing lifejackets and attending to the children just before the ship turned on its side and went down. The remains of Sister Nanette and her companions were never found.

They are buried in the deep of the Surigao waters. Sister Nanette – for whom I had a great deal of affection and admiration – was a member of the Rural Missionaries of the Philippines, an inter-congregational group committed to direct service of the poor and oppressed throughout the Philippines. The shipwreck was sketchily reported, and attempts to have a full investigation proved fruitless.

SISTER NANETTE BERENTSEN

Whether you are young or old, renewal of religious life does not begin with discussions about 'justice and peace', but starts where we take a stand regarding the real conflicts of our society. Justice and peace are not ideals but the fruit of a practical choice. If I look back from where I stand now, then I must say that I lost all my ideals from before. The only ground under my feet is the stern reality of the life of the people who are struggling for survival. Recently I renewed my religious vows at the funeral of Diego, a young pastoral worker who was killed. I stood near his dead body and crying with anger and sorrow because of such brutal killing I prayed: 'My God, I want to go with these suffering people all the way in their struggle, *whatever may happen to me.*' (From a speech delivered before the Association of Major Religious Superiors in Holland at the celebration of their Silver Jubilee on 29 October 1982)

Sister Nanette Berentsen was born on 30 March 1935 at Eibergen, Holland. Entered the Congregation of the Sisters of Julie Postel in Boxmeer on 21 November 1955. Arrived in the Philippines in August 1973 and worked as a Rural Missionary in the provinces of Negros Occidental, Lanao and Agusan.

However, in a 14-page document dated 18 April 1985 the Philippine Coast Guard decided that the cause of the accident was a *force majeure*, or an act beyond human control. The ruling was made by Commodore Brilliante C. Ochoco of the Coast Guard. Citing the testimony of a surviving passenger, Samuel Padilla, who said that two 10-foot to 20-foot waves hit the ship which caused it to capsize, the Coast Guard ruled that the vessel's skipper, Captain Vitor Bayotas, the chief mate, Dulceto Abato, and the third mate, Lilan Cabahug, could not be faulted in the absence of any showing of negligence or incompetence on their part.

The management of the shipping line said the Coast Guard's decision was a vindication because the tragedy was 'an act of God and beyond the will and control of human power'. The statement continued: 'We harbour no resentment against those who unkindly and unfairly accused us, including those who for whatever reasons, sought to take advantage of the tragedy to sully our reputation.'

The year 1985 again ended in tragedy. More than 100 passengers drowned in shark-infested seas on 18 December, when the 152-ton MV *Asuncion Cinco* capsized in the South China Sea some 160 kilometres south of Manila. The ship was on a voyage from Puerto Princesa, on Palawan island to the capital. 'The whole incident happened so fast,' said a survivor, Flor Ybanez. 'There were big waves and the wind was howling. Water was coming into the ship. Then the engines went out and we were informed by the crew that the ship would sink.' Another survivor, Belinda Lopez, said she lost her husband and only child in the disaster. She was in the water for one day and one night before she was rescued.

'We were not warned by the captain,' said Romeo Tayo. 'He was even saying that nothing was wrong. Then he jumped overboard on a liferaft. It was the last time we saw him.' The captain, identified as Edilberto Fermalan, was among the missing. A surviving crewman, Alberto Fabregas, denied that the captain was among the first to leave the ship.

Estimates of the number of people aboard the MV *Asuncion Cinco* varied from 85, made by the ship's owner, to between 200 and 300 by surviving crewmen and passengers. Once again, overloading and a run-down ship may have contributed to the disaster.

Tragedies of this order do not occur every year, but there are regular smaller disasters in which 10, 20, 30 or more people perish with scarcely a mention, even in the national newspapers. 'Near disasters' are even more frequent. On 6 January 1985 more than 500 passengers and crew escaped when an inter-island ferry, the 495-tonne MV *Asia Singapore*, capsized and sank in Butuan city harbour. A 68-year-old woman collapsed and died as the 512 passengers jostled their way to the gangway to the shore before the vessel went down. As in similar incidents, there was a great deal of panic. From personal experience I can confirm the level of individual fear. Arriving at Cagayan de Oro city from Ozamiz city, after a calm voyage, passengers made early moves to one side of the ferry – with their masses of accompanying baggage and cargo – before the ship reached the pier. It started to keel over dangerously. Few people would, or could, move. Only as the most agile leapt from the edge of the vessel, the side just a few feet above the waterline, did the ship gradually settle evenly in the water.

FILIPINO CHARACTERISTICS

Filipinos are an attractive people with varying shades of brown skin. They favour a light brown complexion, young girls especially, and take every precaution against the darkening of their skin, also admiring the longer noses of white people in preference to their own rather flat ones. They take great care of their naturally beautiful teeth. The appeal to consumers is often through Western eyes: dummies modelling clothes in stores, and many photographs in advertisements, have pale skins and Western features. Expensive American-style fast foods cater for an expanding market and, in Manila, the shopping precincts at Makati attract tourists and rich Filipinos alike. Filipino children around Makati, the sons and daughters of some of the country's wealthiest people, are noticeably plump, in contrast to the mass of children struggling for survival elsewhere.

With more than 40 per cent of the population in the Philippines under 15 years of age children are everywhere very much in evidence. Many families have eight or nine children and involvement in the process of childbirth is a natural part of growing up. Filipinos enjoy their children, there is a great deal of physical contact – children are held, carried and caressed – but they also need them: to contribute to the economy of the family, to work in the fields, and to provide for parents in their old age.

Apart from sexual abuse, an equally sinister side of exploitation is found in some parts of the country: drugs. There were, for instance, problems in both the high schools and elementary schools on the island of Jolo. It was necessary to keep the gates of the elementary schools closed as much as possible to keep out 'pushers'. They were paying small children – perhaps only eight years old – two pesos to take a puff of a cigarette. Later, of course, the money flowed in the other direction. The police decided that all pupils would need to register and obtain a card from them prior to school enrolment the following year. This was, it was said, so that children and young people on drugs, or known to the narcotics group. could be identified. The charge for each card was three pesos. When questions were asked about what would happen to the 60 000 pesos collected from the 20 000 pupils, the police became uneasy. Many were believed to be involved, in some way or other, in part of the protection racket. Corruption is widespread throughout the Philippines. Currently, on the island of Jolo, there is an 8.30 p.m.

curfew on those who are 15 years old or younger, a regulation easier to enforce than the parallel one attempted in Manila. In Manila itself drugs are easier to obtain than ever before. They are openly offered to tourists outside the large hotels on the Roxas Boulevard.

Filipinos rarely go anywhere alone. 'Who is your companion?' they enquire. They also frequently ask 'Where have you come from?' and 'Where are you going?' but are content with answers like 'From over there' or 'Around the corner'. 'Where are you going?' is similar to the rhetorical question in the West 'How are you?' Neither a reply nor a direct answer is expected. Not only do Filipinos enjoy physical contact with children but adults often hold the hand or arm of a same-sex companion as they talk or walk along the road.

In the rural areas, particularly, patterns of courtship and marriage remain traditional. Generally there is very little sex before marriage. Girls prize their virginity, making – for some – the tragedy of entry into prostitution that much greater. At *fiestas* girls will still sit demurely on benches arrayed around the square set aside for dancing and be paid for by the man – 5, 10 or more pesos – for each dance. The money goes to charity or towards the general expenses of the *fiesta*.

After the wedding arrangements have been made and the approval of parents has been obtained, a girl may sometimes become pregnant. It is very important for a couple to be able to have children. There is, too, a ritual when, at the stage of the two families meeting to make the wedding arrangements and the bride-to-be is already pregnant, the bridegroom's parents will apologise that their son has made the girl pregnant. The bride's family will then make an expression of anger, but will as quickly forget the exchange and look forward to the wedding. If the married couple are still childless a year after marriage then relatives and people in the community will ask why. Girls in remote areas most often marry at 17 or 18 years, some at 15 or 16. The partner is usually two years older. Both in rural and urban areas there is, however, an increase in births to girls who are not married, despite the strong traditions. Some are rejected by their families, and life then becomes difficult with prostitution too often the answer. If the mother and the newly born remain part of the family then the infant is easily cared for and the girl has the prospect of marriage – to someone who was not the father of her first baby.

Every person from the West appears rich to Filipinos, even to have afforded the air fare for the journey. Many try to forge strong links with people in the West, perhaps hoping that one day they will be fortunate enough to have the money to break out of their poverty, and then to emigrate. A number of Filipinos are successful in this: a high percentage of nurses and doctors trained in the Philippines seek employment abroad.

Advertisements appear regularly in the newspapers, for example, in *Bulletin Today*, inviting Filipinos to marry Westerners. The advertisements are most frequently placed by Germans. Australian men, too, seek Asian wives through the national newspapers. For a Westerner marrying a Filipino, however, there are sometimes problems. They could be expected to offer some support to several members of the girl's family. This is the tradition. If the oldest member of a family is fortunate enough to finish high school or even college and then obtains a regular income from a steady job – or is successful in some other way – then he or she, as a matter of course, will give financial help for the education of a brother or sister, most often the next in line.

The Labour Minister in 1985, Blas Ople, urged regulation of the entry of Filipino women to Australia and other countries. He said that there should be concerted action by the government and the Church to prevent abuses or maltreatment of Filipinos who go to Australia as pre-arranged brides. The 2000 brides who find their way to Australia every year are inadequately briefed, and many become depressed, lonely, unwanted and desperately unhappy.

Education is seen by many as the one avenue of escape from poverty. Occasionally high school girls will look for a 'sugar daddy' in order to ensure the payment of their fees and maintenance during the last few years of their education, thus finding an alternative to dropping out. In some rural areas – where poverty is extreme – families will sometimes 'give away' their adolescent daughters to work for families who are slightly better off and will guarantee to feed them in return for working in the rice fields and about the house. For a considerable proportion of the population the first question of the morning is, 'Have we sufficient food or can we obtain enough money to feed the family today?' Sometimes the answer is 'No' to both parts of the question.

For a Westerner the cost of living is cheap, even though inflation was running at 51 per cent in 1984. It fell slightly in 1985, but was guaranteed to rise sharply after the election. Food, accommodation, travel and laundry make few demands on a tourist's pocket. Prices, the quality of the food and standards of cleanliness do, however, vary a great deal: from the roadside eating houses to the marginally better cafés, to the air-conditioned establishments, to the restaurants in the first-class hotels in Manila. There are what, at first, appear strange practices. For example, on ordering a cup of coffee in many cafés the customer will be presented with a cup of hot water, a jar of coffee, a bowl of sugar and a tin of evaporated milk – with two small holes punched in the top of the tin. Fresh milk is almost unknown. Most purchases are made by buying small quantities of foods in local stores, known as *sari-sari* stores. Most of these have a narrow range of merchandise and sometimes very old stock, reflecting – at the level of the mass of the people – the economic reality of the country.

The tourist industry has virtually collapsed. The huge hotels in Manila along the Roxas Boulevard are only one-third full. Many offer 30 per cent discount for several months of the year. In Davao and Zamboanga, once hoping to attract visitors, there seems little point in keeping the hotels open, except for the custom of a few rich local people. Tourists became frightened to visit many of the major cities. Guns could be seen everywhere. Especially during 1984 and 1985, people died on the streets every day.

A series of hotel fires in Manila and Baguio city, in 1984 and 1985, set the Philippine tourist industry back even further. The first was on 16 October 1984 when a four-hour fire hit the Pacific Hotel on Palanca Street in central Quiapo, injuring three people. Four days later, the Grand Hotel on the same street was set alight, with six people hurt. The first of the most disastrous fires occurred three days later at the historic Pines Hotel in Baguio city when 23 people perished, including eight Americans whose charred bodies were airlifted to the US base at Clark Field and identified there. Four of the dead were US veterans who had just come from attending ceremonies in the southern island of Leyte, where the landing by General Douglas MacArthur on 24 October 1944 had been lavishly commemorated in the presence of Marcos and his wife, the American and Japanese ambassadors, and hundreds of Filipino, American and Japanese veterans of the battle. Without doubt, the Pines Hotel fire was a case of arson.

On 1 November another fire struck the Ambassador Hotel in Manila – frequented by Japanese and overseas Chinese – killing ten people; 30 were injured. A subsequent fire on 9 November killed seven people at the nearby Las Palmas hotel in Ermita, in the heart of Manila's so-called tourist belt.

Twenty-seven foreign tourists and hotel staff died in the blaze which completely gutted the five-star Regent of Manila Hotel on Roxas Boulevard on 13 February 1985. The fire, which started just after midnight, burned for three days. Firefighters interviewed at the scene said that they had been hampered by low water pressure in the hydrants and mains, and reported that there had been an explosion in the hotel's power centre, a failure in the hotel's sprinkler system, a breakdown in the telephone switchboard – making it impossible to arouse sleeping guests – and a collapse of the alarm system after a few minutes of ringing. Survivors among the hotel staff said that almost simultaneous explosions rocked the second and ninth floors of the building. Again, the fire was classified as arson.

Hotels in Manila have, at least, become more fire conscious as a result of the tragedies. Rope ladders are found in many guest rooms. Some hotel fires – and most fires in squatter areas – are started deliberately, in the first instance for the insurance money, and in the second for the land. Only weeks after a fire in a squatter area the foundations will be laid for a supermarket. The plans had already been drawn up.

UNREST AND CONFRONTATION

Militarization was at its height in the two years prior to the presidential election. Tanks and armoured cars were found in city centres, for example, in Butuan city and Davao city. Many soldiers are now dressed in smarter uniforms; and their equipment is more sophisticated. The troops have become accustomed to moving around in much larger groups, having suffered heavy casualties in the few years before the presidential elections of 1986. Not all the soldiers have come to terms with a change of president. Some are corrupt, selling arms and ammunition whenever the opportunity arises. The lower ranks of the military are themselves mostly from poor families – schooled in the brutality of a dictatorship which survived by setting Filipinos against Filipinos in circumstances and conflicts which were mutually destructive.

The assassination of the opposition leader Benigno Aquino at Manila International Airport on 21 August 1983 was a turning point for Filipinos. Each anniversary of his death has been a cause for the expression of further discontent. The election to the *Batasang*

Pambansa (National Assembly) on 14 May 1984 – or, rather, the boycott of the elections – and the dissatisfactions with the poll count, provided additional impetus for those in opposition. The presidential election on 7 February 1986 carried this one stage further, deposing Marcos.

For some time the mood of the opposition had been strengthening, both politically and within the guerrilla movements. The long, winding columns of workers supporting the boycott movement during the run-up to the 1984 elections could never have been envisaged a year previously. The people took to the streets, their red and orange banners large and colourful. Their cries were from the heart. They had moved beyond fear. As one elderly lady said: 'We are marching for the sake of our grandchildren. It is too late for us.' One march I joined was in Negros. Tens of thousands of sugar workers, many among the poorest of the poor, walked defiantly in heavy rain. Their commitment to change in the political structure was powerfully demonstrated. Their efforts finally bore fruit in 1986, at least in the removal of the president.

On the guerrilla front there is still uncertainty about the continuation of the struggle. Against levels of militarization never previously experienced, members of the NPA had an even greater need in 1984 and 1985 for medical and financial help, and for the support of the people in the communities. It is this link between the men and women in the hills and the people in the *barrios* that the army has always wanted to break. Right up to the election the military continued to harass, torture and kill, using – as will be shown later – fanatical groups to massacre whole families. Soldiers and fanatics gave themselves a licence to kill. They were rarely subjected to the process of law as a result of their murderous activities. Church workers became more vulnerable than at any other time. Any association with social action or human rights groups made a worker a target for arrest or 'salvaging', the latter a term used for people who disappear and are subsequently found buried in shallow graves, beheaded or floating in a river. Significantly, on the day following her election as president, Aquino set up a committee to consider the release of political prisoners. As many as 500 were known to be in captivity at the beginning of 1986. Most were freed by the new president within a few weeks of taking office, including four leading members of the Communist Party.

As a short-stay visitor – tourist or businessman – the harsh side of life of the majority of Filipinos is rarely seen: the slum dwellers have been deliberately kept behind the billboards; the propaganda machinery of the Marcos government, though blatant and crude, was extensive; and there were simply no lengths to which the administration, under Marcos, would not go in order to present an image of stability and development to the outside world, an image bolstered by the United States of America – despite its frequent embarrassment – for as long as the need remained to use Marcos in order to preserve and further her own economic and defence interests. This need has not disappeared. The Americans will respond with a sigh of relief to any administration presenting a more humane 'face' and representing the will of the people. They have that today, but perhaps the question of sovereignty and the final expulsion of Americans from their soil is even more important than the exercise of the democratic process.

Tracing the centuries-old struggle of the Filipino people against oppression offers some explanation for their determination to get rid of the two objects of their hatred: the Marcos dictatorship and the distorted US–Philippines relationship. 'Forward, brothers, you have nothing to lose but your chains' was a rallying call which gave heart to many groups of flagging marchers on their way to the demonstrations which became common throughout the country despite military intimidation and brutality. As levels of consciousness were raised and the people were better organised, group by group, they became outspoken and fearless. To have witnessed that progress since the beginning of the decade – especially during 1984 and 1985 – and to have been able to share a little of that experience is to be given some licence to recount part of the very human story of a continuing human struggle.

Notes

1. This account is based on discussions with the residents of the community; with Father Jack Walsh; and on an article which he wrote under the title 'Industrialization and social change: the role of the pastoral ministry', *Tambara*, no. 1 (1984) Jesuit University, Davao City.

2 The Country in Context

Philippine pre-history began as long ago as 500 000 years in a period characterized by the enlargement of the ice caps in the polar region and of the glaciers in the mountainous areas. As they grew larger the sea level went down and, as a consequence, a vast area of land was exposed, forming land bridges to the mainland of Asia. Primitive man arrived in the Philippines during this period.

The proof that man inhabited the Philippines 22 000 years ago came with the discovery, in 1962, of a skull of a man in Tabon, Palawan island. It is believed that the land bridge connecting Palawan with Borneo existed for at least 40 000 years. From the bones dug up in the area of the limestone promontory at Lipuun Point, Palawan, it has been concluded that, at this time, Tabon man hunted wild pig, deer and smaller animal species such as birds and bats. Not a single seashell has been discovered, strengthening the theory that 55 000 to 8500 years ago, the sea level was 100 metres lower than its present level and the coastline was 30 to 35 kilometres away.

About 7000 years ago the ice of the world melted, resulting in climatic and environmental changes and, notably, the raising of the sea levels. The land bridges were submerged and ensured that subsequent immigrant groups arrived by water. They first came from South-east Asia and belonged to the Early Stone Age. Culturally more advanced than previous immigrants, they built grass-roofed houses and practised dry agriculture, producing yams and millet. Physically, they were tall, slender and light-skinned, with sharp thin faces. Classified by anthropologists as 'Indonesian A' they were in contrast to the earlier pigmy people who tramped over the land bridges.

Between 800 and 500 BC another wave of immigrants settled in the Philippines. They brought with them copper and bronze, and probably knowledge about rice culture, building the first rice terraces in the Philippines. These remain remarkable even today, the art of terracing closely resembling methods of building used in southern China. The extent of the terraces and the labour that went into their construction indicate that they must have taken several hundred years to build. They consist of a series of flat platforms of earth with sloping sides fortified with stone walls made waterproof by a mixture of gravel, sand and clay. In Banaue, for example, the terraces cover more than 3000 acres.

The last of the prehistoric migrations occurred between 300 and 200 BC. The immigrants were Malays who arrived in Luzon, Mindanao and the Visayas by way of the Celebes Sea. Their knowledge of agriculture, weaving and the manufacture of iron implements and ornaments must have come from India whence it spread to old Malaysia and reached the Philippines by way of Celebes and Borneo. They introduced the water buffalo and cultivated fruit trees and spices.

THE COMING OF ISLAM

Much later, about 1500 years ago, other immigrants from Indo-China (Vietnam) and South China sailed to Luzon. They also practised dry agriculture, and wore clothing made from beaten bark ornamented with printed designs. Dark, stocky and with thick lips and large noses, they were classified as 'Indonesian B'. Other waves of Malay immigrants came in the 13th, 14th and 15th centuries, laying the foundations of Islam in Mindanao and Sulu.

The spread of Islam followed its introduction to Old Malaysia – the area now covering Indonesia, Borneo and the Malay Peninsula – where Arab traders and missionaries settled to propagate their religious beliefs. Islam was introduced to Old Malaysia by the Arabian scholar, Mudum, who arrived in Sulu about 1380. Ten years later, Raja Baginda, a petty ruler from Menangkabaw, Sumatra, arrived in Sulu and continued Mudum's work with the natives. Baginda was followed by Abu Bakr who subsequently married Baginda's daughter Paramisuli and, on the death of his father-in-law, proclaimed himself sultan. When the Spaniards arrived in the 16th century a great part of Mindanao and Sulu and a part of Luzon around Manila Bay and Lake Bonbon (Taal) were in the hands of the Muslims.

In the fight against the Portuguese for trade rights in the east, Charles and Isabella of Spain sent explorer Ferdinand Magellan with orders to find new trading posts. He dropped anchor off the island of Samar in 1521, giving Spain the western route she so badly needed for trade in East Indian spices. Magellan was killed in Mactan but his ship, *Victoria*, returned to Spain with the news. The Spanish *conquistadores* returned in 1565 and, in a tradition which

32   *The Philippines: People, Poverty and Politics*

was already sweeping through South America, their leader, Miguel Lopez de Legazpi defeated Raja Sulayman, ruler of Manila, and declared the settlement the capital of the new Spanish colony.

SPANISH CONQUEST

The Spanish conquest and colonization of the Philippines may be said to have been a continuous process which ended with the proclamation of Philippine independence in 1898. While it is true that the Spanish *conquistadores* and the friars succeeded in planting the Spanish flag in the archipelago and in consolidating their power, large areas of the country – for example, Mindanao, Sulu, the interior of large islands, and the Mountain Province in Luzon – remained outside Spanish law and religion. Nevertheless, the Spanish rulers continued, throughout their occupation of the islands, to hold on to their beliefs that they would one day convert the inhabitants of these regions to Christianity.

By virtue of 'discovery' and actual occupation, Spain made the Philippines a Crown colony and, therefore, the Spanish king's property. This status continued until 1821 when Mexico, through which the Philippines had been ruled, declared its independence from Spain. As a crown colony the Philippines came under the control of the Council of the Indies which established a highly centralised government revolving around the governor and captain-general. He was given broad executive, legislative and judicial powers, issuing decrees with the force of law.

There were no political subdivisions during the first 70 or so years of Spanish colonization but, thereafter, as practised in Spain and later in Mexico, the country was divided into *encomiendas* and, later, into provinces. During this period the Spanish friars took the opportunity to divide the country into religious spheres of influence. This was done to avoid misunderstandings among the Augustinians who came in 1565, the Franciscans (1577), the Jesuits (1581), the Dominicans (1581) and the Recollects (1606). In the space of about 50 years, the missionary efforts of the friars succeeded in converting a great majority of the people along the coasts and plains to Catholicism. One explanation put forward for this phenomenon – by Teodoro Agoncillo – is that it was due not so much to the efforts of the missionaries as to the Filipinos' precolonial religious beliefs which, from their point of view, differed little from Catholic doctrine. While the alien religious belief taught the existence of one supreme God, *Dios*, the precolonial Filipinos had their *Bathalang Maykapál*; and while the colonizers had their innumerable saints, the Filipinos had their own *diwatas* and *anitos*. Thus, the beliefs of the friars were seen as a reflection of their own. That the two faiths were not fundamentally so much at variance is shown by the fact that, even today, Filipino Catholicism is a unique mixture of precolonial and Catholic religious practices.

In general, the Spanish colonial system has always been noted for its comparatively human characteristics and, certainly, the early Catholic fathers were inspired by missionary zeal – unlike their Anglo-Saxon counterparts who were engaged, almost exclusively, in economic exploitation. Yet, there were ills, and one of the most severe indictments against the Spanish colonial rule was the predominance of the friars in all sectors of life. Thus the parish priest – usually the only Spaniard in the town – became, amongst other things, the inspector of schools (beginning with the last decade of the 19th century); the chairman of the board of statistics, whose duty was to take the census of the parish; the guarantor of the character of every man and woman in his parish; the examiner of students intending to attend the grade school; the censor of plays and all published works to be staged or to be read by his parishioners; a member of the provincial board and, most often, its auditor; and the person charged with certifying the physical condition of any man in the parish who might be impressed into the service of the colonial army. This growth of power in the hands of the priestly class led to corruption; and corruption led, first, to opulence and demoralisation; secondly, in some instances, to conflict between the clerical and civil authorities; and, lastly, to native sufferings and discontent.

The beginning of the 18th century saw the first cracks in the image of Spanish invincibility. Dutch and British fleets frequently harassed Spanish ships and, by 1762, the British were occupying Manila and its suburbs. Through the efforts of Simon de Anda y Salazar who organised a resistance army – first in Bulacan and later Pampanga – the rest of the colony was kept loyal to Spain, but it was not until April 1764 – nearly a year after the Seven Years' War – that the British handed the city back to Spain.

NEW IDEALISM

When the Suez Canal was opened in 1869, the distance from Spain to the Philippines was shorter, leading to the exodus of liberal Spaniards to the islands and to the introduction of new ideas and reading materials from Europe. Conservative Spanish power was now considered fallible, and sporadic Filipino uprisings surfaced throughout the country. The battle for independence strengthened, worrying the Spanish administrators, who began to torture and kill hundreds of rebels. The unjust execution of three prominent Filipino priests in 1872, while not purely political – but part of the secularisation controversy between the Spanish friars and the Filipino priests over the control of the curacies in the Philippines – became the rallying point of the propaganda movement which the Filipino intelligentsia sustained for more than two decades. Young Filipino students abroad were in the forefront of the movement, some of whom are today's revered heroes.

JOSÉ RIZAL

The most notable of these was José Rizal, a writer, and leader of the non-violent *La Liga Filipina*. He had a gift for irony that exasperated the friars whom he exposed to ridicule with his subtle attacks. Leaving the Philippines at 21 years of age, he studied medicine, literature and languages in Spain, five years later writing his socio-historical novel, *Noli Me Tangere* (*Touch Me Not*) which exposed the ills of Philippine society. The immediate popularity that the novel enjoyed, both in Spain and in the colony, forced the friars to condemn it and the colonial government to ban it – thus adding to its popularity. On his return to the Philippines Rizal's movements were carefully watched by the government. On the advice of his relatives and of the Spanish Governor-General he left for the second time.

During Rizal's absence his father and relatives were driven from the farm they were leasing from the Dominicans and, when they refused to vacate their lands, their houses were burned down and the occupants driven away at bayonet point. Rizal became more bitter than ever and, in 1891, finished his second novel, *El Filibusterisimo* (*The Subversive*). In this politically more mature work, Rizal projects his revolutionary tendencies and predicts a revolution in which all the suffering and oppressed elements of society would be involved. With the publication of further papers, the Spanish friars and officials could no longer tolerate him and, in 1892, when he returned to the Philippines for the second time, he was arrested and sent to Mindanao. He was later on his way to Cuba, via Spain, to serve as a volunteer physician when the colonial authorities ordered his arrest. Rizal was immediately returned to the Philippines and taken to Fort Santiago in Manila where he awaited trial. He was charged with rebellion and organising illicit associations, found guilty and sentenced to death. At seven o'clock in the morning of 30 December 1896, the prisoner was taken to what is now Rizal Park to be executed. With his elbows tied behind him he was shot by a squad of eight native soldiers. Calmly, he turned halfway round and fell on his side with his face turned up to the sky. His execution heralded him as the martyr of the revolution, making independence from Spain more inevitable. Filipinos had become bonded with a sense of nationality.

KATIPUNAN

Meanwhile, on the very day that a decree was being signed banishing Rizal to Mindanao – 7 July 1892 – a small group of men met in Manila and formed an association known as the *Katipunan* (*Kataastaasang Katipunan nang manga Anak nang Bayan* – Highest and most Respectable Society of the Sons of the People). The leader of the group was Andres Bonifacio, a poor man from Tondo fiercely dedicated to the cause of the people. He had a single objective: to unite Filipinos into one nation and achieve independence through revolution.

Initially, the *Katipunan* was a secret society but, by August 1896, when the first battle of the revolution took place – where there now stands the Pinaglaban Monument in San Juan, Metro Manila – the membership was 100 000. This battle was led by Bonifacio and, thereafter, the revolution spread. The Spanish Governor-General declared a state of war in Manila, the Spaniards mounted a reign of terror that merely inflamed the revolution. The early victories of the revolutionaries brought to the fore a Cavite leader, Emilio Aguinaldo, who challenged Bonifacio for the leadership and won. On 10 May 1897, Bonifacio and his brother Procopio were executed on Mount Buntig, Macapagal, Cavite. Bonifacio is today honoured as the greatest hero of the Philippines.

AMERICAN DOMINATION

Two years after Rizal's death the Spanish–American War broke out over Cuba. The United States eyed the Philippines as a stronghold in the Pacific. Admiral George Dewey sailed his fleet into Manila Bay and invited Aguinaldo to join him in the fight for liberation. Thousands of Filipino rebels flocked to enlist in the revolutionary army and the Spanish army gave up Manila with scarcely a shot being fired. Aguinaldo had every expectation that the Americans would recognise Philippine independence, but they had no intention of doing so. Following meetings between American and Spanish representatives, the Treaty of Paris was signed in December 1898. Under this, the cession of the Philippines was agreed in return for compensation amounting to US$20 million. Within a short while a large number of American troops landed in Manila.

Aguinaldo's hopes were dashed. He had inaugurated the Philippine Republic on 23 January 1899, amidst the people's jubilation, and took his oath of office as president of the revolutionary government. But it was not to be. An angry Aguinaldo led a new resistance movement and the Filipino–American War that followed lasted three years. When the fighting was all over – Aguinaldo was captured on 3 March 1901 in Panalan, Isabela – the Philippines was once more in alien hands, this time American.

Aguinaldo swore allegiance to American sovereignty on 1 April. Two weeks later he explained his action, saying:

the effects of the war which only recently have come to my knowledge have fully convinced me that complete termination of hostilities and the establishment of lasting peace are not only desirable but absolutely essential to the welfare of the Philippines . . . The time has come when we find ourselves faced by an irresistible force which while impeding our progress, nevertheless enlightens our minds, pointing out to us another path, the cause of peace which the majority of our country have gladly embraced, confident that, under the protection of the American people, we would obtain all the liberties promised to us and which we are even now beginning to enjoy.

IDEALISM: AN ANALYSIS

In respect of these years of revolutionary fervour, Agoncillo makes a number of points relevant to today in his book, *A Short History of the Philippines*. Rizal and his followers, and Bonifacio and his followers, approached 'revolution' from different standpoints. In many ways, the *Katipunan* succeeded where the middle class and their reformists had failed. The intelligentsia, Agoncillo suggests, were not truly radicals but conservatives, for they insisted, even in the face of Spanish obstinacy, on winning freedom through reforms. From the start these were perhaps impossible to realise given that the enemies of native aspirations for a better life, namely, the friars, were as securely entrenched in Spain as they were in the colony. There was something naive in the reformist group which made them fail to see the restlessness of the masses, for they were at heart too cautious to recognise the ability of the masses to respond to adequate appeals. Since the reformists wrote in the language not of the masses, but of their masters, they failed to establish rapport with the people of the country without whom no movement for freedom could succeed. It is to the credit of Bonifacio that, though almost illiterate, he was able to penetrate the hearts and minds of the masses and so he made them feel the need for unity and action. Bonifacio employed the medium of expression that he correctly thought would establish an intimate dialogue with the people. There was, therefore, mutual understanding on two levels: on the level of language used, that is, Tagalog; and on the level of ideas which were as simple as they were fiery: Spanish brutality, greed and injustice on one hand, and the need to remove the Spaniards through force, on the other. In summary, the reformists were conservative, although the friars considered them radical, for they demanded in essence no more than making their country a province of Spain, with the natives enjoying the rights and discharging the duties of Spanish citizens. The revolutionaries, however, stood for armed confrontation with the colonizing power, believing that only force could produce freedom and independence.

An analysis of the events leading to the execution of Bonifacio is also important, offering a glaring example of the abnormal psychology that dominated the revolution at a crucial stage. As Agoncillo points out, the *Katipunan* that accumulated its power out of the violent impulses of the masses had become unwieldly. The people, thinking and acting under the pressure of the moment became suspicious. All shades of action and thinking contrary to their own became a potential danger to their existence. And so Bonifacio, who had himself become distrustful and suspicious of his colleagues in the movement, became the victim of their suspicion and distrust. Thus, it was the very revolutionary movement which he had created that misunderstood him. He and his colleagues in Cavite had no conflict of ideals. There was only a clash of interests. Not unnaturally, he sought to continue as the head of the group that he had initiated; his erstwhile followers saw fit to change allegiance at a significant moment. Agoncillo concludes that as an organiser, Bonifacio was indeed great, but, as a military leader he was inferior to Aguinaldo.

TOWARDS INDEPENDENCE

For 48 years – from 13 August 1898 to 4 July 1946 – Filipinos waited for independence. The Americans were slow to grant it, believing that Filipinos had neither culture nor civilisation and were not, therefore, able to manage their own affairs. And, while the majority of Filipinos accepted American sovereignty, the colonial administration remained nervous about those who opposed it. The Sedition Law was passed in 1901. Section 8 provided that 'Every person who shall utter words or speeches, write, publish or circulate, scurrilous libels against the government of the United States or the insular government of the Philippine Island . . .' shall be punished by a fine of not more than US$2000 or by imprisonment not exceeding two years or both. Heavy penalties were imposed upon those found guilty of sedition, rebellion, or of advocating independence. The provisions of the law were so broad that any Filipino who uttered the word 'independence' or who conversed with anybody suspected by the government of putting forward ideas repugnant to the colonial government, could be fined or imprisoned – or shot. Thus, the development of political consciousness and individual freedom, two of the cornerstones America presented to the world as its contribution to the Filipino people were, for the most part, superficial. Unlike the Spanish, the Americans left a legacy of economic exploitation. They remained in control of the Philippine economy; American goods entered the Philippines free of duty, making the country its principal market in the Orient; and all roads, bridges and other construction work were made with American equipment, materials and vehicles.

Certainly, the Americans established the framework of a universal education system, leading to new levels of literacy among the people, but they more destructively conditioned the minds of Filipinos to a subtle acceptance of the American way of life as 'good', and as a model to be followed. In effect, the Americans tried to rewrite Filipino recent history, neglecting indigenous languages and literature, and leaving unmentioned Filipino heroes who – especially if they had fought the Americans – were given the status of bandits.

Throughout this period of American domination, however, there were those who held on to their ideal of independence. The feelings of the nationalists found expression in 'subversive' newspapers, notably *El Nuevo Día* (*New Day*) and *El Renacimiento* (*The Renaissance*), editorials and articles bringing to the attention of the people the defects of the American colonial regime, and attacking the institutions and practices that had been imposed upon the country. Agoncillo draws attention to an editorial, referring to an American official, Dean C. Worcester, which appeared on 30 October 1908. Entitled *Aves de Rapiña* (*Birds of Prey*) it read:

The eagle, symbolizing liberty and strength, has found the most admirers. And men, collectively and singly, have ever desired to copy and imitate this most rapacious of birds in order to triumph in the plundering of his fellowmen. But there is a man who, besides being an eagle, also has the characteristics of the vulture, the owl, and the vampire. He ascends the mountains of Benguet ostensibly to classify and measure Igorot skulls, to study and civilize the Igorots, but, at the same time, he also espies during his flight, with the keen eye of the bird of prey, where the large deposits of gold are, the real prey concealed in the lonely mountains and then he appropriates these all to himself afterward, thanks to the legal facilities he can make and unmake at will, always, however, redounding to his benefit.

MANUEL QUEZON

The main step toward independence was made on 15 November 1935 when Manuel Quezon was sworn in as President of the Philippine Commonwealth. While the Commonwealth was conceived as an experiment in self-government, and an interim period of adjustment in the political, social and economic spheres, it was again largely motivated by American self-interest and not altruism. The arguments, and confusions, were principally concerned with exports, immigration and the labour market. American labour unions resented the increasing immigration of Filipino workers – and, thus, cheap labour – to the West Coast; and there was a decreasing demand for American manufactured goods. Farm groups believed that it was Philippine products, especially sugar and coconut oil, which were responsible for the plight of American farmers. By giving independence to the Philippines it was felt that the USA could impose sufficiently high tarrifs on Philippine products to put them out of competition.

THE SECOND WORLD WAR

There is no doubt that, but for the Second World War, the movement towards full independence would have been accelerated. However, following the attack on Pearl Harbour by the Japanese on 7 December 1941, and the paralysis of American's military strength in the Pacific, Manila was declared an open city. Japanese troops landed unopposed in Luzon and converged on Manila, entering the city on 2 January 1942. The day after the occupation, the end of American sovereignty over the Philippines and the imposition of martial law in all occupied areas were announced by the Japanese Military Commander.

Filipino and American soldiers held out for three months, fighting their last days in Bataan, where they were finally defeated. The island of Corregidor, a fortress in Manila Bay, fell shortly afterwards and the Japanese started their impossible task of 'emancipating Filipinos from the domination of the United States of America'. Meanwhile, many Filipinos took to the hills and became the most formidable resistance force in Asia. Stranded American forces were channelled through well-organised escape routes, or stayed to fight alongside the resistance groups. The guerrilla activities were varied. Where arms and ammunition were available, the enemy was engaged in skirmishes, and military installations were sabotaged. The extent and nature of guerrilla warfare is reflected in a typical letter of instructions circulated among the fighters:

1. Groups will be organised to exceed 30 riflemen.
2. Groups will keep on moving from place to place to do battle with the enemy and to avoid difficulty of supply.
3. Hit and run tactics will be employed. Not more than six rounds will be expended during ambuscades and raids, except in successful encounters where annihilation of the enemy is possible.
4. Never fight in places selected by the enemy. Fight only on the ground you have prepared for him.
5. Pigs, chickens, cows, rice, corn and other supplies will be moved

to places that are unlikely to fall into enemy hands. Supplies in danger of actually falling into enemy hands will be destroyed.

6. All roads leading into and out of places occupied by the enemy will be barricaded with barbed wire entanglements. Solid barricades will be placed in depth behind the barbed wire.
7. The enemy must be placed under constant surveillance. Spies, scouts and patrols must be sent out daily. Every day snipers must fire at least once or twice on the enemy.
8. Patrols going out will be provided with grenades, sufficient ammunition, *bolos*, and molotov cocktails.
9. Stop all sorts of lawlessness, looting and banditry.
10. Fifth columnists and spies of the enemy will be dealt with severely. Any Filipino who works directly or indirectly for the enemy becomes our enemy and will be dealt with accordingly.
11. Kill at least one Japanese daily.

In addition to fighting, collaborators had to be ferreted out, there was counter-propaganda to be disseminated, and information about the enemy to be sent to MacArthur – who had 'escaped' to Australia to prepare for the later recapture of the islands. By this time, Quezon – and his earlier rival for the presidency, Sergio Osmeña – had been moved to America, via Australia, where the refugee Commonwealth had been established.

Life under the Japanese was difficult and dangerous. As in their other occupied territories, they were ruthless, arrogant and cruel; their reign of terror in the Philippines lasted for a little more than three years. The smell of death, decay and starvation was everywhere. The Japanese perpetrated the worst evils. Fort Santiago came to be associated with intimidation and torture. Nobody could be sure that he would not be arrested for, say, not bowing properly to a Japanese sentry at the street corner, or for not carrying his residence certificate. There were, of course, those Filipino opportunists who took advantage of the moment to engage in business with both the Japanese and their fellow citizens, which reinforced the wholesale graft and corruption permeating government, business and military circles – in effect, most of Filipino society – to the present day.

MACARTHUR RETURNS

The early months of 1944 proved to be the beginning of the fall of

Japan's original idea of a Greater East Asia Co-prosperity Sphere. Inching his way north from the New Guinea, MacArthur had taken the Central and South-west Pacific, putting his forces within striking distance of the Philippines. In June, the Battle of the Philippines Sea was fought, resulting in one of Japan's costliest defeats, virtually isolating the enemy in the Philippines. MacArthur had earlier planned the invasion to begin in Mindanao, thinking that he could establish an air base for the air umbrella of the forces that would strike Leyte. He decided to push straight on to Leyte on 11 October when sorties in September revealed the vulnerability of the enemy position in the Visayas. With the approaches swept of mines, the Central Philippine Attack Force consisting of 650 ships and four army divisions entered Leyte Gulf. The Japanese resisted in vain. On 20 October 1944, MacArthur, accompanied by President Sergio Osmeña, waded ashore in fulfilment of a solemn promise to return. Quezon had died in America on 1 August of the same year. On 4 July 1945 – and after the massacre of thousands of Filipinos by the retreating Japanese – MacArthur proclaimed the liberation of the entire Philippines from the enemy.

The end of the Second World War found the Philippines a devastated battleground, a victim of a holocaust that would long remain. The ravages of war left their imprint not only on the physical appearance of the country, especially Manila, but on the national economy. Poverty brought death to thousands and disease to thousands more; agricultural production was at a standstill; hoarding and blackmarketeering were rife; and the price of essential consumer goods rose astronomically. MacArthur – who had installed himself as 'proconsul' – made no secret of his impatience with Osmeña, and openly supported Manuel A. Roxas, who had sat at Osmeña's feet as a political novice, for president of the Commonwealth, and later the Republic which was declared on 4 July 1946. Roxas headed a government made up of many former collaborators – having previously granted amnesty to all political prisoners – and, once again, power was vested in the pre-war lords of Philippine economy, with all the associated intrigue and corruption. Roxas died on American soil at the Clark Air Base on 15 April 1948. He had been invited by the Americans – fearful of Russian interest in the country – to make a public statement about the loyalty of the Philippines to the United States. He became ill soon after finishing his speech in defence 'of justice, of freedom, and the other principles which we both love and cherish'. Vice-President

Elpidio Quirino, who immediately took over from Roxas, although well-intentioned, also failed in his mission to improve not only the economy, but morality inside and outside the government.

THE HUKBALAHÁP

Mention must be made of a vast peasant organisation which, while having its roots in smaller organisations dating from the 1920s, was at its height from 1942 until 1962. It was called *Hukbó ng Bayan Laban sa Hapón* (People's Anti-Japanese Army) or *Hukbalaháp* for short, which later became *Huk*. Peasant leaders took advantage of the war to bring together groups of tenant farmers who, for decades, had been angered by the poverty and degradation they suffered at the hands of the landlords. The *Hukbalaháp* had a three-point platform – economic, political and military – with a determination to work for a free and democratic Philippines. The *Huk* organisation had a wide mass base and a political sophistication that other resistance groups in the Philippines never had. Its leaders, who came from the lowest stratum of society, were zealous fanatics who understood the needs, customs and aspirations of the people. A strict code of discipline was imposed on its members, demonstrated, for example, when the *Hukbalaháp* Amazon, Felipa Culala, was executed by her own men after investigations showed that her activities were contrary to the rules and principles of the organisation and endangering the movement. The method of indoctrination in the aims and purposes of the *Huk* was so thorough – ranging from lectures to writing textbooks and preparing historical pageants – that the people under the *Huk* sovereignty grasped the simple message and could not help believing that a new vista had been opened up in which they, and not the landlords, were in control. This was reinforced when, on occasions, they witnessed their landlords fleeing before them to seek refuge in Manila.

Roxas tried to solve the *Huk* problem with force – and failed. Quirino attempted to win over the *Huk*s by peaceful means, even granting absolute amnesty to all leaders and members; he, too, failed. Quirino, however, continued to hope that the *Huk* problem could be solved and appointed Ramón Magsaysáy, a former guerrilla, as his Secretary of National Defence, giving him all facilities to deal with the *Huk*s. Magsaysáy approached the fugitives with understanding and concern, acknowledging their grievances and their long history of degradation at the hands of the landlords. Little by little, they surrendered, tired of running, fighting and being hunted. Magsaysáy, supported by the Americans and especially the CIA, became a national figure and, at the next election, defeated Quirino overwhelmingly.

MAGSAYSÁY

Magsaysáy understood the problem of the rural areas and embarked upon a programme of improving the land-tenure system, giving credit to the peasants, building roads, and community development. Despite the new faith in his leadership he was not a man of great vision and most projects turned out to be temporary expedients. Magsaysáy – who, in effect, paved the way for a society dominated by the masses through their legitimate leaders – did little to improve the daily life of peasant farmers while he was alive. Vice-President Carlos P. Garcia succeeded to the presidency, and was elected in his own right in November 1957. Although the *Huk* movement was by this time losing momentum, Garcia was no more successful in restoring peace and order in central Luzon than in his attempts to eradicate graft and corruption. He was defeated primarily on these very issues in 1961 when Diosdado Macapagal, a man from a very poor background, became president. He, too, was moved by the plight of the peasant farmers – still suffering since Spanish times – and on 8 August 1963 signed into law an Amended Land Reform Code.

It was not, however, until 1964 and 1965 – before the election of Ferdinand Marcos and during the first months of his tenure of office – that, with a lack of ideology in the movement and the promise of land reforms and social and economic programmes, the power and influence of the *Huk* petered out. The question of tenancy remained, however, and continues to remain, one of the most serious in the Philippines.

HISTORY DISTORTED

The history of the country can be written and re-written – and has been written – many times. While most 'facts' and dates provide a measure of common agreement, the interpretation of events and the motivation for most actions become increasingly distorted as the present is approached. This must be true, to some extent, of the outline of Philippine history presented in this chapter, but is nowhere more apparent than in the differences to be found in the 'history' presented by Marcos and the reality of the people he sought to manipulate and control. One 'official' account of events makes interesting reading:

On 21 September 1972 President Ferdinand E. Marcos invoked Martial Law. Reforms and innovations were immediately initiated which re-established political stability and gave unprecedented impetus to economic development. Major programmes were undertaken to achieve the goals of a changing social order. Among these are the integration of the country's regions, land reform, industrial development, infrastructure, tourism and education.

Industrial development is being pursued primarily to promote employment through labour-intensive programmes, by way of encouraging export-oriented and domestic industries. Traditional exports are being further developed, while the policy of economic dispersal has seen fruit with the setting up of the industrial complexes in the various regions. In this context, the first export processing zone has been established in Bataan to provide domestic and foreign investors with the necessary infrastructure and tax concessions to enhance manufacturing in the Philippines. Integration of regions has led to further unification of national ideas, making the implementation of land reform and vital educational programmes an easier task to fulfil.

Tourism and infrastructure complete the national programme for development. Tourism, now developed into one of the country's top dollar earners, has become a significant economic booster. Its promotion is expected to increase annually tourist arrivals to the Philippines and, as a consequence, the much needed tourist dollars. On the other hand, infrastructure has affected the socio-economic conditions of the country enormously. Under the national plan, it is now being intensified to meet the needs of agrarian reform, rural development, industry, tourism and the expansion of employment opportunities.

In January 1981 President Marcos voluntarily lifted Martial Law in the first steps to return to normalization in the political arena . . .

ECONOMIC AND POLITICAL REALITY

This 'image' of stability was very far from the truth, the 1965 election being the last one – until 1986 – in which Marcos did not have almost complete control of the electoral machinery, and the start of a 20-year reign of protest, repression and economic decline.

As economic decline accelerated, protests became more frequent. In response, repressive measures were even more apparent. 'Clever', by some standards, Marcos surrounded himself with 'cronies', gave power to an enlarged and ill-disciplined army, courted the Americans who – despite their embarrassment – needed to maintain bases in the Philippines, and left a legacy of poverty and anger, which erupted at the beginning of 1986 after 400 years of domination and, more recently, brutal oppression.

IBON, a fortnightly publication making comment on current issues – and furnishing facts and figures – provided a helpful framework for the analysis and assessment of contemporary Philippine society in the issue dated 15 April 1985. Several areas were considered: for example, the quality of life; the prices of basic goods; unemployment; economic realignment; industrialisation; agriculture; foreign debts; agriculture; and graft and corruption. As pointed out in *IBON*, 20 years is a long time. A great deal happened during that period. The USA had five different presidents – Johnson, Nixon, Ford, Carter and Reagan. The Russian leadership changed four times – from Brezhnev to Andropov, to Chernenko to Gorbachev. Roman Catholics had three different popes – Paul VI, John Paul I and John Paul II. And in all this time, three countries – Vietnam, Iran and Nicaragua – won their revolutions.

What happened to the people of the Philippines? They increased in number: from 30 million in 1965 to more than 54 million in 1985. Those born since 1965, the year Marcos came to power, numbered 25 million in 1985: they are the 'martial law babies' who grew up knowing only martial law, and its parallel sequel, as a way of life.

QUALITY OF LIFE

An ultimate goal in developing a country is the improvement of the quality of life of its people. Most indicators point to the fact that for most Filipinos this has never occurred. There has, indeed, been a steady deterioration in the quality of life. As will be seen in Chapter 3, communicable diseases, caused by poverty and poor sanitation, still rank among the top killer diseases. These diseases accounted for 45.6 per cent of total deaths in 1965. From 1966 to 1983 their share in accountability fluctuated between 37 and 47.3 per cent. Pneumonia remains the top killer disease, and a resurgence of malaria, typhoid, measles and leprosy has been noted during the last ten years.

Filipinos, too, have been eating less food, and of inferior quality. Per capita annual consumption of protein-rich foods, for instance, dropped from over 90 kilograms in 1970 to just over 50 kilograms in 1981. This is only 45 per cent of the recommended amount of this food group.

The 1980 Census of Population and Housing revealed that almost one out of two households lived in buildings with roofs made of *cogon, nipa,* and makeshift or salvaged materials. Migration to the cities, 'hamleting' (the forced movement of people by the army) and an increase in the proportion of families falling below the poverty line – from 66 per cent in 1965 to 71 per cent in 1983 – worsened this figure. There are nearly three million squatters. There has been a deterioration in income distribution: the poorest 60 per cent of families received only 23 per cent of total incomes in 1983, down from 24 per cent in 1965; the richest 20 per cent of families, however, increased their share from 55 per cent in 1965 to 56.5 per cent in 1983.

PRICES AND WAGES

For the eight-year period 1965–72 inflation averaged 8.4 per cent yearly, perhaps not too much out of step with other economies, but

Table 2.1

	Price in pesos		
	1972	1984	1985
Rice, special, *wagwag*, per kilogram	1.28	5.29	7.78
Corn, white, milled	0.94	3.79	5.92
Condensed milk, Senorita, 14 ounces	1.42	7.99	10.27
Fresh eggs, medium, per dozen	3.34	13.74	17.02
Galunggong (fish), medium, per kilogram	2.21	19.19	22.20
Beef, pure meat, per kilogram	8.94	50.64	64.62
Pork, pure meat, per kilogram	7.60	30.71	43.00
Sugar, refined, per kilogram	1.35	7.12	7.60
Beer, 350 cc	0.56	2.61	3.30
Coca-cola, 8 ounces	0.25	1.74	2.30
Cement, Republic, sack	5.23	48.97	53.17
Tuition fee, Bachelor of Science in Education, 1st year, 1 semester	185.00	633.74	690.00
Minimum fare, jeepney, 1st 5 kilometres	0.15	1.20	1.50

climbed to 16.3 per cent by 1983, reaching a peak of 51 per cent in 1984. Increase in the nominal wages of workers could not keep up with inflation. In fact, it was a part of government policy to ensure that increases in nominal wages lagged behind inflation. Cheap labour was a necessary part of an export promotion strategy designed to attract foreign investments. And when inflation could not be stemmed, even greater pressure was put on wages. The increases noted over a 13-year period are shown in Table 2.1.

Real wages of skilled workers in Metro Manila fell by almost 60 per cent from 1965 to 1980; those of unskilled workers by 48 per cent. By 1984 effective minimum wages barely covered half the cost of living.

UNEMPLOYMENT

Millions of Filipinos are either unemployed or underemployed, probably about 50 per cent of adults of working age in urban areas, with slightly reduced figures in the countryside. What has emerged is a distorted employment structure indicative of an economy at best in limbo, at worst in decline. The slack in employment in industry and agriculture has been taken up by the proliferation of superfluous jobs in the service sector. As noted earlier, vendors and peddlars jostle for space and custom in every major thoroughfare. Prostitution – considered in some detail in Chapter 4 – has established itself as a reliable though poorly-paid employment, less unacceptable to society than it was not too long ago. In this respect, children become a source of income.

Industrialisation in the last 20 years has not affected the unemployment problem. Reliance on the manufacture of non-traditional exports to the neglect of heavy industries has failed to generate enough jobs for a growing population. In fact, the share of industry in total employment has been declining: from 16 per cent in 1971 to 14.7 per cent in 1984.

When export-led industrialisation failed to produce enough jobs, the government turned to exporting labour itself. The Philippines exports Filipinos: labourers, skilled technicians, nurses, doctors and domestic servants. Hong Kong, Singapore, the USA and the Middle East are attractive overseas destinations, and the overall number of Filipinos working abroad jumped from 12 500 in 1975 to well over a million in 1985. There are 17 000 Filipinos employed in London – mostly in hotels and hospitals – and 30 000 in Hong Kong.

ECONOMIC REALIGNMENT

Soon after Marcos was re-elected in 1969 he announced a *de facto* devaluation of the peso in exchange for a standby facility from the International Monetary Fund (IMF). This was the country's seventh such loan, and set the stage for the reversal of previous policies that placed restrictions on imports as well as on the outward flow of foreign exchange, opening the economy wider to foreign goods and foreign investments, principally those of the USA.

Before long 'export-led industrialisation' became the economic catchword. Investment incentives and preferential credit were given to exporters; rules on foreign investments were relaxed; export processing zones were set up; schedules to lower import tariffs were drawn up and wages maintained at low levels, not only through wage legislation but through a ban on strikes. Foreign markets took precedence over the domestic market. Bananas and shrimps went to the Japanese; huge plantations were established, for example, in Mindanao, ruthlessly displacing hundreds of families without compensation and sometimes at the point of a rifle; sugar had to be rationed at times among local consumers; and even rice was exported – as people starved in both the urban and rural areas. Employees in the export processing zones worked under inhuman conditions to complete orders for foreign companies and foreign buyers.

Export promotion strengthened – rather than lowered – import dependence. This and the unrestricted outflow of profits and capital by foreign investors (57 foreign banks were trading in the Philippines in 1982) led to frequent foreign exchange crises. The government's response was to borrow more. As a result, the IMF and other creditors lent more in return for stricter control over the economy and a pledge to maintain export promotion, thereby worsening the overall economic plight.

Today the focus of the IMF, the World Bank (WB) and the government has moved from industry to agriculture. The emphasis on exports remains. Thus, the Filipino farmer, as well as the Filipino factory worker, continues to accumulate profits for the few at whatever cost to the majority.

INDUSTRY

During the Marcos era, Philippine development plans generously provided for the expansion and progress of industry. Visions of a strong, self-reliant industry invariably unfolded between the pages of official documents. More often than not, as in the case of numerous projects announced in the national daily newspaper, *Bulletin Today*, the plans never left the pages. Beyond official rhetoric, no serious efforts were made to develop basic and heavy industries during the last two decades. The focus on 11 major industrial projects in 1981 was a related and short-lived attempt to set up a solid foundation for Philippine industry. They were promptly opposed by dominant foreign interests led by the WB. In 1983, 11 of the official projects were officially deferred. So far, only three have started operations, and each may be considered a failure. The country's smelter plant quickly broke down with technical problems after two months of operation; the fertiliser plant was similarly affected by technical problems; and coal has to be imported to fuel the country's major cement plants ever since these were converted to coal.

One particular failure in industrial development plans was found in the car industry. The Philippine Car Manufacturing Programme, designed in 1973, was flaunted as a model car programme in Southeast Asia. In March 1985 Prime Minister Virata himself announced that the programme had failed. He admitted that since 1975 not one of the five companies in the programme had produced a single car that could be stamped 'Made in the Philippines'. The remaining three car manufacturers – CARCO, General Motors Pilipinas and Pilipinas Nissan – were only producing, in March 1985, four or five units a day in plants designed for an output of 280 each week.

More will be said about the drugs industry in Chapter 3. There have, however, been restrictions for the past 17 years. The government imposed a ban on the licensing of distributors of locally manufactured medicines: since 1968 only distributors selling imported medicines were licensed to operate. In 1985, because of the scarcity of foreign exchange, the ban was lifted 'to encourage the entry of Filipino capital into the industry'. But Filipinos must compete with transnational drug firms in the Philippines which compose 70 per cent of the 508 registered firms.

AGRICULTURE

The agricultural industry in the Philippines employs 52 per cent of the labour force and supports 70 per cent of the population.

Although providing food for the people and raw materials for industry, small farmers carry the heaviest burden in the economy, crisis or no crisis. Long neglected by government, abused and cheated by landlords, merchants and money-lenders, small farmers have continued to sink into debt and into poverty. More than 70 per cent have incomes below the poverty line.

In 1979 a farmer's income was only 60 per cent of the value of his income five years previously. The increased crop production resulting from the Green Revolution, launched eight years before, only enabled farmers to buy more overpriced fertilisers and pesticides, and to pay for more farm necessities like irrigation services and hired farm labour. The emphasis on commercial crop production also had lasting effects on the agricultural landscape. The land area planted with commercial crops expanded by 1.7 million hectares from 1965 to 1983, and this resulted in the displacement of small, self-sufficient farmers, forcing them to become plantation and contract workers.

The land reform programme achieved nothing. By 1981 only 1799 farmers had been granted full ownership of the land they worked. However, a growing rural population increased the demand for the land available: in 1970 the average farm size was 3.6 hectares while by 1980 it had contracted to 2.6 hectares; and, although the number of farms rose by 46 per cent over a five-year period, the total farm area only expanded by 6.36 per cent. The number of landless agricultural workers increased dramatically, from 800 000 in 1971 to two million in 1985. Most of these workers receive less than 20 pesos a day.

FOREIGN DEBT

By mid-1984 the country's total external debt amounted to US$25.6 billion, equivalent to 42 times its debt in 1965; over 11 times its debt in 1972; and 483 per cent of its total export earnings in 1984. Throughout 1985 further loans were negotiated by the government as part of its recovery package.

This heavy borrowing was a consequence of the export-led industrialisation policy, supported by the IMF, the WB and private international commercial banks. The policy failed, many traditional markets for Philippine exports setting up protectionist barriers to limit the entry of goods. Nevertheless, borrowing continued;

creditors became less confident; the country's credit rating began to fall; public and private borrowers were given less time in which to repay new loans; and bank charges and interest rates were raised. The country remains in debt; the cost of rescheduling loans imposes an even heavier financial burden; and gives greater control to the IMF, the WB and transnational banks.

Mismanagement of the economy also resulted in the proliferation of government corporations and monopolies. Trading agencies such as the National Sugar Trading Agency (NASUTRA), the Philippine Coconut Authority and the National Food Administration were created through presidential decrees and given immunity from public accounting. The interrelationship between these monopolies, big businesses and the state banks, reinforced the concentration of power and wealth in the hands of a few favoured families. Disini, Cuenca, Silverio and Cojuangco were among the most powerful names when Marcos was in power.

GRAFT AND CORRUPTION

In all presidential elections graft and corruption has always been a consistent issue against the incumbent, no president before Marcos winning his bid for a second term in office. Macapagal lost to Marcos in 1965 partly on this very question. Marcos, subsequently, proved the most astute of them all, using the funds, personnel and other resources of the government to cement his power, to control his enemies, to buy support and to ensure his re-election. Less than two weeks after the announcement of the 1986 election – originally scheduled for 1987 – the Deputy Prime Minister placed orders in Hong Kong for one million children's watches (at HK$5 each) and one million transistor radios and alarm radios (at HK$30 each) to be shipped immediately. Other election bribes offered in Manila included tinned foods and medicines; while in the rural areas 50 peso and 100 peso notes were used. The latter were widely distributed – by Imelda Marcos herself in Rizal Park – during the 1984 election to the *Batasang Pambansa*, and again in 1986.

Graft and corruption has always been commonplace throughout the government – from policemen to generals, from the *barrio* to the presidential palace. I have myself, on occasions, found access made much easier by a 'tip', for instance, in getting into a prison or another secure building. The *'tong'* system – whereby policemen collect 'taxes' from jeepney drivers on street corners – is found throughout Metro Manila. Firemen attending some of the major hotel fires in 1984 and 1985 would not connect their hoses until they had been bribed. While graft and corruption has always been a problem in Philippine society it has become even more widespread as poverty has bitten deeper. In the Philippines – and especially in anything remotely connected with government – it is a way of life. Such practices are difficult to control and perhaps impossible to break.

AMERICAN DOMINATION

Thus, the country ailed during the Marcos dictatorship. But yet there is more. Apart from poverty, sickness and disease (considered in Chapters 3 and 4) and questions of human rights and oppression (considered in Chapters 5 and 6) the Philippines must be seen within the context of the United States, and of its need to safeguard its economic and defence interests. Even following the election there seem to be no limits to which the USA will not go in order to protect these. Of course, they would prefer not to be embarrassed by the poverty to which they contribute; by the excesses of the dictatorship which they supported; and by the associated brutality and killings, but nowhere else in South-east Asia can offer such a strategic position for their military bases, such a comparatively docile workforce and such a government capable of being manipulated and controlled. Immediately following the election Aquino said that she would honour the bases agreement until 1991, and then reconsider the position. The determination of the USA – as shown later in this chapter – is to maintain security and defence goals, whatever the cost. Aquino will be unlikely to drive the Americans out.

When Marcos declared Martial Law in 1972 the USA immediately doubled its military aid to the Philippines. US military aid to Marcos in 1982 was US$140.1 million, plus US$100 million as rental for US bases. During the 1983 review of the US–RP Military Bases Agreement (MBA), American negotiators promised to extend US$900 million to the Marcos government in exchange for the continued use of US military bases in the country. This aid enabled Marcos to increase the number of troops from 60 000 in 1972 to nearly 300 000 in 1985. The 16 American bases, five of which are major military installations, are the most visible manifestations of US political and strategic interests in the country and in the entire Asia–Pacific region. Some bases are used to store nuclear weapons. Since 1947 when the MBA was signed, the USA has ensured a continuation of its economic and military control even after formally granting independence to the Philippines a year before. The Subic Naval Base, headquarters of the US Seventh Fleet, and Clark Air Base, home of the US Air Force's 13th Squadron, are two of the most important US military installations overseas. These, together with an undetermined number of other sites being used by the Americans, serve multiple aggressive functions. Not only are they springboards for the rapid deployment of conventional forces in East Asia and the Indian Ocean, they are also staging areas for covert operations directed at both the Philippines and its neighbours. In the past these bases have been the launching pads for intervention in Korea, Vietnam, Laos and Cambodia. They are also potential support bases for US operations in the Indian Ocean as far as East Africa. The presence of 16 000 well-equipped US troops on the bases always paved the way for US intervention in the Philippines in the event of any threat to the Marcos regime. Recently, the bases have assumed an important role in the 'counter-force' or 'first strike' strategy of nuclear warfare aimed at the Soviet Union. Additional forces were on hand – in ships outside Manila Bay – during the two months prior to the election.

SPECIAL OPERATIONS

Another sign of US military activity in the Philippines is the building up of two 'special operations force' (SOF) units. In addition, a 'special warfare group facility' at Subic Bay has been constructed. The information about the SOF activity was gathered from issue no. 2 of the *Defence Monitor*, a publication of the Centre for Defence Information, which is headed by former US Navy Admiral Gene la Roque. The US embassy in Manila, in an apparent effort to minimise the negative implications of these activities, issued a statement on 12 June 1985 confirming the information but adding that 'there is nothing secret about their presence'.

The SOFs are known as America's 'secret soldiers' and are military command units trained for anti-guerrilla warfare, psychological warfare ('psy-ops') and covert clandestine and unconventional warfare. In the Philippines, the two SOF units are the Special Warfare Unit 1 – Sea, Air and Land Services (SEALS) – at Subic Bay, and the 1st Operations Squadron at Clark Air Base. Even though the US embassy claims that 'there has certainly been no involvement of these units . . . in any combat or combat support operations in the territory of the Republic of the Philippines', it also admits that their primary mission is to maintain readiness through training. Another source of information is the transcript of the US House of Representatives hearings on military construction appropriations. The transcript revealed the construction of the 'special warfare group facility' at Subic Bay for the SOFs. The construction project, coded P-832, was estimated to cost US$780 000.

SOF units led US troops in the invasion of Grenada in 1983, and are now training Contra bandits in Nicaragua. Unlike its other military assistance appropriations, the Pentagon is not required to report to Congress, and is exempt from congressional enquiry, where SOF units and their clandestine operations overseas are concerned.

American troops in the Philippines have for some time engaged in joint war exercises with the AFP as part of the security defence plan under the US–RP Mutual Aid Defence Treaty. The war exercises include training in 'psy-ops', torture techniques and jungle survival.

The US$900 million compromise agreed upon in 1983 apparently satisfied both parties. From the US point of view, the money would buy sufficient stability to maintain vast US economic interests manifested in US$1.5 billion in investments spread over more than 105 American corporations all over the country. The US$900 million was initially allocated no differently from previous financial assistance handed out by the US government: US$475 million for economic assistance; US$300 million as military sales credit payable in 20 years with a ten-year grace period; and US$125 million for direct military assistance. However, before money even started flowing, Congress altered the mix of the Reagan administration's first payment, taking about US$45 million from the US$85 million in military aid and adding it to US$95 million of economic assistance. For the fiscal year 1986, the House of Representatives foreign affairs committee recommended a repeat of this move, cutting US$75 million off military aid and adding US$60 million to economic assistance. Stephen Solarz, the head of the Asia–Pacific sub-committee which first proposed the change, said the move would indicate clearly to Marcos that he should make the reforms sought by the USA. The move, of course, upset the Philippines government and brought retaliatory threats from Marcos that he might be inclined to do without military assistance altogether – and without the US bases – when the current agreement runs out. If the move by the foreign affairs committee also irritated the Reagan administration it was at least in line with the thinking of US policy.

INTER-AGENCY REPORT

That the US government has had a 'get tough' policy for the Philippines there is no doubt, and this is shown in the following abbreviated version of a US government inter-agency report issued in Washington DC in November 1984:

US policy towards the Philippines
The problem
The United States has extremely important interests in the Philippines:

— Politically, because the US nurtured the independence and democratic institutions of our former colony, the Philippines must be a stable, democratically oriented ally. A radicalized Philippines would destabilize the whole region.
— Strategically, continued unhampered access to our bases at Subic and Clark is of prime importance because of the expanded Soviet and Vietnamese threat in the region. Fall-back positions would be much more expensive and less satisfactory.
— A strong ASEAN that includes a healthy Philippines allied to the US is a buffer to communist presence in Southeast Asia and a model of what economic freedom and democratic progress can accomplish.
— Economically, we benefit from a strong investment and trade position.

Political and economic development in the Philippines threaten these interests. Long-standing political and economic problems came to a head following the Aquino assassination in August 1983, which destroyed most of the political credibility the 19-year old Marcos Government enjoyed and exacerbated a shaky financial situation. A positive political dynamic in the direction of greater openness has developed in the wake of the Aquino assassination, but many question whether President Marcos can or will allow sufficient revitalization of democratic institutions to prevent a full-scale polarization of Philippine society.

Meanwhile, although the Philippines is likely to overcome the current financial crisis with considerable outside help, medium-term economic prospects are quite gloomy and in the absence of major structural economic reform the longer term outlook does not permit such optimism. At the same time, the communist New People's Army, taking advantage of the depressed economy, the weaknesses of the Philippine military and its abuse of civilians, popular fear and resentment of the military, and the government's inability to deliver economic and social development programs, has continued to expand significantly. This threat will doubtless continue to grow in the absence of progress toward credible democratic institutions, military reform including the curbing of abuse, and basic economic reform. In the absence of political and economic stability, continued steady progress toward an insurgent communist take-over is a distinct possibility in the mid-to-long term, and possibly sooner.

However, reforms are likely in the short run to weaken some bases of support for the current government, which will resist many of them. While President Marcos at this stage is part of the problem he is also necessarily part of the solution. We need to be able to work with him and to try to influence him through a well-orchestrated policy of incentives and disincentives to set the stage for peaceful and eventual transition to a successor government whenever that takes place. Marcos, for his part, will try to use us to remain in power indefinitely.

US goals
Politically, the US wants a strong, stable, democratically oriented, pro-US Philippines. However, without a healthy economy, the Philippines cannot achieve political stability. Thus, specific US *economic* goals remain:

— to strengthen the Philippine economy through our multilateral and bilateral assistance programs;
— to move the Philippine economy toward a free market orientation; and
— to maintain and expand current levels of trade and investment (US exports: $1.8 billion; imports $2 billion; direct investment $1.3 billion).

Our security and *defense* goals are to maintain US military presence and to fulfil treaty obligations and commitments made operational through our naval and air bases at Subic and Clark. Through military assistance and training provided to the Philippines Armed Forces our objectives are:

— to assist in maintaining internal defense and conventional deterrence capability;
— to continue to support military, civic and social action activities; and
— to assist in defeating the ongoing insurgency.

Strong people/cultural relationships and broad existing institutional ties over many years assist us in achieving all our goals.

Premises underlying US policy
The US does not want to remove Marcos from power. Rather, we are urging revitalization of democratic institutions, dismantling 'crony' monopoly capitalism and allowing the economy to respond to free market forces, and restoring professional, apolitical leadership to the Philippines military to deal with the growing communist insurgency. These efforts are meant to

stabilize while strengthening institutions which will eventually provide for peaceful transition.

Our approach assumes that our interests in the Philippines are worth a high-priority and costly effort to preserve. At the same time, and although we have important influence and leverage *vis-à-vis* the Philippines, we cannot take the lead in reforming the Philippine system; the Filipinos must do this themselves. Our influence is most effective when it is exercised in support of efforts that have already developed within the Philippines.

We must pursue a comprehensive approach to the triad of challenges affecting our interests because the problems themselves are interlinked. This will require:

— a more open economic system that ends or substantially alters 'crony capitalism' and agricultural monopolies;
— a more open political system that offers a credible promise of democratic reform; and
— an effective military capable of carrying the fight to the communist insurgency while controlling abuses of its own.

Our assets include not only the economic and military assistance that we are able to provide but also the respect and sympathy that we continue to enjoy with most segments of the Philippine population. Our support could be lost if we come to be seen as favoring a continuation of the Marcos regime to the exclusion of other democratic alternatives.

In considering how this policy can be strengthened in the future, we have examined approaches differentiated primarily by the level of resources we would be prepared to devote to encouraging needed reform in the Philippines and by the level of the US profile in the effort. We have also examined negative approaches:

— a 'no sale' option to be followed should Marcos fail to agree to our proposals for assistance in return for reform; and
— a 'non-feasance' option should Marcos agree to undertake reform measures but fail to comply.

Military measures

To impress upon President Marcos the seriousness with which we view the insurgency and the deplorable state of his Armed Forces to deal with it, we may need to provide private briefings for Marcos by a US military intelligence team. This would be a sensitive undertaking. Marcos is not uninformed about the NPA threat or the deficiency of the AFP to deal with them. However, he is probably unwilling to admit either fully to the NPA threat or to the deficiencies of the AFP because to do so would be an indictment of his nearly twenty years of rule.

Major US efforts to halt any further deterioration in the Philippine military will be hampered by the Philippine military's structural weakness: poor, uninspiring leadership; corruption; mismanagement of resources. Given the growth of the insurgency, military assistance is nonetheless essential. A restoration of professional, apolitical military leadership could significantly alter the situation.

At the outset, substantial new funds beyond those envisaged in the bases-related commitments may not be needed. What is needed is a better utilization of already planned funds.

An overriding consideration should be to avoid getting ourselves caught between the slow erosion of Marcos' authoritarian control and the still fragile revitalization of democratic institutions, being made hostage to Marcos' political fortunes, being saddled with ultimate responsibility for winning the insurgency, or being tagged with the success or failure of individuals in the moderate leadership. A strong case can thus be made for security assistance which concentrates on practical programs such as logistics, maintenance, training programs, and equipment for mobility and communications. Specific measures to:

— ensure that the provision of military aid at least equals that outlined in the presidential commitment over the five-year period;
— ensure the most efficient use of military assistance;
— improve communication capabilities;
— re-orient Philippine participation in joint exercises to concentrate on tasks which will advance civic action capabilities;
— assist the AFP to fulfil their perimeter security responsibilities;
— consider means of assisting the AFP with their cash flow problems by, for example, seeking greater concessionary loan authority and enhanced grant assistance;
— make a major effort to assist the AFP in improving the existing logistics system and in upgrading their transportation capabilities; and
— assist in re-establishing training programs throughout the AFP, ranging from basic to advanced programs.

Political measures
(a) Private diplomacy
In the Philippine cultural context, the way we convey our policy messages to the government leadership, the opposition, the Church, and the business community is almost as important as the policy.

An effective, low key approach involves no special efforts at communication other than the normal – an occasional presidential letter, regular visits by administration officials, close Embassy contact, and regular one-to-one meetings between President Marcos and Ambassador Bosworth. This has the advantage of moving issues along one at a time in ways that clearly spell out US intentions. Occasional visitors and regular communication at the Ambassadorial level, particularly with President Marcos, would be geared to making sure our messages are received, understood, and placed in the appropriate policy context. This mode is appropriate for expressing US support for initiatives needed to move the Philippines successfully through the transition period such as strengthened/reformed election bodies (NAMFREL and COMELEC), a stronger independent judiciary, and revitalized rural development efforts.

A presidential letter would be the key to setting the stage of linking increase in economic, military, and financial assistance to major reform. The same message could be sent by a high level emissary such as Secretary Shultz or NSC Director McFarlane. A third option would be to ask one of several private sector leaders known to the Philippine leadership (a 'Wisemen's mission') to carry the message. This would be particularly advisable if a high level trade/aid/investment initiative effort is made.

(b) Public diplomacy
Public diplomacy involves both Philippines and US audiences and is an essential part of our policy. As a first step, we would have to spell out our Philippine policy through a high level Administration speech, followed by regular policy statements in Washington and Manila.

Since appearances and the perception of personal ties are a most important factor in the Philippine relationship, US officials will have to take care not to appear too close to the Marcos regime. At the same time, of course, US officials will have to maintain a relationship which permits us to continue to exercise influence positively. This is a thin line to walk but it can be done.

Consensus approach: pros/cons
The *advantages* of the consensus approach are:

— Continuation of a policy that has yielded positive results over the past year.
— Enables us to build upon and reinforce positive trends emerging from within the Philippines and avoid over-identification with success or failure that would accompany a more dramatic, high resources/high-profile policy.
— Large-scale commitment of new funds would not be necessary.
— It gives us the flexibility we need to deal with the Filipinos and the Congress.

The chief *drawback* to the consensus approach is, of course, the risk that it might not be sufficient either to prod or entice the necessary reforms. If the quid pro quo policy should fail to bring about needed reform we would be open to criticism that we are not doing or have not done enough to protect our long-term interests in a stable, democratically-oriented Philippines.

Our option in such event would be to step up the pressure or enhance our assistance as necessary in the light of internal developments.

Enhanced military assistance
A prerequisite for seeking a more favorable military assistance package than called for by the base-related commitment is sufficient movement toward military reform to indicate that the Philippine Armed Forces is coming to grips with its fundamental problems and is carrying out its role in a more professional manner . . . Our presentation to President Marcos for enhanced military assistance would indicate that we would expect the following:

— restoration of professional, apolitical leadership of the Armed Forces in order to deal with the NPA threat;
— improvement in dealing with military abuse;
— improved training; and
— more military equipment for logistics, communications, and basic military needs.

'No-sale' non-feasance options
Our strategy options rest on the premise that the Marcos government will begin to undertake, accelerate or adjust to the reforms needed to correct the deteriorating situation. We, thus, need to consider what we would do if Marcos refuses to undertake or blocks reform ('no-sale') or, more likely, agrees to the reforms but fails to follow through (non-feasance). All proposals for new assistance should include benchmarks and discreet but plain deadlines for agreement in principle and execution in practice. If there is no agreement, or if agreement is dilatory, we should:

— reiterate our concerns;
— send signals that non-cooperation in Manila leads to non-cooperation in Washington, e.g. delayed disbursement of funds, delayed program approvals, negative notes in multilateral forums; and
— discreetly publicize the fact that cooperation is not forthcoming on matters important to the welfare and security of the Philippines. These signals should increase pressure on Marcos from the public, opposition, business leaders, and even from his own close associates. If economic assistance is not forthcoming, the deteriorating situation itself should increase the political and economic pressures on Marcos.

Experience tells us that agreement in principle followed by non-feasance is probably as likely as agreement followed by faithful execution. To guard against this, our tactical approach to assistance must include:

— clear definition of the elements composing agreement in principle;
— clear definition of acceptable performance criteria;
— periodic in-house evaluation of progress; and
— periodic review of compliance and results with the Philippine Government.

If a review established backsliding, we would take the steps outlined above under the 'no-sale' option.

The Americans became increasingly nervous throughout 1985, sending – amongst others – the CIA Director, William Casey, in May 1985, and Senator Paul Laxalt, a personal friend of Reagan and chairman of his three presidential campaigns, in October 1985, to meet Marcos in Manila. The message remained the same: bring about political, military and economic reform, and stop the growing communist insurgency. Marcos, as we now know, was unable to respond to the message to bring about change. He left the country, discredited, on 25 February 1986. The uncertainty and turbulence which surrounded the end of his presidency are recorded in Chapter 8.

3 Poverty, Sickness and Disease

To a Westerner, never far from medical care, there is one aspect of the widespread sickness and disease that strikes home forcibly: the plight of people unable to obtain or to afford the services of a doctor or nurse, and even less able to purchase the highly-priced medicines and pills produced by the multinational drug companies and controlled through the ever-increasing number of retail outlets found in the towns and cities.

This initial, sophisticated reaction, however, is scarcely relevant in a country where involvement with sickness, disease, accidents and death forms a major part of the everyday experience of the mass of the population struggling to ensure their children's and their own survival. Only by living with a community of 30, 40, 50 or more families in a rural area on one of the islands or in a fishing village or in a remote mountain area is it possible to see how the frequent absence of medical care, the poverty of the people and the high levels of sickness and disease interrelate to produce conditions for living not dissimilar from the accounts we have of life in Europe in the early years of the 19th century.

'HOUSING'

Slums and squatter areas are found throughout the towns and cities of the Philippines, dwelling places of tin, wood, *nipa*, plastic sheeting or concrete blocks built around open sewer drains and pitched anywhere a family can find space to erect a shack. Ten or twelve people may sleep on the floor of a tiny room, the same few square feet being used by day to prepare and cook food, to nurse a sick child or to mend a bicycle.

In Manila, too, there is little hope. A report by the Metro Manila Commission (MMC) dated March 1985, noted that almost half of the city's seven million plus people live below the poverty line. Shantytowns proliferate on waste ground, under bridges and along canal banks and rivers. Crime, disease and hunger are rife. The closely packed hovels and crumbling buildings are, as noted earlier, fire hazards. Two hundred and forty-five of Manila's 415 listed slums are designated as priority areas for development. Figures mean little. The Ministry of Human Settlements launched a 'house-building programme for the poor'. Imelda Marcos was the Minister of Human Settlements. Few, however, could afford the houses, families needing a monthly income of nearly 4000 pesos to meet the mortgage. Fifty per cent of Manila's households earn, at best, half this amount. Those 'resettled' from slums often drift back to the central areas of the capital: there is no means of earning a livelihood in the new environment and it is impossible to find the money for travelling each day. They are provided with neither electricity nor piped water, and most often relocation is to yet another piece of waste ground.

Tondo forms part of Manila and is the largest slum in South-east Asia. The land is part of the foreshore of Manila Bay and was reclaimed in 1932. Nearly 130 000 families live there, many of them for 30 years. Sixty-five per cent of the adults are without regular employment, living on their wits or by casual labouring. Although the area now serves as the Philippines' show window for transforming a slum into a 'model town', much remains to be done elsewhere. And it must be remembered that the policy adopted in Tondo was one of slum upgrading and maximum retention, rather than demolition and relocation.

Shack communities are found on and around the garbage mountain, the largest rubbish tip in Metro Manila. The stench is overpowering, the mud is ankle-deep, young children play in the rotting filth and, as elsewhere, the shacks often provide shelter for several families. As the blinding rain and howling wind of a typhoon prevented movement outdoors on one of my visits to the 'Smoking Mountain' I sat for two hours in a small hut with several members of a large family – the children in grime-encrusted clothes – learning about life in the community. The people are scavengers, even working by torchlight at night to collect and separate tins, bottles, paper, scrap metal and boxes. Children join in. People say that they no longer notice the smell and have built up some immunity to the diseases which ooze from every muddy pool. Ear infections among the children, together with frequent diarrhoea and respiratory illnesses, contribute to the high mortality rate in the zero to five age group.

As I walked away from the garbage mountain knee-deep in disease-ridden water and following my conversation with those who scrape a living from the leftovers of the consumer society, I became aware of social injustice to a degree never previously experienced. Yet, on a day-to-day basis many of the scavengers regard themselves as fortunate. Some days they are able to earn 30 pesos. Families eke out their usual meal of rice and fish with kitchen leftovers from restaurants and other eating houses.

HEALTH CARE

Health is one of the indicators of the stage of development of a society. If there is change in the Philippines it has been in the continuing deterioration of already meagre services. Government health clinics with broken front entrances and swinging cupboard doors inside, especially in the rural areas, reflect what is happening: nurses not being appointed and no supplies of medicine. Over 800 towns lack health centres. Yet the Philippines is the world's largest 'exporter' of nurses and the second largest 'exporter' of doctors. In health provision, as elsewhere, grand schemes have been prepared but little or nothing has happened. Marcos and his wife loved personal acronyms, for example, Medical Assistance to the Rural Communities and Other Sectors (MARCOS); and Integrated Medical Expeditions to Less Developed Areas (IMELDA).

DENTAL CARE

Dental care in Third World countries is a problem that needs continuing attention, especially as Western-style sweets and soft drinks grow in popularity. The Philippines is no exception. The poor suffer through inadequately funded government dental programmes, shortages of equipment and dentists. Fillings, extractions and false teeth are easily available only for those able to pay. Financial difficulties beset those who live in the rural areas. The bus fare sometimes costs more than the treatment, even though dentists are very poorly paid. One woman, a qualified dentist with nearly 20 years' experience, recently moved to Hong Kong to work as a domestic helper. Her salary more than doubled.

I had a valuable experience in Mindanao, in the south of the country. One Sunday I accompanied two nurses, Dolfs Bunag and Jim Kurtz, one Filipino, the other American, to Kitcharao in Agusan del Norte. Here, as part of their community-based health programme, and after a seminar on dental care and tooth extraction with local health workers, the two men decided to help the local people 'put their knowledge into practice'. Untrained, non-professional health workers were moving into the field of 'tooth-pulling'.

By Western standards conditions were crude, but the nurses ensured that the rudiments of hygiene were observed, especially in respect of the injections and the sterilizing of instruments. The latter were boiled in a large pan heated by an open fire, a pig sleeping contentedly beside.

The ten extractions took most of the day, progress being slowed by the need to sterilize the instruments for 30 minutes after they had been used, and by the opportunities that had to be taken to teach new skills. Giving injections and extracting teeth were nerve-racking for both patients and amateur dentists.

There were adults and children, including a boy aged four. Filipinos have naturally beautiful teeth, and many keep them in good condition, but some of the teeth for extraction were in an advanced state of decay, especially in the case of one adolescent girl. With advanced decay – and a soft inside – the top of the tooth is inclined to break off, leaving the roots to be taken out later. This can be a painful and lengthy procedure.

The 'clinic' offered no privacy. Children wandered in and out. At one point there were about 15 watching. When there was pain friends would hold the hands, head and jaw of the patient. If he or she cried out – and that was rare – both nurses and onlookers would identify whether there was real suffering or only anxiety and respond accordingly. Flies soon descended on any blood-stained swabs that fell to the floor.

The nurses and their trainees were so much a part of the community that there was absolute confidence in them, and the nurses themselves were largely self-taught in this area of their work.

Such was the agony suffered previously by some of the patients that the relief could be seen on their faces soon after the extraction. It was a tiring day for Bunag and Kurtz. They had travelled a long way in intense heat, and were far from the support of colleagues had anything gone wrong. They felt bound to attend to all the patients who had sought treatment, they had to be mindful of the risk of infection and had to teach and create an anxiety-free environment. Gaining insight into the conditions under which workers and patients work and receive treatment is a powerful reminder to a Westerner of our own good fortune and of the need to reach out more frequently to those in underdeveloped countries. Shortly after spending the day with Bunag he was arrested. Stopped by the army at a checkpoint, his bags and boxes were searched. When dental instruments, and antibiotic and analgesic medicines were found he and a colleague, a medical assistant, were taken for interrogation. It took four hours to convince the 'investigators' that they were on their way to Buenavista to hold a free clinic in the local parish.

PRIMARY HEALTH CARE

Fortunately, primary health care is not exclusively in the hands of the government, the real organisation of the people stemming from community-based health programmes provided by concerned and committed health professionals like Bunag and, above all, the people themselves. In the rural areas a great deal of initiative has come from a group of Catholic nuns – Filipino, European and American – who, with funding from overseas, harness the skills and energy of the health professionals to maximum effect. Sister Nanette, whose death was recorded in Chapter 1, was among their number.

The health professionals are used for the selection, training and organisation of health workers, ordinary people from the *barrios* who later each take charge of the health care of ten families. The basis of training is self-reliance; using herbal medicines, acupuncture and acupressure; mobilising community resources in the face of the sickness of an individual; and making the families responsible for the training of their health workers.

I have attended numerous training sessions of health workers, many of whom travelled miles from remote areas, bringing food and sleeping mats to spend a week together in a hall attached to a church to learn the rudiments of health care; to practise first aid; and to improve their often considerable knowledge of herbal remedies. Alongside the health workers, the health professionals and programme coordinators learn and relearn about the medicinal and curative use of plants together with work on microscopy, minor surgery, acupuncture and acupressure. Acupuncture is part of the later training of health workers and is fundamental to the concepts of health care on which the programmes are based. Health professionals, often traditionally trained in hospital settings, receive minimal wages, about 900 pesos a month.

The training sessions for health workers, taking place at regular intervals, are lively, intense and reflect the personal investment of members of the group to serve their communities. Training in health skills – and this includes learning how to deal with snake bites – means time away from the farm or fishing ground, sacrifice indeed in such a depressed economy. Training involves identifying, picking, preparing and boiling a range of herbs and plants. There is, too, a social aspect of training and the very long sessions are punctuated with humour, guitar playing and action songs, enlivening some very hard work on the part of people unaccustomed to note-taking and academic learning.

In one *barrio* I noticed that many of the dogs had scars and stitches, and remarked upon this. The workers told me that they were 'auxiliary' health workers, used by those who were learning minor surgery to practise how to give injections and stitch wounds. The workers first inject melons, papayas and other fruit in order to get the 'feel' of the needle as it is inserted , and then 'sew' a variety of skin-like substances as part of their training before turning to the animals. All the dogs had recovered satisfactorily.

In evaluating community-based health programmes in the Philippines, a number of lessons have to be learned. For example, there is a need to redefine self-reliance. *Barrios* cannot operate on their own in meeting the health needs of their people. They are too poor. Genuine self-reliance can only come about through a more even distribution of health services in the country. And this means a more even distribution of monetary income for each family. While the development of herbal remedies remains most desirable – and I have seen how these are used to good effect for both internal and external conditions – it is wrong to suppose that certain groups should have to depend on a simplified 'cheap alternative' health care system. Community-based health programmes can never be micro solutions to macro problems. That is why throughout each programme, workers are helped to analyse the causes of their sickness, to think about why so many people die before their time and are encouraged to seek solutions to their problems outside the narrow band of health care.

Health workers have thus become involved in far wider political issues, and were increasingly regarded as 'subversives' by a government concerned only with the cost–benefit ratios of health care as part of its national and economic developmental schemes.

HOSPITAL CARE

In a 20-bed hospital in a river town in Mindanao, two nurses attended to the needs of the patients: 12 hours on duty, 12 hours off, seven days a week. Little wonder they took time off to saunter through the village during their period of duty, to chat and to do their shopping. Neither had been paid for two months, and they had been told that there was no money for the appointment of a third nurse. The hospital was without medicines. In keeping with tradition, relatives provided most of the patients' care, and brought in their food. The corridors and the small wards were dirty. There was little equipment. The building was more a gathering place for sick, dying and injured people rather than a hospital in the recognised sense.

Blood for transfusions is often difficult to obtain. People will wait outside hospital gates, willing to sell their blood as the need arises. Sometimes the donors themselves become ill – they have sold too much blood from their already malnourished bodies. Prisoners are always a source of blood for hospitals. When a supply is not available outside the hospital gates, inmates of the local prison will often sell the requisite number of pints.

There are, of course, better hospitals. Forty-six per cent of the beds are in Metro Manila where the ratio of beds is 1:640 people. Even in the city, however, health care is only for the rich. In Mindanao the ratio is one public health physician for every 38 520 population and one hospital bed for 1148 people. Seven out of ten Filipinos in the rural areas are born and die without ever seeing a doctor.

A friend of mine took his infant son to a government hospital. The child was seriously ill with a high fever. The administrator demanded 1000 pesos before he would agree to an admission. The child's parents had no money; they promised to find the money 'within a few days'. Their offer was refused, and the child died shortly afterwards.

Some hospitals staffed by missionary sisters ensure better standards, receiving medicine and equipment from funding agencies overseas. Occasionally, too, it is possible to come across a small provincial hospital providing adequate care. I had one experience in Luzon. A companion was overcome with exhaustion at a place high in the mountains on a visit to the Bontoc tribe. She hallucinated and eventually fell unconscious. Members of the tribe carried the girl hour after hour up and down the mountain slopes and across rivers and streams, her body wrapped in a blanket slung between two poles. On arrival at Bontoc Hospital two large bottles of saline drip were purchased, the tubes were connected, and 24 hours later the girl had recovered sufficiently to be discharged. In this case there was a simple solution to what was initially quite frightening, and could so easily have resulted in death.

For one other young girl the outcome was different. At a mental hospital in Luzon, on the edge of Mariveles, there are 900 patients, 700 male and 200 female. About 200 patients wander almost unsupervised about the open campus and into the adjacent *barrios*, where they are responded to with friendship by the local people. Some earn a few pesos a day by working in the grounds of the hospital. All wear T-shirts with the insignia of the hospital on the front and the word RESIDENT in two-inch capital letters on the back.

Two doctors look after the patients, one recently qualified and dedicated to serving the needs of the people of his region of origin, together with medical and other assistants, few in number. Some patients live in hide-outs in the crumbling ruins of a building half-destroyed by air attacks during the Second World War. Others are permanently locked up, even chained, as many as 12 to a cell 'designed' for four. They never leave their cells.

In the female section some women stretched through the thick wooden bars of one cage to touch me with calls of 'Hi, Joe!' and 'Hi, man!' Their cries, looks and dishevelled appearance were reminiscent of the most horrific American films about life in mental hospitals. Three women were naked. One was masturbating. Dignity and respect had been abandoned.

Outside the cage on a wooden board a girl in her later teens lay unconscious. The young doctor connected a saline drip as the flies settled freely on her legs, arms and face. Somebody pulled down her dress in an attempt to cover her knees. The girl was severely dehydrated. Apparently she had not been communicating for some time (the orderly could not recall whether it was for days or hours) and had subsequently collapsed. The care and attention needed for her survival were just not available. I found it difficult to walk away. Later it was learned that she had died.

MALNUTRITION

The health situation of the Filipino people is of serious concern both because of the types and magnitude of illnesses suffered and because much disease can so easily be prevented. And the prevailing health conditions must always be viewed within the context of the interrelationship between the existing economic and political crisis, and the abject poverty of so many people at the level of the family.

The most common health problem is malnutrition. While this may not necessarily kill its victims, it makes people highly susceptible to other common diseases. It is estimated that at least 70 per cent of the population are malnourished. Despite their rich agricultural lands Filipinos have a very low per capita calorie intake. Even government surveys show that for the population as a whole the average daily diet contains only 87 per cent of the recommended daily allowance of calories. Two-thirds of families are generally too poor to afford a nutritionally adequate diet. Young children are most affected by malnutrition as is clearly seen in Table 3.1.

Table 3.1

Pre-school children (%)	Degree of malnutrition
46	first degree
26	second degree
7	third degree (causes severe underdevelopment or death)
Total: 79% malnourished	

Pregnant women most often receive only 64 per cent of the necessary calories, while nursing mothers have only 46 per cent of their requirements met. Breastfeeding until the infant is two or three years old exhausts the women, most of whom also try to make some contribution to the family income. Women breastfeed their older infants simply because there is no money to buy milk or food.

I had one meal in the company of 11-year-old Bernadette, with a weeping tropical ulcer irritated by sand on her right leg. She ate only rice and soy sauce, the diet to which she had become accustomed.

COMMON CAUSES OF DEATH

The five most common causes of death in the Philippines are pneumonia; tuberculosis; heart disease; gastro-enteritis and colitis;

and vascular diseases. Eighty per cent of these and other diseases in the Philippines can be prevented by good diet and proper sanitation. These killer diseases illustrate the significance of malnutrition, poor housing, and inadequate sanitation and waste disposal in the spread of communicable diseases. Both pneumonia and tuberculosis, for example, are airborne, and affect only those people within close range of the original carrier. Overcrowded living conditions combined with low resistance due to poor diet ensures a permanent pool of contagion. Pneumonia, often suffered by infants, kills one out of every two of its victims in the Philippines. Long before reaching adolescence 40 per cent of children die, mainly as a result of drinking unsafe water. Since only 40 per cent of the population have access to potable water, and only 5 per cent have a sewerage system, gastro-enteritis is a constantly recurring and debilitating disease. Infant mortality is placed at 65 out of every 1000. After gasping for breath for two days, six-month-old Beni (a word from the Manobo tribe meaning 'seedling') died at 4 a.m. He received a blessing from the chapel leader – the priest was too far from the remote village – and was buried the same afternoon. The sight of small, home-made coffins being carried to the cemetery – in one case being transported in a shoe box on a bicycle – is a powerful reminder of the deprivation of the people.

PHILIPPINE HEALTH IN FIGURES

- 79 per cent of Filipino children suffer from malnutrition.
- 62 out of every 100 Filipinos die without any medical attention.
- The Philippines has the highest rates in the world for whooping cough, diphtheria and rabies.
- In the entire Western Pacific region, the country has the highest rates for tuberculosis, schistosomiasis and polio.
- According to the Asian Development Bank, Filipinos have the lowest average food intake in Asia, lower even than in Bangladesh.
- Of the 70 per cent of Filipinos who live in rural areas, only 10 per cent benefit from the services of medical doctors. Yet, the Philippines is the world's largest exporter of nurses and the second largest exporter of doctors.
- 46 per cent of all hospital beds are in Manila where only 12 per cent of the population lives.
- 808 towns lack health centres.
- In Mindanao there is only one public health physician for 38 520 people.
- Fifteen million Filipinos belong to families with incomes of less than 6000 pesos a year or 500 pesos a month.

The story is told of Carlo, a young worker, father of three, who was sacked from his job for his role in leading a strike in a Manila factory. As jobs were hard to find, especially for a militant unionist, his family had to make do with very little. One evening, his youngest son, barely two years old, was crying loudly and could not sleep. The poor boy was very hungry. Carlo lifted his arm and with all the strength in him, whacked his son on the back until the boy finally stopped crying and fell asleep, all thought of hunger forgotten. Then, it was his father's turn to cry.

Tribal Filipinos, who make up 16 per cent of the population, are among the most disadvantaged groups. Childbirth in some of the 60 tribes is a painful and difficult experience. Among the Dumagats, for example, only the traditional birth attendant assists the mother during labour. To cut the umbilical cord a sharpened bamboo stick is used.

Many of the Muslim poor remain out of reach. It is known that they suffer from chronic protein deficiency, and that the mortality rate in the 0–12 months age group may be as high as 60 per cent in some communities; nobody really knows. Large numbers suffer from tuberculosis. Concepts of hygiene are primitive and a great deal of disease is communicated by the practice of mothers masticating food for their young children.

Parents are constantly faced with decisions about the care of children: whether to spend money on a sick child or to buy food for those who have a chance of survival. I was present in a community when such a decision was being made. The previous year the family, in a remote rural area, had spent, for them, a considerable sum of money in transporting their 8-year-old son to hospital and buying medicines. The boy died three days after admission. A great deal of money had been used. Faced with a parallel situation a year later – this time their 12-year-old daughter was ill – the same decision was made. They would put themselves into debt in order to provide the necessary medical care. On this occasion neighbours came to the aid of the family, sharing the costs. Tata, the young girl, recovered and returned to her community within two weeks.

While specialist drugs are, of course, essential for the treatment of some illnesses and the recovery of the patient, Western approaches to health care and Western concepts of the doctor–patient relationship are, generally, less relevant. I accompanied a Filipino doctor on one of his infrequent '*barrio* rounds'. The surgery was held in the open-sided chapel. The altar became the doctor's table.

The pews were filled by those who wanted diagnosis or treatment, and by others who merely came to watch. I met Luerte. He was a fortunate patient who recovered. Following an accident at home his damaged leg was untreated and later had to be amputated above the knee. This 10-year-old boy had then been neglected and gangrene had set in. In Luerte's case money was also found to pay for injections and admission to hospital.

There were many children present in the chapel, more onlookers than patients. One mother brought her very sick child (meningitis was diagnosed); a man was concerned about his very large scrotum, and in terrible pain; two people had goitres; several people were suffering from high blood pressure (many Filipinos live almost exclusively on rice and *ginamos*, dried salted fish); and an 18-year-old youth had schistosomiasis.

SCHISTOSOMIASIS

Schistosomiasis is endemic in 22 provinces. The eggs of the parasite, *Schistosoma japonicum*, are passed with the stools of an infected person or animal, and hatch into larvae when they contact water. These larvae live in tiny snails for 4–5 weeks before multiplying into several hundred cercariae which then secrete a toxic substance to penetrate the skin of a human, a rat or a farm animal, and enter the bloodstream. Rice fields, irrigation channels and shallow, slow-flowing rivers where people wash and swim are sources of schistosomiasis. The parasites attack the intestines and the brain of both young people and adults, and death is painful. Stick-thin legs, yellow skin, pale eyes and, above all, a distended stomach are the principal outward signs of the disease. To ease the pain of a dying person, unable to stand or lie comfortably in any position, a cradle is sometimes made to support the patient in a leaning position. To ease the pressure and the pain in her stomach one woman drove a knife into her belly in order to release the huge amount of fluid inside her.

There are probably more than one million cases of schistosomiasis. In Gandarra, Western Samar, in one of the worst affected *barrios*, out of a population of 334 people, 280 suffer from schistosomiasis, that is, 84 per cent. The river is infested: the main source of water for irrigation of the rice fields, for washing, and the only means of transport to the outlying *barrios*. The nurse responsible for the schistosomiasis eradication programme received only 400 pesos instead of the 1800 pesos she was originally allocated for the scheme. The money just 'disappeared' on its way to the people. Health workers are paid an 'incentive' equal to the total cost of implementation, but corruption – as in other areas of public spending – drains away money from the government's rural health programme. Thirteen-year-old Perlita was cured – with financial help from a charitable organisation. She was proud of herself. She went to hospital and, although running away once, was persuaded to return and receive treatment. A companion who refused to stay in hospital died. Perlita's slightly older neighbour, Lawin, showed me his 'fat tummy'. His parents had no money for hospitals. There was no medicine in the village. He, too, is probably now dead.

RESPIRATORY INFECTIONS

Respiratory illnesses are the biggest, most ruthless killer of Filipinos. Throughout the world such illnesses are an enormous public health concern, and death rates in developing countries like the Philippines are often 20 to 50 times higher than in countries in the West. This is largely explained by the severe disparity in living conditions and health resources between rich and poor countries.

Like all communicable diseases, the occurrence of respiratory infections is the end result of two opposing factors: on the one hand, the strength or virulence of the germs causing the infection and, on the other, the capacity of the individual to resist the infection. Both factors are influenced by biological conditions. But more important, from the public health point of view, are the social and environmental determinants of respiratory infections, for even biological conditions are, to a large extent, influenced by them. For instance, polluted and congested environments are excellent breeding grounds for germs. Transmission from one individual to another also occurs more easily under such conditions. On the other hand, patient resistance is hampered by poor living conditions which adversely affect nutritional and immunological status. The capacity to resist is lowest among infants and young children whose biological defences against germs are not yet developed; and among frail, elderly people.

This point was proved by an extensive study recently conducted by the Ministry of Health among children aged four years and below from a poor community in Quezon city, Metro Manila. The study isolated four major risk factors which predisposed children to contracting respiratory illnesses: (a) low socio-economic status; (b) malnutrition; (c) a congested home environment; and (d) the absence of immunisation. Respiratory illnesses were found to occur more frequently among low-income compared to middle-income families; among second and third degree malnourished children compared to normal and first degree malnourished subjects; among households with sleeping densities of more than three per room; and among children with no vaccination for diphtheria, pertussis and tetanus. Malnutrition also increases the chances of fatality in cases of acute respiratory infection.

Other risk factors include domestic and environmental pollution, low birth weight, parental smoking and the absence of breastfeeding. The increase in cigarette smoking is important. Many Filipinos just buy one or two cigarettes at a time; they are very cheap. As in other Third World countries there are no restrictions on their sale, and 'government health warnings' are unknown.

Socio-economic conditions are a crucial factor, determining to a large extent the patient's nutrition, access to health services and household overcrowding. In short, respiratory infections breed on poverty. This is the main reason why in the Philippines, where poverty and underdevelopment prevail, acute respiratory infections continue to claim tens of thousands of young Filipino lives.

Aware of the severity of the problem, the government has slowly taken steps towards the reduction of respiratory infection. A National Committee was established by the Ministry of Health in 1979 to undertake the formulation of a national programme of management and control. The long-term objective is a tenfold reduction in mortality from acute respiratory infection as proposed by the World Health Organisation in line with its goal of 'health for all by the year 2000'. To meet this objective three phases of work have been identified: (a) the improvement of patient management by using primary health care structures; (b) prevention through the use of vaccines; and (c) stimulation of social and environmental change to prevent infection and enhance resistance to disease.

Whether or not a genuinely community-based programme can be formulated by the national government on the basis of its researches, and whether or not such a programme will be implemented effectively on a nationwide scale, remain to be seen. Meanwhile, the following is re-enacted day by day, month by month, as the battle for life continues:

A young woman in rags cried as she cradled the cold, limp body of her firstborn. The provincial hospital's admitting doctor had just pronounced the baby dead after less than three hours' struggle to save him. Beyond the continuous administration of oxygen, the massive intravenous medications and finally the frantic efforts of revival, nothing more could be done. Only a few days previously the mother was convinced that her child was afflicted with nothing more than a common cold. It seemed to make no difference that the baby's resistance had just been drained by a bout of measles, that he was pitifully malnourished, or that he had never been immunised. Only when the fever failed to subside and the breathing became increasingly laboured did the woman and her husband decide to take their child on the difficult four-hour journey from their *sitio* to the *barrio* proper and from there to the hospital. By then it was too late. Pneumonia, the dreaded infant killer, was claiming another victim.

BLINDNESS

On one of my first visits to the Philippines I noticed that very few people seemed to wear spectacles. Naively, I thought that they must have good eyesight and contrasted what I saw with the situation in Hong Kong, less than two hours' flying time away, where a very high percentage of the population has glasses. I soon realised, however, that in the Philippines the absence of spectacles, the poor eyesight of the people and the high incidence of blindness were further manifestations of the poverty experienced by so many.

In 1970 the number of blind Filipinos was no more than 380 000. Today the figure is 1.3 million. By the year 2000 it is expected to reach two million. Children are especially vulnerable. Nearly 11 per cent of those affected are no more than ten years of age. This high percentage is particularly alarming in view of the fact that a survey made in the mid-1970s showed zero prevalence in the same age group.

By the time a Filipino reaches the age of peak productivity the chances of going blind are much greater. Close to 47 per cent of blind Filipinos are of working age. Some manufacturing processes in which Filipinos are engaged – for example, working through microscopes for long hours each day in the Bataan Export Processing Zone, Mariveles, Luzon – can destroy the eyesight of young girls in two years.

Why are so many Filipinos going blind? Official surveys up to 1969 revealed the following leading causes of blindness in the country: cataract (31 to 36 per cent of cases), eye injuries (25 per cent), corneal scars, glaucoma, diseases of the retina and optic nerve, and phthisis. Data compiled in 1975 and 1976 showed essentially the same pattern but with an increase to 51.5 per cent in the case of cataract.

BLINDNESS IN THE PHILIPPINES: TEN FACTS

● Today 1.3 million Filipinos are blind.
● Blind people make up 2.5 per cent of the population, that is, one in 40 Filipinos.
● The Philippines has the third largest number of blind people in the world (next to Saudi Arabia and Yemen).
● By the year 2000 two million Filipinos are expected to be blind.
● Almost half of those who are blind are of working age. One out of every ten is only 10 years old or less.
● Half of the cases of blindness in the Philippines are preventable. Six out of every ten are remediable, if treated early.
● Three out of every ten Filipinos need spectacles. Of these, only 7.5 per cent actually wear them.
● More than 8 per cent of Filipino children have untreated eye problems.
● There is only one eye specialist available for every 200 possible Filipino eye patients.
● Almost nine out of ten of these eye specialists practise in Metro Manila.

In 1982 the World Health Organisation expressed concern about the spread of four eye diseases which threaten to double the number of blind people by the next century, particularly in developing countries. These are: (a) trachoma, a contagious disease caused by a virus; (b) xerophthalmia, a condition caused by vitamin A deficiency; (c) onchocerciasis, river blindness due to a water-breeding parasite; and (d) cataract.

It has been estimated that 50 per cent of the causes of blindness in the Philippines can be prevented. Up to 60 per cent of these diseases are remediable, if seen and treated early. Take the case of xerophthalmia. In the early stages, lack of vitamin A, which is needed to nourish the outer linings of the body including the eyes and the skin, manifests as night blindness and drying of the outer surface of the eye. When the deficiency is not corrected the cornea becomes hazy and the eye surface softens. In the final stage the eye literally pops out of its ruptured enclosure, a condition called phthisis bulbi.

It seems that, in every village community, there are blind people. Sometimes whole families are blind. More than 80 000 people could have had their sight saved had they been treated early enough. However, too often there are also accidents. Seventeen-year-old Isaleo is blind, his eye cavities mutilated. Both arms are severed below the elbows. He lost sight and limbs 'dynamite fishing', a few hundred yards from his home on the shore. Young children lead blind adults around as guide dogs do in the West.

I met one blind family in Cagayan de Oro city: father, mother and their three young sons. Their blindness had been traced directly to vitamin A deficiency. They were being cared for by a Filipino nun who, single-handed, ran a small community for those experiencing extreme deprivation: a limbless man; a badly-scarred 10-year-old girl, the victim of physical abuse; a mentally handicapped mother and her adult daughter, also mentally handicapped; two tiny infants lying in boxes covered with muslin under the shade of a tree; and an 80-year-old woman on the point of death. Mr and Mrs Callad and their sons sat silently, the boys aimlessly making 'patterns' with sticks in the dust. They were bewildered and anxious, trying to make sense of a world that had gradually become black.

LEPROSY

Leprosy has been known in South-east Asia since the 14th century. Worldwide there are thought to be about 15 million cases. Feared since biblical times because of its disfiguring results, it is prevalent in several areas of the Philippines. The incidence in males is greater than in females, and children are more susceptible than adults. Figures are available showing an increased number of cases in the Philippines during recent years, but the government is not prepared to release them. Because of poor data collection it may well be that the number of people suffering from the disease has reached alarming proportions.

I visited one leprosarium in the south of Mindanao, near Zamboanga city, housing 700 patients. It proved a unique experience: coping with the disfigurement of the patients; their poverty; their alienation from the mainstream of society; their natural desire to shake hands, embrace and be touched – difficult but possible, and so rewarding; and the fact that the 700 people included whole families, Christian and Muslim, with many children at risk.

The prognosis is poor without treatment, but a wide range of treatments is currently available. The lack of money in the Philippines prevents many people from receiving medication, and thus the disease spreads. And very old fears live on. Men and women described how, when the leprosarium was moved to its present location a few years ago they were jeered, stoned and spat upon by residents of the surrounding area. Only slowly have very strong feelings begun to subside.

THE DRUG INDUSTRY

The multi-million drug industry makes vast profits from the poor health of the Filipino people. Fifty per cent of the total health expenditure goes on drugs, none of which can cure poverty. Seventy per cent of the market is in the hands of 26 different multinational corporations; 26 per cent is owned by one Filipino company, United Laboratories, which has international links; and the remaining 4 per cent is controlled by several Filipino businessmen. So lucrative is the industry that 28 of the drug companies rank among the top 1000 corporations in the Philippines. Multinationals operating in the country include the world's leading drug companies which control and undertake most of the research and developmental work in the pharmaceutical sector and dominate the drug industry worldwide, except for the socialist countries. Among these companies are Pfizer, Bristol-Myers, Squibb and Upjohn.

In the Philippines the huge profits are made by various means. Ninety-five per cent of raw materials for drug manufacturing is imported, even though most of the materials can be found in the Philippines. Importation enables the companies to manipulate the cost of the materials to their utmost advantage. The gross overcharging enables the company to repatriate large profits to the mother country without having to pay taxes on this portion. In addition, royalty payments are made to the mother company, enabling the company to withhold taxes in the Philippines. Drug companies make a further profit by using cheap labour to package and distribute the drugs.

The Philippines has the highest drug prices in South-east Asia. Some items are even more expensive than in the United States or Europe. Librium and valium, for instance, are sold at prices as much as 1000 per cent higher than in the UK. Often the same drug is sold under a different brand name, but the newer brand is sold at a higher price.

Promotion costs also increase the price. This promotion, as elsewhere, is mainly through distributing free samples to doctors, organising health seminars for health personnel, and even providing world trips for doctors. The advertising campaigns are so fierce that people are led to believe that the more expensive the drug the better it is.

Besides paying for overpriced drugs, Filipinos also consume hazardous drugs which are banned in the home country of the multinational and dumped in the Philippines and other Third World countries. Many of these drugs can be fatal if misused. Multinational corporations market these products aggressively in the Philippines, unhampered by government regulations which exist in their home countries. Such dangerous drugs as dipyrone, clioquinol and chloramphenicol – an antibiotic which is known to cause aplastic anaemia – are recommended for wide usage in the Philippines. Under supervision some of these drugs can be valuable, but their side-effects are so devastating that their use is severely restricted or banned in Europe or the USA. Yet, these drugs are dumped indiscriminately in the Philippines and many of them can be bought over the counter. It is not unusual for drugs which are prohibited abroad to be registered with the Food and Drug Administration in the Philippines and easily available.

Chloromycetin is a typical example of drug dumping. This is a valuable antibiotic which is effective against typhoid fever, but it has such enormous risks to the user that there is very restricted use of the drug in the United States where it is manufactured. This, combined with the fact that there is a much lower incidence of typhoid in America, has led to an aggressive campaign in the promotion of the drug in the Philippines. It is now used indiscriminately as an antibiotic against a broad range of infections because no warning as to its side-effects has ever been given to consumers. Some years ago, following a typhoon disaster, the Philippines received a huge consignment as relief aid. When questioned about its side-effects the answer was given that Filipinos have a different reaction to the drug from Europeans and Americans.

Fifty per cent of all drug sales are in Manila which has only one-fifth of the total population. In 1984, nine million pesos was spent on weight-reducing drugs while only 150 000 pesos was spent on anti-leprosy drugs, or less than 15 pesos on each patient with leprosy. More than five million pesos was spent on cholesterol reducers while 70 per cent of the population suffers from malnutrition. Expenditure on drugs depends on purchasing power rather than on individual needs. Because of this, vital drugs which can arrest disease are unavailable to the vast majority who cannot afford the high cost of medicines.

Towards the end of 1985 the US President, Ronald Reagan, proposed that Congress should repeal an existing ban on the export of drugs not approved for use in America, the proposal being part of a trade policy that focuses on the opening of foreign markets to American goods, rather than the protection of domestic industries. Those advocating the repeal say that the USA should not 'refuse to allow another country to buy drugs it believes will help its people'. It is important to note that the United Nations and the World Health Organisation support the policy that drug restrictions are the responsibility of the importing, not the exporting, country. The Philippines does not have the scientific capability to evaluate the hazards of certain drugs. Why should Filipinos become the guinea-pigs of the American drug industry?

BREAST- AND BOTTLE-FEEDING

The promotional efforts of milk companies in Third World countries urging women to bottle-feed rather than breastfeed their babies has been well aired during recent years. The industry in the Philippines is 100 per cent foreign-owned. The aggressive sales campaigns are similar to those used by the drug companies, demonstrating how unscrupulous multinational corporations increase their profits at the expense of people's health and well-being. In a country like the Philippines with its growing population there is a ready market.

Among poor people the choice between breastfeeding and bottle-feeding is often a choice between health and disease, between life and death. Bottle-feeding is expensive and requires hygienic facilities for preparation. Many mothers endeavour to make a can of milk last longer by feeding their babies with over-diluted milk. Infants fed with over-diluted milk prepared under unhygienic conditions often develop diarrhoea which may later lead to protein–energy malnutrition. Diarrhoea is rampant among bottle-fed babies and is the prime cause of mortality in children under one year of age.

Although many milk companies have today modified their

promotional strategies, their advertisements continue to mislead and discourage breastfeeding. The new theme is 'mixed feeding', bottle and breast, with the formula presented as a supplement to mother's milk. Local milk cans carry labels endorsing this mixed feeding approach. One product says: 'Breast milk is best for your infant and is preferred feeding whenever possible. This product is a sound nutritious substitute or supplement for breast milk, to be used *when breastfeeding is unsuccessful, inappropriate or stopped early.*' Another states: 'Breast milk is the preferred feeding for newborns. Infant formula is intended to replace or supplement breast milk when breastfeeding is not possible or is insufficient or when mothers elect not to breastfeed.' The mixed feeding concept offers the companies several important advantages. Breastfeeding can be openly encouraged, earning for the companies public service recognition. At the same time these companies can effectively discourage breastfeeding by implying that a mother may not have enough milk to breastfeed or may prefer not to do so.

The supply of milk to nearly every hospital in Metro Manila remains an effective method of promotion. The arrangement varies from hospital to hospital. Some hospitals are exclusively supplied by only one milk company. In most cases, however, the 'flavour of the month' arrangement prevails. In this the patronage of different milk companies is rotated on a monthly basis. Sometimes the rotation happens on a ten-day period. For instance, Product A will be given to the infants in the nurseries during the first ten days of the month, Product B will be fed for the next ten days and Product C for the last ten days.

This arrangement also prevents mothers from breastfeeding, hospital authorities suggesting that babies must be confined to the sterile surroundings of the nursery to avoid infection. The association of promotional and educational materials with hospitals and the medical profession gives 'respectability' to bottle feeding. In rural areas, however, where promotional activities are equally strong, mothers do not always have the benefit of instruction in the preparation of the formula, increasing the risk of disease.

Apart from the economic exploitation of the poor, there is the continued practice of 'dumping' items other than medicines. Products deemed unfit or harmful to Caucasian babies are sometimes exported for consumption by Filipino infants. There have been instances of imported milk arriving without a date stamp. In other cases the product was to be sold beyond the expiry date, or the date stamp had been tampered with. When discovered, the company involved merely regrets an 'error' and offers to ship back the consignment to the country of origin.

BATAAN EXPORT PROCESSING ZONE

The 'open door' policy of the Marcos regime which brought so many multinationals, eager to avail themselves of cheap labour and raw materials, to the Philippines has had a profound effect on the health of the Filipino people, particularly on workers and farmers. Many factory workers die or are injured because of poor working conditions. Health and safety standards – where they exist – are violated at will. The cost of 'development' is often paid for by even lower health standards.

Export processing zones, offering benefits and incentives to overseas multinational corporations are a comparatively new phenomenon in international trade. They are found throughout Asia. The Bataan Export Processing Zone (BEPZ), situated about 170 kilometres by road from Manila, was created in 1968 under Republic Act No. 5490 which declared 1029 hectares of Mariveles in Bataan to be administered by the Export Processing Zone Authority. Operations began in 1975. Over 60 companies now have factories and industrial concerns there, manufacturing, among other things, heavy metal products, electronics, plastic and rubber goods, fibreglass boats, food products and clothes.

The BEPZ administrator once said that living and working conditions and facilities would be 'consistent with international standards'. Indeed, for the Zone executives, many of whom are foreigners, and for visiting dignitaries, every comfort is available. There is, too, an elaborate church, and luxury hotels and a spacious administration building provide the image designed to attract investors and the multinational corporations. A wall plaque extols the virtues of the enterprise, 'where labour and dignity can stand side by side'. On one visit to the Zone I posed as a buyer, intent on placing a huge order for jeans. The comfort I experienced in the administration building – in contrast to that of the workers I had left minutes previously – was quite unsettling, but served to reinforce the reality of life for the 70 000 or more workers and their families who have flocked to the Zone. About half of the workers are under 25 years of age, 80 per cent of them women.

The 'housing' BEPZ claims to provide for its workers accommodates less than 10 000 workers. In the Sampaguita Dormitory (*sampaguita* is the national flower of the Philippines) there are about 600 women workers, groups of eight women sleeping in narrow bunk beds in a room eight metres by four metres. Their laundry hangs on clothes lines criss-crossed all over the room. Water comes only during specific hours of the day. This gives the boarders a difficult time in coping with the washing and cleaning they have to do. The stench from the toilets pervades the length of the corridors. In the Cadena de Amor dormitory, 14 girls sleep in one room, and the complete lack of privacy has reportedly had an adverse effect on the emotional stability of the women workers who endure considerable stress in the factories.

Most workers live in the town of Mariveles, in squatter-type huts. With the arrival of thousands of workers, shanties mushroomed all over. Girls buy 'bedspace'. The smaller homes have 10 to 20 boarders while the larger ones have 50 to 60. Water is expensive and again, 12 or more people may sleep in a small room. One girl told me of her difficulty and embarrassment when she was suffering from diarrhoea and shared the use of the primitive toilet with 60 other people. At the end of a long shift most workers are stunned and exhausted, resting in their bedspaces on the floors of their shacks for as much as two hours before finding the strength to prepare a meal or wash their clothes.

Bronchitis and influenza are again easily spread in these overcrowded conditions. Gastro-enteritis and other faecally-related diseases arising from inadequate sanitation and contaminated drinking water are also leading causes of infant mortality. The mortality rates in Mariveles are revealing. The parish register shows that the death rate of children below six years of age has continued to rise since 1972. The percentage of deaths in the 0–5 years age group was 35 per cent in 1975, 63 per cent in 1977 and more than 70 per cent in 1983. There is also a high death rate among the 16–25 age group with an abnormally high incidence of deaths due to heart attacks, violence and bleeding ulcers.

Once inside the factories the workers have to suffer even worse conditions. Medical treatment is inadequate, many factories not even having a separate room for a clinic. Sometimes the nurses double as ordinary company employees. Minor injuries handled in the BEPZ hospital, and the cost of hospitalisation following accidents, are charged to the workers or to their social security system insurance. For more serious ailments it would cost more than 500 pesos for the one-way journey from Mariveles to Balanga where the nearest hospital is situated.

Common health problems cited by the workers include (a) fainting: from lack of food, poor ventilation, high stress because of quotas, continuous overtime, and the refusal of the supervisors to allow them to use the toilet; (b) eye strain: especially in watch-making and electronics factories; (c) poor breathing: resulting from fibres in the air which irritate the lungs, notably in the textile factories; and (d) headaches: from fatigue and the continuous noise of machines.

The common diseases of BEPZ workers are tuberculosis, ulcers, anaemia and urinary disorders. The number of tuberculosis victims is difficult to ascertain. No X-rays or sputum tests are conducted. Most workers do not return because they cannot tolerate the working conditions. The companies operating on the site have little concern for their employees. There are always 10 000 other young workers 'waiting in the wings' for employment.

However, the most insidious health hazard is stress. A common practice among many companies when export shipments are being prepared is forced overtime. Usual patterns are two to four hours overtime, 12-hour shifts or 14-hour shifts. Double (16 hours) and triple (24 hours) shifts are not unknown. Some factories demand prolonged overtime – 12 to 14 hour shifts each day – without any day off, for weeks at a time. The girls have to ask permission to go to the toilet – and they are often kept waiting; the high noise level in some factories is difficult to tolerate; and the workers only have a 15-minute lunch break. I spoke to one worker in a textile factory. She described how, just before the end of the shift, she was told of the need to work overtime. The huge sliding doors were locked and armed guards posted at each exit.

BEPZ is not far from a large AFP encampment, and some girls supplement their earnings in the beer houses in Mariveles, or are 'used' sexually by supervisory staff in return for favours during the physically and emotionally tortuous days at the workbench or on the assembly lines. Most girls are committed to sending money home in order to support their families and to help younger brothers and sisters, especially in respect of education.

Some of the young women are married and separated from their children. Their daily wages barely enable them to exist without the prospect of having to provide for dependants. Prostitution may bring in an extra 50 pesos a night for a girl working in the beer houses. Pregnancy for the factory girls is a tragedy, and they are immediately dismissed. Attempted abortions are common, and many abandoned babies are discovered, simply thrown away at birth by their desperate mothers. Leonie hid her pregnancy until very late. Her labour commenced unexpectedly. She was rushed to hospital in Balanga where her child was born. Leonie agreed to give the infant away to 'a man from Manila' – for adoption, it was said – and she was back at her workbench within a week.

Working in the Zone gives the girls an illusion of being better off. Each week they have cash in their hands. However, after deductions for food, water and bedspace they are, in effect, no more prosperous than their sisters who have remained in the *barrio* or on the farm. Above all, they are no longer free women, distorting Filipino values and traditions.

THE MINING INDUSTRY

Miners are among the hardest hit by occupational hazards. Apart from the high risk within the mine tunnels – and a number of recent incidents are detailed in Chapter 1 – miners are constantly exposed to mineral dust particles which predispose them to skin and lung cancer. At the Benguet Consolidated Mines, the largest gold mine in the country and US-owned, miners are further exposed to radioactivity when they are made to pass a detector each time they leave the mine pits. The detector checks whether they have been stealing gold ore from the mines.

Copper mining

The Atlas Consolidated Mining and Development Corporation, Asia's largest copper mining company, and the seventh biggest in the world operates in Toledo city in Cebu, Visayas. Here, too, the miners work under stressful and unhealthy conditions. Tuberculosis and lung diseases are common. There are also cases of gas poisoning, and of nystagmus, an eye ailment characterised by the inability to control the movement of the eye, uncontrollable shaking of the head and the inability to tolerate naked light. This condition is caused by spending too much time underground.

POLLUTION

Pollution is a growing hazard in the Philippines, and not only as a result of the urban congestion noted in Chapter 1. Many multinationals establish companies in the country partly to escape pollution controls in their own countries – controls which reduce profits. The Kawasaki sintering plant, for example, exported its pollution from Chiba, Japan to Mindanao after successful protests in Japan by environmentalists. Sintering is the second and most polluting stage of processing steel. During sintering, various impurities such as sulphur, arsenic, zinc and lead are removed from the steel in order to prepare it for the smelting process. Sulphur oxides, nitrogen oxides, arsenic acids and other pollutants are blown into the atmosphere and are extremely hazardous to the environment, and to health. Tuberculosis, bronchial asthma, chronic bronchitis and other pulmonary ailments are common illnesses suffered as a result of living near the plant.

Pollution of the sea is becoming an increasing problem. In Cebu city, for example, each year fishermen find it more difficult to earn their livelihood because of pollution caused by the many industries there. Rivers, too, become increasingly polluted. The copper mine in Cebu, for example, has caused extensive damage to the local rivers and surrounding land.

It is difficult to protest. Father Pedro Lucero, whose torture is described in Chapter 5, was imprisoned from 1983 to 1985, principally because he voiced over the radio the dangers of the 'red tide' in Samar. Thousands of fishermen lost their livelihoods as the river and coastal waters were poisoned.

NUCLEAR THREAT

In 1976 the Marcos regime started its preparations for the construction of the Bataan Nuclear Power Plant (BNPP) with the encouragement of the US government, backed up with generous loans from the Export–Import bank. The reactor is a 620 megawatt Westinghouse pressurised-water plant, originally meant to be operational in 1982. Delays resulted from protests and further negotiations, and in 1985 costs were already twice the first estimate.

The original estimated cost of the BNPP was US$883.3 million plus 1.7 billion pesos. The present cost has jumped to US$1.5 billion plus 4.16 billion pesos (*Business Day*, 29 August 1985). This translates to the oft-quoted price tag of about $1.9 billion. In order to operate the nuclear plant the Nuclear Power Corporation (NPC) needed another $22 million loan (which the US Export—Import Bank granted) to pay for spare parts and foreign consultants (*Business Day*, 22 August 1985). The loan cost is also huge. The interest payments on the loan amount to $350 000 a day. The cost of the BNPP makes up about 9 per cent of the country's foreign debt of $26 billion. Clearly, the BNPP is the costliest investment the Philippines has made. The country has no need for the reactor; it has been built for prestige, and creates an illusion of industrialisation. There is nobody to care for it.

The reactor is an obsolete 1970s model which Westinghouse, in an effort to increase its falling profits, exported to the Philippines, thereby escaping many of the safety regulations required in the USA. The absence of clear environmental regulations for such reactors, coupled with political repression in the Philippines, allowed Westinghouse and the NPC to proceed without opposition. The reactor is located in a community of about 14 000 people in Morong, Bataan. The energy generated is primarily for use in BEPZ, but also by US military installations, namely, at Subic Bay and Clarke Air Base.

One of the most serious hazards relates to the site selected for the nuclear plant, an area where earthquakes occur. The great Manila trench is only 60 miles off the coast and a major earthquake fault-line runs through Bataan province out to the South China Sea only 16 miles from the site. Furthermore, the US Department of Defense aerial imagery supplied to the National Power Corporation revealed faulting on the plant site itself but this report was suppressed. In addition, the Bataan coastline has experienced tidal waves, and the plant site is in the vicinity of five volcanoes. The town of Morong is on the slope of Mount Natib which is classified as a 'passive volcano'. The whole of the Philippines is part of the Pacific Belt, a ring of intense volcanic and earthquake activity. In the event of an earthquake or volcanic eruption, a meltdown could occur, causing a catastrophe. Hundreds of square miles would be contaminated and thousands would die. Survivors would suffer the effects of radiation.

There is a further hazard posed by the fact that the reactor had 200 safety faults. Many but not all of these have been remedied but a major shortcoming remains in relation to the cooling system. Its ineffectiveness can cause a meltdown.

The issue of waste disposal and storage has not yet been solved. There is no provision for the disposal or storage of nuclear waste in the Philippines. The reactor itself can supposedly handle 30 years (the lifetime of the reactor) of accumulated spent fuel rods and two and a half years of low level waste. The present plan is for waste to be sent to the USA for processing, for uranium enrichment and plutonium manufacture. Waste not wanted by the USA for processing will be shipped back to the Philippines. The annual cost will be enormous. After 30 years the reactor itself becomes nuclear waste, and will have to bc kept isolated for scores of years to avoid contamination of the surrounding area.

Already the local people are experiencing the effects of the plant on their lives. Rice fields and fish-spawning grounds have filled with sediment from the site and the fishing catch has declined by over 95 per cent. The reactor requires hundreds of gallons of water for cooling, the water being returned to the sea at a higher temperature. Gradually the ecology of the area will change, destroying the traditional livelihoods of the Morong people. The reactor is essential for US and other foreign interests. It will, therefore, eventually go ahead. Uranium ore from Australia will make the plant operational. Plans have been made for secret shipment. However, following the accident at the Chernobyl plant in the Ukraine in April 1986, the new government agreed to 'mothball' the plant for the time being.

Nuclear arms

The US bases in the Philippines have a stockpile of nuclear arms. The US Seventh Fleet carries nuclear missiles, posing a threat to the Filipino people. Because there are actual storage sites for nuclear weapons on the bases, the Philippines are an immediate target in the event of nuclear war.

FERTILISERS AND PESTICIDES

The Green Revolution, hailed as the salvation of poor farmers, has had devastating effects on the land and the people of the Philippines. Thousands of farmers are now faced with the choice of either using pesticides and fertilisers and risking poisoning, or not using these chemicals and facing starvation. This narrow choice is the result of agricultural developments pursued and encouraged by the WB and the Food and Agriculture Organisation. These two agencies, along with regional development banks have been pinpointed as the main agencies responsible for starting agricultural projects and programmes that involve the overuse and abuse of hazardous pesticides.

Miracle rice

Farmers have been encouraged over the past years to grow a new fast-growing variety of rice, developed by the International Rice Research Institute (IRRI), which was founded in the early 1960s by the Rockefeller and the Ford Foundations. The rice, known as 'Miracle Rice' because of its fast growing capacity, requires large amounts of fertiliser in order to be grown successfully. However, the hybrid seeds have been found to be highly susceptible to pests, so farmers are now forced to use pesticides to protect the plants. Besides being a constant financial drain, the pesticides also pose a serious health and environmental hazard.

The 'Miracle Rice' has institutionalised the use of fertilisers and other chemicals in farming, to the point where the industry has become extremely lucrative. Of the 17 fertiliser and 18 pesticide firms in the Philippines, 18 belong to the top 1000 corporations.

The largest fertiliser firm is Planters Products, on whose board sit top officials. Planters supplies 50 to 60 per cent of the country's fertiliser needs, followed by well-known names like the Maria Christina Fertiliser Corporation and the Atlas Fertiliser Corporation. But many of these firms, such as Planters, though Philippine-owned, merely package foreign-made products.

Several studies point out that 'Miracle Rice' and high-yield varieties have been developed in response to the heavy use of fertilisers and pesticides. Many of the US companies are supported by financial agencies like USAID, the Export–Import Bank and the WB, all of them controlled by US capital. Investing heavily in foreign interests these agencies' global operations provide loans to purchase pesticides and other agricultural products while completely ignoring the environmental impact of their loan projects. Many loans are closely tied to the fertiliser industry. Masagana 99, the Marcos government programme which aimed at rice self-sufficiency, uses only foreign pesticides. A total of 80 different brands of pesticides being used in Masagana are all foreign-based.

The National Rice Convention of rice farmers from Luzon, Visayas and Mindanao, held in July 1985, concluded that by linking rice and technology in the way that it did, the IRRI brought about the *Kumunoy ng Kahirapan* (Whirlpool of Poverty). Those attending the convention compared the 'slow white death' in the rural areas of the Philippines to the Bhopal tragedy in India. They pointed to the erosion of precious protein foods, namely frogs and fish; of the Philippine environment; and of cultural values and traditions. More directly they said: 'Thousands of Filipinos die in the countryside, unnoticed and unheralded. Thousands of Filipino people are dying even without a nuclear war.'

Pesticides and herbicides which are banned or have restricted usage in the USA and Europe are often exported and used extensively in the Philippines: 2-diprono 3-chloropropane, used by Del Monte to prevent worms from attacking pineapples, causes cancer and sterility and has been banned by the US Environmental Protection Agency. Phosvel, a brand name for an organophosphate, causes loss of coordination and lowers the ability to work, talk and think clearly; it has killed more than a thousand water buffaloes, and paralysed and asphyxiated an unknown number of farmers. Heptachlor, chlordane and endin, household names in agriculture in the Philippines, are associated with a range of chemically-induced diseases and birth defects.

The British government, too, is involved in the exposure of workers to spraying operations which would not be tolerated in the UK. Since 1982 the Commonwealth Development Corporation has been investing more than £6 million in palm oil plantations on the island of Mindanao. The project has been surrounded by controversy and the investment has been condemned by Amnesty International, the Anti-Slavery Society, the Philippine Support Group and others. Talking to workers just completing their shift demonstrates the disregard for safety on the plantations of those engaged in spraying the palm oil plants. Their reports clearly indicate the ways in which their health has been affected.

Environmental and health hazards

Environmental contamination and pollution are other dangers from fertilisers and pesticides. Only 28 per cent of the nitrogen of chemical fertilisers is absorbed by plants while the remaining 72 per cent goes into the air or seeps through the soil. Nitrogen wafted into the air becomes nitrous oxide which can destroy the ozone layer that gives protection from the ultra-violet rays of the sun. When the

Plate I: Children of the Philippines

(a)

(b)

Plate II: Everyday life: (a) Making rice cakes; (b) The pump is often the centre of the community

(a)

(b)

Plate III: (a) Mantoganoy; (b) During the mass wedding at Mantoganoy

(a)

(b)

Plate IV: (a) Pedal power in Jolo; (b) Mysterious fires often destroy large squatter areas

(a)

(b)

Plate V: (a) A farmer's small house made of *nipa*, near Lake Mainit, Agusan del Norte; (b) The Muslim communities are among the poorest. These children are Badjaos, a timid people who build their homes on stilts and flee easily in the face of danger

(a)

(b)

Plate VI: (a) Genus *Carabao*; (b) Sister Nanette (second from the right), to whom this book is dedicated, with the author and a group of health professionals

Plate VII: The memory of José Rizal lives. The painting depicting his life and death is in the museum at Fort Santiago, Manila

PHILIPPINES HISTORICAL COMMITTEE
1959

PRISON CELL OF JOSÉ RIZAL

IN THIS CELL JOSE RIZAL WAS DETAINED PRISONER FROM 3 NOVEMBER TO THE MORNING OF 29 DECEMBER 1896 FALSELY CHARGED WITH REBELLION, SEDITION AND FORMATION OF ILLEGAL SOCIETIES.

AFTER THE READING OF THE COURT SENTENCE AT 6:00 A.M. 29 DECEMBER, HE WAS KEPT IN AN IMPROVISED CHAPEL UNTIL HIS EXECUTION AT 7:03 A.M. 30 DECEMBER 1896 ON THE LUNETA, BAGUMBAYAN FIELD, MANILA.

(a)

(b)

Plate VIII: (a) The garbage tip in Manila is known as the Smoking Mountain; (b) Children and pigs rummage along the river bank

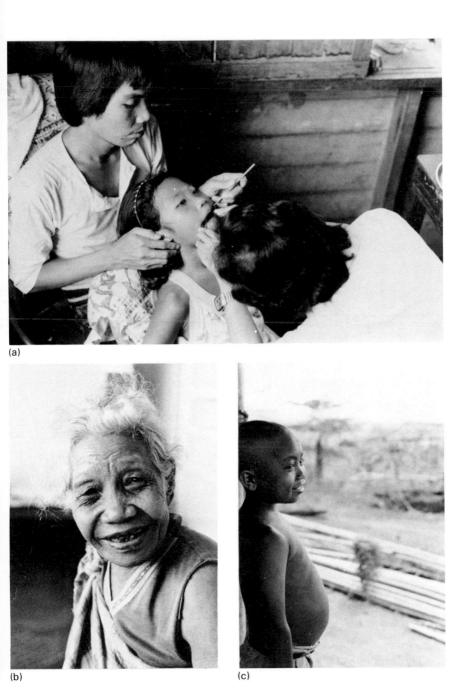

(a)

(b)

(c)

Plate IX: (a) Dolfs Bunag teaches a health worker to pull teeth, in Kitcharao; (b) A leper woman; (c) This boy's fat tummy is caused by schistosomiasis

(a)

(b)

Plate X: (a) Olongapo, a centre for prostitution; (b) Santa Monica, Manila, a centre for child prostitution

(a)

(b)

Plate XI: (a) Tribal woman and child. Tribal Filipinos are among the poorest people in the rural communities; (b) Attending a *bodong*, in Bontoc

(a)

(b)

(c)

Plate XII: (a) Father Brian Gore celebrating mass in prison. He was held on false charges of multiple murder for more than a year; (b) Father Pete, the smiling priest; (c) A loyal church worker, Albert Garrido

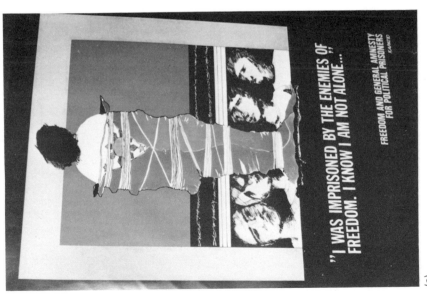

Plate XIII: (a) A KAPATID poster in the TFDP office, Manila; (b) A TFDP poster from Mindanao, where some of the worst atrocities have occurred

(a)

(b)

Plate XIV: (a) Informers, intelligence, insurgents or innocent bystanders? (b) Prison conditions are very poor

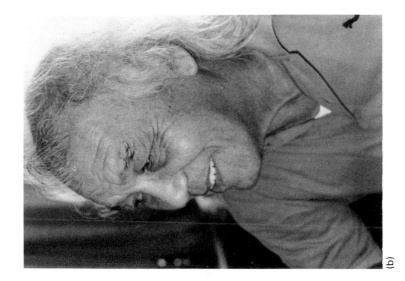

Plate XV: (a) Father Tullio Favali; (b) Cesar Climaco

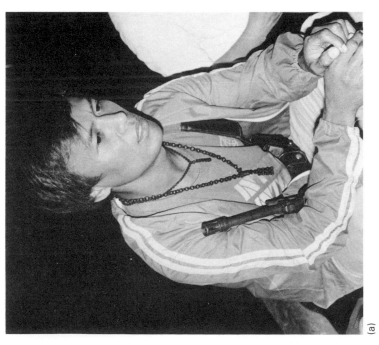

(b)

(a)

Plate XVI: (a) Conrado Balweg; (b) Marcos, tested in crisis: poster for 1986 election

concentration of nitrous oxide exceeds 45 parts per million it causes asphyxiation in infants. The same infants could later become victims of genetic deterioration since many studies reveal that the progressive build-up of lethal chemicals can alter a person's genetic make-up and also cause infertility. Cellular and tissue changes which lead to diseases like muscle paralysis, nervous system disorders, blurred vision, and speech and memory blocks, are other likely effects, as is cancer. The US National Cancer Institute links 20 chemicals and compounds to cancer, and pesticides and fertilisers are high on the list.

Chemical fertilisers also destroy the soil's organic matter, creating a barren agricultural environment that again requires more pesticides. The diminishing financial returns per acre put pressure on the government to devote more land to export crops in order to generate greater income.

Although toxic enough to rid crops of unwanted insects, most synthetic pesticides have produced resistance and immunity in these pests because of abuse and misuse. Increasing amounts are being applied and stronger compounds are being formulated. The resulting dosage, however, has a pronounced effect on friendly parasites and predators. Insecticide reduction appears an obvious solution, but this often entails loss to farmers who are already dependent on this system and who have not developed alternative organic programmes for coping with pests. Friendly insects are likewise eradicated, their natural functions in helping curb infestations discarded. Resistant species thus multiply faster.

The use of pesticides and fertilisers is certainly in the interests of the multinational chemical companies, and of the exporters of the crops which they help to produce. From the point of view of the people, however, the profits are reaped from poison.

A CULTURE OF POVERTY

In this chapter the interrelationship between sickness, disease and poverty has been described, showing how, for many people, the daily task is merely to find enough money to buy food to stay alive, to feed the children, and to pray that sickness and disease are kind enough to pass them by. Without money, without adequate food, without medical attention, people are rendered powerless. Theirs is a culture of poverty with its attendant affront to human dignity.

Living in a culture of poverty, sharing with the people of the Philippines the hazards and fears of their existence, and moving into the hearts and minds of some of the tens of thousands of men, women and children fighting for survival in the muddy, insanitary squalor which city dwellers – as well as peasant farmers, fishermen and tribal minorities – have to endure throughout their lives, and talking to the prostitutes who seek an alternative source of income for themselves and their families, has been for me, on every occasion, a painful and salutary experience.

The helplessness in their existence; the viciousness of their environment; and the absence of alternatives – except, perhaps, for some, prostitution – bite deeply. The predominant feeling is one of anger, anger present in all those people thus trampled on by society, and anger waiting to be released, harnessed and channelled into mass action.

NEGROS: A CASE STUDY

Various groups in the Philippines come to the fore at different times, evoking the concern, worldwide, of those who become aware of their plight. There seems no limit to the impoverished minorities, and majorities, in the Philippines: fishermen, tribal people, Muslims, the urban poor, the rural poor, beggars in the streets, the victims of disasters – natural and otherwise – political prisoners and grossly handicapped people included. In 1985 the spotlight was on Negros, a volcanic island in the central Philippines, whose two million inhabitants were reeling from the effects of a collapse of the world market price of sugar which stopped sugar production in the Philippines from the second quarter of the year.

The island of Negros – a beautiful island – has a sad history. With the arrival in 1856 of Nicholas Loney, a British colonizer, the port city of Iloilo fell into decline; a province was raped; local industry and initiative were destroyed; and an economic system established which ensured a life of increasing poverty for the vast majority of the people, and huge profits for the rich. Prior to Loney's arrival Iloilo was one of the most progressive cities of the New World comparing in size to Sydney, Chicago and Buenos Aires, and more than twice the size of Manila. A visiting historian at the time said it was 'the largest in agricultural production, the most active in manufacturing and one of the best instructed among the provinces'.

Iloilo survived the Spanish invasion successfully. As well as having an abundant rice crop, it had a shipyard, a fishing port and, most important of all, a textile industry that had 'reached a remarkable degree of development'.

It was one of the textile centres of the world at the time, having 80 000 looms at work each day. Said Loney: 'Almost every family possesses one or two of these primitive machines made of bamboo, while the majority of the *mestizos* and more well to do Visayans kept from six to one dozen looms at work.' So famous were their weaving mixtures of silk, cotton, pineapple and hemp that their markets were worldwide. Loney, a classic imperialist, did his homework well. The Western market needed sugar, the rich land of Negros was admirably suited for growing it, and Iloilo had all the human resources needed to be enslaved for its production. He studied the weaving industry and pirated its best patterns. Returning to Britain, where he was an agent for several Manchester textile firms, he had the patterns mass-produced by the cheap labour and machines of the Industrial Revolution. He then sent a shipload of the cheap textiles directly to Iloilo for export to its markets.

In one stroke he destroyed an independent industry and put an end to a way of life that had developed over generations. Twenty years later textiles were Negros's biggest import, constituting fully one-half of its total import by value.

Loney followed up his shipment of textiles with another ship loaded with coal and machinery for sugar production. The silenced looms had given him an educated elite of small capitalists and an army of hungry and jobless workers for the sugarcane fields. He inflamed the appetites of the elite with stories of vast fortunes to be made from sugar and gave them generous crop loans. He even gave them machinery at low cost and on an instalment system.

Then he led them and their private armies to sparsely populated areas round the slopes of 8000-foot high Kanla-on, where settlers from Panay had been farming small but viable lots for generations.

Life for the settlers had been peaceful and free with an abundance of foods. But now they were forcibly driven from their land to make way for the invaders, who bought for a pittance or 'landgrabbed' their holdings, and set up the *hacienda* or sugar-farm system which lasts up to this day.

Many of the leading Philippine families acquired their wealth in this way. For instance Teodoro Benedicto, a textile merchant, is on record as having acquired almost 10 000 hectares along the foot of

Kanla-on after 1871, by driving out the settlers by force of arms, killing many of them and burning their homes. In a unique historical document in the National Archives, 21 of these settlers give testimony that Benedicto's armies drove them off their land and deprived them of all their properties, even their standing crops. He assured continuous possession of these vast properties by paying off the local politicians and law-enforcing agencies.

Most Negrenses are accustomed to the *tiempos muertes* – the dead season – from April to September when most of the sugar mills are silent and the people out of work and hungry. In 1985, however, the 'dead season' took on a new meaning as most of the 350 000 sugar workers faced starvation, reduced to eating sweet potatoes and bananas once or twice a day. Others existed on meals of mice, frogs and snakes boiled in water with a sprinkling of salt.

Production of refined sugar in 1985 for both export and domestic markets dropped to 1.6 million tons from the previous year's figure of 2.3 million. In 1986 only 60 per cent of the 1985 hectarage is to be planted to sugar. The extremely depressed world market price of sugar is not helped by savage infighting at a local level. Massive graft and corruption, and abuse of government power, continued within the Philippine Sugar Commission (PHILSUCOM) and NASUTRA during 1985, both controlled by the former Ambassador to Japan, Roberto Benedicto.

A sugar worker in the *haciendas* of Negros is a third or fourth generation labourer in the canefields, knowing nothing but cane – as his father and grandfather before him. Some families in the nation's 'sugar bowl' trace their lineage back two centuries on Negros and, for most workers, the living conditions are similar to those found in the plain plantations of the West Indies and North America in the 1800s. People are trapped by feudalism. I spoke to one worker. 'What is your name?' I asked. 'I'm one of Tolentino's men,' he replied.

The regulated wage for agricultural workers is 32 pesos a day but in Negros less than 5 per cent of the *hacienderos* pay this amount. Most use the *pakyaw* system, operating their farms on piecework. *Pakyaw* rates vary but in Hacienda Javelosa, 50 kilometres from Escalante town in northern Negros, the workers still receive only four pesos a day, the same rate they were being paid in 1965.

At best, workers endure slave-like conditions:

(a) For loading cut cane, ten tons of it into a truck, 60 pesos is paid.

Since six people are required to finish the job in a day the average wage is 10 pesos for each worker.

(b) For weeding, the rate is 180 pesos per hectare. Gangs of 40 people finish two hectares a day, meaning that each worker receives 8.50 pesos.

(c) For ploughing a hectare of canefield, which a single ploughman can complete in three days, the total pay is 18 pesos, or 6 pesos a day.

(d) For fertilising, three sacks of fertiliser must be spread over a hectare of land. The pay is 10 pesos a day.

(e) For planting, which involves pushing cane stems into the earth, the rate is 4.50 pesos per thousand. The average daily earning is 13.50 pesos.

(f) For *pamatdan*, which is preparing the cane sticks for planting, the pay is 34 pesos per 10 000. A person usually averages about 3500 a day, giving daily earnings of 11.50 pesos.

Almost half the sugar workforce is younger than 15 years. In Binabuno town, for example, children start working at six or seven years old. Child labour is an integral part of life on the *haciendas* and is a by-product of the *pakyaw* system. When a man has work to complete – for instance, weeding – he cannot usually complete the task quickly enough so has to get help from members of the family in order to obtain the minimum daily wage needed for survival.

Working in the canefields, under the blistering Negros sun, is torture. Sweat drips into the children's eyes and blinds them. The sugarcane machete feels heavier and heavier. Many of the young people wear garments with long sleeves. The cane has very fine hairs along the stem which causes irritations and itchiness. Children are trained for nothing else but being a *hacienda* worker. The conditions under which they labour become worse each day.

People were starving to death in Negros in 1985. In a hospital serving Bacolod city and nearby areas, child deaths from malnutrition rose from 79 in 1983 to 172 in 1984 with nearly twice that figure in 1985. And that, of course, represents only those children whose parents could afford to transport them to hospital. In any case, the public hospital turns away victims of starvation every day because some 25 emaciated children already occupy its 14 beds. On the wards, the living skeletons lie two to a mattress, most suffering from nutritional diarrhoea, an advanced stage of malnutrition when the intestines cease functioning. These are children of our time.

The United Nations International Children's Emergency Fund (UNICEF) expressed alarm at the conditions people were experiencing. A spokesman for UNICEF, Bituin Gonzales, said in August, 1985 that a house-to-house weigh-in of children in two Negros towns and a city had revealed that from 8 to 14.4 per cent of all the children weighed were suffering from what the organisation described as protein–calorie malnutrition. A 2 per cent average of severely malnourished children is considered a public health problem. In Negros the rate is more than 5 per cent. The government made no response of any significance during 1985 to the appeal for massive food aid.

4 Prostitution

Prostitution is commonly associated with low incomes, and is attracting more and more girls – and children – in the Philippines. Sexual relationships outside marriage have traditionally been unacceptable to young people and their families within the framework of everyday religious life in the country. Of course, as in almost every town and city in the world, prostitutes have always been available, but the wholesale movement of Filipinas into prostitution is a comparatively new phenomenon. About 500 000 Filipinas are prostitutes – either full-time, or as a supplement to other employment. All run the risks associated with prostitution: venereal disease, psychological problems, violence from the clients, and even death at the hands of their employers – or clients. Yet, for the poor, and their families, there is also, except in the worst cases, access to food and health care – and to life itself.

There is, too, in the Philippines a ready supply of *bakla* (homosexuals), and cases of AIDS have now been confirmed in Manila.

It is often difficult for Filipinas to enjoy ordinary relationships with foreigners. Sadly, most girls seen with Europeans in certain parts of Manila, for example, are regarded by their compatriots as prostitutes. 'Now you will be all right for money' is a not uncommon remark from some passers-by to a local girl and her Western companion in downtown Manila, a comment deeply wounding to Filipinas sensitive to human values and human relationships.

Prostitution is by no means confined to Manila: Butuan city, Bacolod city, Zamboanga city, Cebu city and Davao city all have well-known areas where prostitutes can be found. In Magsaysay Park and Rizal Park, Davao city, for example, girls in their early teens seek customers from about six o'clock until midnight 'at prices that are lower than the price of pork and fish sold by the kilo'. Girls in Magsaysay Park have been known to offer companionship to men for less than 10 pesos an hour with an additional 5 peso charge for the use of a room in the slum area along Quezon Boulevard. On Davao city's Anda Street, just near busy San Pedro Street, Anda prostitutes are very much in evidence every evening. Enjoying higher status than the girls working in Magsaysay Park, the Anda Street group charge their customers from 50 to 250 pesos. At least

20 per cent of each girl's earnings goes to *bugaw* (pimps). Most policemen, themselves equally poor, either ignore the girls, looking to the left when the girls take up their road positions to the right; or settle for cash rewards or sexual favours.

In the Philippines there are three groups of clients: local men; 'tourists' – especially from Japan, Australia and West Germany; and American servicemen, stationed at or visiting the US bases. The main centres, in addition to Manila, are Cebu city, Olongapo city, and Angeles city – with Pagsanjan the focus of child prostitution. Angeles city nuzzles next to Clark Air Base; and Olongapo is adjacent to Subic Naval Base. Girls rarely work in their own part of the country; they nearly always move elsewhere, say, from Cebu to Manila, or from Samar or Leyte to Olongapo. In this way they feel able to hide at least some of their activities from their parents and neighbours. Entertainers in the bars in Tacloban city and Catbologan, Western Samar – both places with regular 'exports' of their own girls – have been recruited from Angeles city or Cebu city. Businessmen from Cebu will take their girls from Cebu for the weekend, staying at the popular Leyte Park Hotel.

The Chinese, too, are involved. Five girls were brought to Manila from the island of Palawan by a Chinese businessman and later raped, chained, tortured and imprisoned. One girl had her tongue cut out, another had her hair shaved. A third girl managed to escape, shouting 'I'll undress – don't kill me!' Some Chinese are pimps, or control other pimps. Many have strange beliefs and practices. One Chinese youth firmly believed that by going to bed with a virgin he would be cured of venereal disease.

It is foreigners who are responsible for the rapid development of prostitution, now posing a serious threat to the whole social fabric of the country. In Cebu city there are 2610 registered masseuses, catering for a large Japanese clientele. In 1984, there were 99 000 visitors to Cebu. Half were Japanese. In the same year there were 59 charter flights from Tokyo to Cebu – 'singles' tours. Visitors are met at the airport and driven to one of the many hotels situated in a picturesque area where – in addition to provision for Catholic mass twice weekly at 5 p.m. – there is a 24-hour massage service available. Most hotels have their own girls. Even from Hong Kong, travel agencies arrange 'special' tours, advertised as 'Forces singlemans [*sic*] tours to the Philippines'. In Manila, visitors on package tours will be taken to a bar during the evening where, often through a one-way screen, they may personally select their escorts and then leave the numbers of their hotel rooms. If desired, a different girl each night is part of the bargain. Prostitution – except in Olongapo – is illegal, but, as in other fields, the law is rarely enforced. In Cebu city, for instance, there is a byelaw which allows the police to remove girls from the bars – in their bikinis, or when they are found naked. It is common practice for the police to be given sexual favours by the girls in return for being released.

Manila, of course, remains a principal centre of prostitution, with Ermita the main red-light district. Two streets run parallel through the heart of it: M.H. del Pilar and Mabini. At night they come 'alive', offering every kind of bar, hostess and service. Girls hang around outside the bars during the early part of the evening, hoping to entice customers. Those who enter are persuaded to buy expensive drinks for themselves and their new escorts. But the main purpose of the bar is prostitution. In the peak season around December and January nearly 10 000 Australian men can be found patronising the whole range of establishments: from the dingy massage parlours to the lively ago-go bars where on mirrored stages girls in bikinis – or less – leap, tumble and gyrate all over the place, pushing their naked areas into the noses of patrons. Walking along M.H. del Pilar Street and Mabini Street the girls can sometimes be seen performing their routines – rubbing themselves against poles – through clear-glass windows. For customers with more money, there are night clubs with immaculately dressed hostesses, and it is even possible to be taken to a rented yacht where similar 'high-class' girls entertain their clients.

For most men the ago-go dancers on the mirrored stage have the greatest appeal. Having chosen a girl, the tourist beckons the mamasan, asking to speak with Louise or Carol or Pearl. Soon the girl leaves the stage. He buys her a drink, and soon the mamasan is being signalled again, this time to arrange the 'bar fine', that is, the amount that will secure the girl's services for the evening, or whole night. This is usually about 250 pesos. The girl goes to the back of the bar to change, and the couple later depart; or both will go upstairs to one of the several rooms – some mirrored – which are available for the girls and their clients. The girls in the foreign-owned establishments are more likely to be 'clean'. They have medical check-ups at least twice a week, or in the most expensive bars, often once a day. The girls pay for these check-ups themselves, about 50 pesos each time. According to her performance, the girl will usually receive a tip from her client at the end of the evening, or the next morning: probably about 250 pesos. The girls dislike Indians, and hate Arabs. Although most girls are on the pill, they will always encourage their clients to wear a condom: for extra security, and as protection against disease. Most prostitutes have the poorest living accommodation: as many as 20 girls in bunk beds in a small, shabby room. Often their 'leisure time', that is, mornings until about 12 noon or 3 p.m. is also strictly controlled.

Romeo's bar, at 11 p.m. on 17 January 1986, was probably little different from many other nights. The 12 bikini-clad girls took turns in groups of four to dance on the small stage for periods of 20 minutes, the others sitting at the bar – bored – or chatting to customers. One 40-year-old, thin-looking Australian sat near the stage; three much younger, 'beefy' Australian men stood behind him, drinking at the bar. Two Europeans sat in a far corner, with their arms around girls. One dark-skinned, swarthy man drank alone.

Some girls, 18 to 20 years, had exceptional vitality. Two were exceedingly attractive. Three others were much older, 'hard' and unhappy. The three men at the bar showed signs of nervousness, perhaps matching what they were experiencing as their own sexual inadequacy with the abundance of sexual energy displayed by most of the women. The man seated near the stage spoke with the most beautiful girl during one of her breaks from dancing. He caressed her. She returned to the stage. Thereafter, the man's eyes never left the girl, except for a few moments of negotiation with the mamasan. Susie was the prostitute's name. It was embroidered on her bikini bottom. She flirted with the Australian from the stage, from time to time lifting the edge of her brassiere or stroking her crotch. During the next change of dancers she went straight to him. The mamasan brought a tissue, and wiped the perspiration off the girl's back. Susie then took the tissue, handed it to the man and 'discreetly' lifted her orange-coloured bikini, inviting him to wipe her breasts. His hand moved down her body. She opened the front of her bikini pants and, more cautiously and embarrassingly, he wiped the sweat from her pubic hair. They talked further. The transaction was completed. It was time to go.

There was both camaraderie and rivalry among the girls. A sense of desperation was present in the voice of the girl who sidled up to me and said, 'Help me'. Several less attractive girls watched the one who was engaged with the lone Australian. Those who fail to make money for the owner of the bar for too many nights in succession soon find themselves on the streets.

OLONGAPO CITY

Olongapo, about three hours' drive north of Manila, must be a contender in any competition for the world's biggest brothel. With 17 000 prostitutes operating in a small geographical area, the girls meet the huge sexual appetite of the US Seventh Fleet based at the adjacent Subic Bay Naval Base. The sailors 'love' Olongapo. They express their affection bluntly: 'It's easier to get a piece of ass in Olongapo than a drink of water'; or 'Three hundred pesos for overnight and she loved me from head to foot, copping my joint four times between screws'; or 'From Subic you need to walk less than a mile for good hard sex'.

Olongapo is the most sordid city I have ever visited. Street upon street of human flesh. Every taste catered for: short term, medium term, long term, in the bar or on the bed. There is a street for black sailors. I never did discover whether the girls charge more or less than in other streets, but their clients appeared well satisfied.

The history of prostitution in Olongapo is traced to 1901 when US President Theodore Roosevelt issued an executive order designating Subic Bay and 70 000 acres of land, including what is now Olongapo, as a military reservation area. The Second World War, the Korean War and the Vietnam War all increased the importance of the base. It provides for the upkeep and maintenance of ships; supplies the Seventh Fleet with food, fuel and ammunition (there is a huge airstrip next to the base taking the largest aircraft); and gives the fleet personnel an ideal haven for rest and recreation.

And rest and recreation means sex. The playboy mentality of the American culture has reduced sex to a physical activity, a leisure accessory or plaything which can be bought or sold like any commodity in the market, and disposed of after using. Functional, instrumental and exploitative sexual encounters are the kinds of sexual experience that men are looking for on arrival in port. The woman prostitute, who has learned to reduce herself to being a mere object or tool for sexual gratification apparently meets the needs of the sailor-customer. Often there are 10 000 or more sailors on shore leave at the same time. It is perhaps fortunate that – at the last count – there were only 30 000 fatherless American children throughout the Philippines. The 'bar fine' routine is also operated in Olongapo, although prices – and competition – are even keener in this city, leading to clients expecting the most perverted behaviour.

There are groups and agencies – government, civic and religious –

that are trying to serve the hostesses, especially in respect of the prevention and control of venereal disease. Most of the 17 000 'regular' women are registered with the Social Hygiene Clinic which provides them with check-up certificates. The clinic, under the jurisdiction of the City Health Officer and supported by major financial, material and technical assistance from the US Naval Base, gives an impression that the government has a concern for the welfare of the women. In fact, however, the Olongapo city government serves as a legitimising agency for institutionalised prostitution, part of the façade to cover up the organised and systematic way in which the economic and political elites of the city – many Chinese among them – manipulate and exploit those working in the field of 'rest and recreation'. Selling human flesh – or rather renting it – has become a large industry in Olongapo where the majority of the prostitutes are certified clean by the government. It is an industry which is not only a product of, but an essential cornerstone in, the prevailing structure of injustice and dehumanisation in the city.

The Social Hygiene Clinic has as its main function the control of venereal diseases. Specific objectives are:

(a) to reduce to a minimum the incidence of venereal diseases through mass screening of probable reservoirs of infection;
(b) to manage and treat all cases found in the clinic;
(c) to intensify contact tracing; and
(d) to strengthen the educational component of the prevention and control of venereal diseases.

The clinic conducts smear tests for hostesses every two weeks and serological examinations of target populations every six months. Despite efforts, however, gonorrhoea has for many years remained one of the leading communicable diseases in the city. One problem is that many of the women working from street corners fail to register with the clinic and easily spread disease.

The most thorough investigation of the rest and recreation industry in Olongapo city was undertaken by Leopolo Moselina of the Asian Social Institute, Manila. In his findings he pointed to the depravity, the trickery and the human tragedy which surrounds the industry in Olongapo. He described what goes on inside some bars:

Stripteasers are reportedly paid fifty pesos a night for performing such acts as *coin-sucking*, *banana-* or *sausage-*, *cigarette-smoking* and *egg-breaking*. The coin-sucking act, in particular, is sometimes done with the participation of the customer who, lying down, puts several one peso coins on his nose or mouth from where the stripteaser 'sucks' the coin by means of her vagina. After sucking, she releases the coins from her vagina and picks them up afterwards as her prize. This way she also earns extra money. Unfortunately, only a few months ago, one of the stripteasers suffered from severe uterine infection as a result of her coin-sucking acts.

In this same club, a customer sometimes does the stripteasing himself. He removes his pants (several customers go there in short pants) and, standing on the table, or dancing on stage, exhibits his erect penis. Or there are occasions when the stripteasers, naked all over, dance on stage with a customer who is also naked. With these lewd and lascivious acts as regular features, which no doubt build up desires for sexual intercourse, it is not surprising that this particular establishment maintains rooms for short time or overnight sexual engagements.

Accounts of hostesses reveal that the sexual transactions between them and their clients are varied: from normal sexual intercourse to any number of perverted acts. Sometimes they resist the extremes, but are frequently forced to give in. They feel powerless and need to make money. Occasionally the woman will enjoy the man's company, and they will arrange to meet again. Always there is a great deal of bargaining between the couple, the charge for services depending on the age of the girl; their emotional–psychological state; the length of time the prostitute has been operating (whether she is still 'cherry' – meaning virgin – or already 'horse', having been in the job a long while); and how desperate the girl is for money. Sometimes the hostess will tell her client about her child – that he is sick, needs medicine or the services of a doctor. But she has no money. Often this works out in her favour. Money is given. For her this is one way to earn – all she has to do is to appeal to her client's emotions and arouse his pity about her sad and wretched life.

The bar girls learn to play tricks on their clients in order to maximise their incomes. Cecile gives an account of her behaviour:

I get the first customer who is very drunk to pay the bar fine at 10 p.m. While he is at the counter I tell my second customer I will meet him at 11 p.m. at the club. Then I leave with the first sailor. Upon arriving at the hotel I insist that he takes a shower. While he is taking his shower, I quickly take from my bag a tube filled with chicken blood and apply it on the appropriate area of my body. Then I moan and groan as if I am in great pain. This gets the attention of the sailor who will ask, 'What's wrong, honey?' I will reply, 'Oh, I am sorry sailor boy, it is my menstruation – I think I must go home, as I feel abdominal pain.' The sailor, disappointed but understanding the situation, gives me his last 20 dollars, which he is saving to give me in the morning, for my taxi fare.

Hurriedly, I put on a sanitary napkin, leave the hotel and rush to the club. I immediately go to the comfort room to wash and powder – just in time to meet my second customer before others get ahead of me. This customer, since it is almost closing time, I will take to my apartment for overnight. Thus, besides collecting the supposed bar fine, I can get the amount usually paid to the hotel and the customary 20 dollars. In one night, if I start early enough, I can do the chicken blood trick twice and am still able to get a customer for overnight.

There are clients who say that they prefer massage clinics to night clubs. These are, of course, fronts for prostitution. Without having to pay bar fines they can obtain whatever sexual favours they wish from willing attendants. Since they can have sexual intercourse inside the massage cubicle, it also means less expense on the part of the client who does not have to pay for a hotel room. All he pays is the amount for the massage plus whatever he agrees with the attendant for extra services. Doris, a massage clinic attendant, describes what occurs inside a massage cubicle:

Seldom does a customer come for the sole purpose of having a massage. Very often, customers ask for extra services from 'hand job' to 'blow job' to sexual intercourse. Customers who know about massage clinics do not pay any more for the hand job because it is part of the massage – usually it is referred to as a 'sensation' . . . So perhaps we spend only about 10 or 15 minutes for the actual massage; the rest of the hour is the extra services. For these extra services, we charge additional payment which is entirely ours – the owner of the massage clinic does not get a share from this any more, although there may be some owners who demand something from their attendants. Some kind of a bargaining process takes place . . . Attendants, however, do not charge a uniform amount. It depends on how good an attendant is in naming and exacting her price for the services requested . . .

One cannot blame a massage attendant for engaging in sexual acts which may appear perversions to the conventional members of society. To us, these acts have become routine and normal – they are expected as part of the job of a massage attendant here in Olongapo. Only perhaps in the beginning, an attendant may be shocked and may therefore raise the question why such things have to be done. Anyone who wants to earn more will be forced to do them. We will not be able to support our families – most of us here have families to support, some have their own children – if we rely only on our commission. We get four pesos out of 20 pesos . . . If our customers stay overnight we get extra commission from his additional payment.

Despite the predisposing factors, both on the personal and

structural levels, affecting the women, their basic value orientation makes it difficult for many to accept themselves as prostitutes. Moselina collected a range of comments from the women working in Olongapo:

Who would be genuinely happy in this kind of work when you feel you are only being used as a plaything? I feel I have become less and less of a human person.

I have learned to be untrue to myself. I have to pretend; if not, I cannot go on with this job.

I have become callous deep inside me. I feel I don't know any more how it is to love and be loved.

The actual act of dropping one's panties, spreading one's legs and doing all possible motions during a sexual encounter with a customer in order to earn money is easy to do. What is difficult is to convince oneself to do it and to keep doing it.

Of course, I'm beginning to enjoy a bit my sexual encounters with customers – especially those whom I like. This is because I am now resigned to being a prostitute. But the enjoyment, perhaps, will never be as total as one would have with a man you really love and who really loves you.

Oftentimes, I do not feel anything during sexual encounters. There are times when I am hurt. If I keep doing it, it is because I need money for myself and my children. I have learned to do the motions mechanically in order to satisfy my customers. If you do it very well, they will keep coming back to you, and that means money.

Outwardly, you may see us apparently enjoying what we are doing. Yes, we may be happy when there are ships around, when we have customers, when we are busy in the clubs. But we dread those times when ships are gone, when there are no customers – for these are the moments when we are forced to reflect on ourselves, to confront ourselves which we keep avoiding. It has been a painful experience to be here and we don't want, if possible, to be reminded of it again and again. That's why most of us resort to various forms of escape – drinking, drugs, excessive eating, sleeping and talking.

Club owners, and clients, prefer young girls, and with a constant supply available from the Visayas particularly, women approaching 30 years of age may find themselves out of a regular job. There are now in Olongapo quite a number of slightly older prostitutes who compete unequally with the newcomers arriving nearly every week. As in Manila, it is generally the older women who can be persuaded to engage in the most perveted behaviour. Even then, with increasing age, they will gradually find themselves doing any of the following:

(a) joining the ranks of the streetwalkers and plying their trade for as long as they can manage;
(b) being forced to work as laundrywomen, or babysitters for the younger hostesses with children;
(c) becoming street vendors, or scavengers;
(d) initiating their own daughters into the trade, thus starting a second generation of entertainers (this often happens to young Amerasian girls);
(e) finding courage to go back home and start life anew;
(f) finding a common-law husband to support them; or
(g) with all other possibilities exhausted, turning to begging, and the absolute poverty that perhaps first encouraged the original movement into prostitution.

ANGELES CITY

What Subic Bay is to American sailors, Angeles city is to American airmen. Clark Air Base – 43 000 hectares of plains and hills, 4000 of which are fenced and are the heart of the air facility proper – is reputedly the largest military airbase outside the USA. Angeles is located about an hour's drive from Manila. Here, too, thousands of hospitality girls take care of the servicemen's needs, often teenage students moonlighting in the oldest profession when tuition-paying time draws near.

The scene differs little from that in Olongapo city: a few more porno films being shown on Betamax, some live sex shows, and private rooms never far away for group sessions, or couples. There are probably more expensive cocktail lounges in Angeles city. Certainly, the ghettoes are to be found where, on small benches in airless rooms, women sit casually, vying for interest. Some girls are young and attractive. A fair-skinned Amerasian with auburn hair, wearing an abbreviated see-through outfit, plays with her ample breast to catch attention.

The rates are uniform: 50 pesos short time: 100 pesos overnight. The cubicle is narrow and cramped, scarcely enough to hold the bed. There is neither a toilet nor running water. The common comfort room is at the back of the house. Most of these tiny brothels do not allow their workers to go out unguarded. They remain virtual prisoners. Food intake is controlled, in order to prevent the girls from becoming fat and ugly. The net profit for these prostitutes is small. They remain trapped in an alternative form of poverty.

SAMAR AND LEYTE: RECRUITING GROUNDS

Very many hospitality girls in Manila, Olongapo and Angeles come from the Eastern Visayas region. Typically unemployed, students or working as domestic helpers, they are easily recruited, most often not knowing that they are to become prostitutes. The picture of working in the tourist and entertainment trades is the one presented by the recruiters. However, both in Samar and Leyte there are now groups engaged in preventing the recruitment of young girls into the prostitution industry. Prevention work of this nature is as dangerous as any other sort of human rights work. The recruiters are often powerful men and in southern Leyte, for example, the military harrassment of church groups has been so intense that campaigns of this sort – when army officers themselves are involved in recruiting – have been too risky. One intelligence officer in the area is known to have two daughters working in Japan as entertainers; one is now a recruiter. Another senior military officer keeps a photograph album of girls 'to order'. One ordinary paratrooper is a recruiter.

There are many reasons why an individual girl chooses to go to Manila to work in the 'tourist and entertainment business' or, knowingly, as a prostitute. First, parents need and expect financial contributions from their children. Peasants and poor fishermen, with large families, are unable to maintain unemployed adolescents. Fishermen live in the poorest communities. There is very little work for daughters in the provinces and, what there is, is badly paid and marginal. Young women do not have much access to the economic life of the region, except in the sense of helping tenant farmer fathers on their farms – unpaid work. Farm work, heavy domestic work and the lack of health facilities, together with malnourishment, rapidly age the women who remain in the region, and lead to frequent family tragedies, the early deaths of parents or breadwinners. Secondly, rural life is incompatible with socially-accepted norms for young women. Even in the poorest *barrios*, the requirement to be beautiful and the expectation of some leisure time – and therefore money – is present. The young feminine ideal promoted by society at large is unattainable by rural women: to have a completely dysfunctional body, and to be an artistic object of beauty.

These and other factors make young girls easy prey for recruiters, many of whom are themselves prostitutes or ex-prostitutes. It is clear, as Sophie Dick reports in her study of the region, that 'respectable' middle-class members of society are those who are making the 'big money'. They insure themselves against disapproval of their activities by church donations and public works of generosity; this, in turn, institutionalises the trade in young women and makes it respectable.

There arc indications that recruiters are, in some cases, protected by military personnel. In Catbalogan, Samar, the military arc certainly the major patrons of the night clubs. There are prostitutes in Tacloban and Catbalogan – despite the massive 'export' to Manila, Olongapo and elsewhere. The girls in these cities often come, as mentioned earlier, from Cebu. In this context, too, recruitment is just another means for landlords to exploit the landless. It demonstrates the lack of importance given by some men to women's issues that, in a region where all kinds of pressures may be put on exploitative landlords by peasant groups or the NPA, the recruiters are most often left to flourish unhindered. The guerrillas have a problem. They are aware of the evils of recruitment, but realise that – given the circumstances – poor people have to live, a further example of the current distortion of values.

There are two groups concerned with prevention in the region, both connected with the STOP (Stop Trafficking of Pilipinas) campaign. The group in Leyte – Sisters of St Joseph based in Tacloban – is primarily concerned with preventing girls from going to Manila. They are at present concentrating on north-east Leyte; for the reasons stated earlier, it has not been advisable to work in the southern part.

The sisters have initiated core groups in towns which are known – from research in Manila, and from local and national news reports – to be fertile ground for recruiters. They work closely with the priests to learn more about the affected *barrios* and to make links with key individuals. The different core groups operate in different ways, according to the decisions of the members. In one town, the core group is organising skills training – in hairdressing, dressmaking, tailoring and cosmetics – while, in another, the core group works with the priest, teachers, catechists and women's groups, giving the message during mass and in schools, even with the youngest children. Their aim is value formation. This group, and the sisters, base their teaching on biblical texts on the 'dignity of man'. Sisters of St

Joseph are able to provide training for young women to improve their skills – and therefore their earning power – as domestic helpers. This scheme is funded through a group called LINKS. The sisters will find suitable local placements, but if the trainees are determined to go to Manila, they are referred to the Good Shepherd Sisters at Rose Virginie House, Makati, who will give them temporary accommodation on arrival and help them to find work. The sisters in Leyte have been disappointed by the poor response to their training scheme: 'It seems as if the recruiters are still getting there first.'

In arranging for girls to stay in Manila with the Good Shepherd Sisters, the sisters are attempting to overcome the major problems facing young women going to the cities: loneliness, and the lack of money and accommodation. Girls easily fall into the hands of *bugaw* who provide food, shelter and companionship – and then trap them into prostitution in order to pay their debts.

In Samar – where the work is also new – it is equally difficult to organise local people. During mass, the congregation is warned of the deceptions of recruiters – even though an armed soldier has traditionally stood at the back of the church – and efforts are made to increase the level of awareness among young people. The church in the area has a reputation for militancy, however, but it has been difficult to obtain support for church programmes. One church worker said that she could not even persuade people to stay behind after mass while she briefed them about the dangers of recruitment to 'domestic work' in Manila. To be seen in church outside the mass has been dangerous. For that reason the topic of prostitution could only be introduced into the homily and the 'community concerns' sections of the mass.

Recruiters are often generous church donors. In Leyte, there lives a major recruiter who is usually Hermana Mayor at the local *fiesta*, and an important supporter of her local church. One churchwoman from Leyte tells the story of a visit to Manila by the local STOP group, carolling among the Manila Leytenos to raise money for the anti-prostitution campaign. Accommodation was kindly offered by a *kababayan* (townmate) who also owned a house in Manila. It was not until the group arrived at the door in Avenida that they discovered that the 'house' was a bar. It was on four floors: the restaurant (where they were expected to sleep) and, above that, areas for drinking, for dancing, and for 'other activities'. Patronage of the church is insurance for the recruiters. Where the recruiters are the only people in the area able to support the church financially, it is difficult for the church to refuse their donations.

Sophie Dick met a *barrio* captain in one of the 'worst-affected' areas who has given full support to the STOP campaign – yet she owns a bar in Olongapo. Sometimes she entertains other recruiters in her home. Other local people own bars – or chains of bars – in Manila. One man was known to have sold his wife to a recruiter.

Many girls who travel to Manila, Olongapo and elsewhere – and who become full-time or part-time prostitutes – remain desperately poor, become diseased and eventually – as we have seen – turn to scavenging or begging. Others, for whatever reason, do manage to send money home regularly to support their families; and to pay occasional visits to their *barrios* where, in contrast to local girls who have not been away, they are well-dressed and not without money. Some 'sexys' – the name given to those returning from Manila on vacation – come from middle-class families. A number of girls from Manila have earned sufficient money to build wooden houses for their parents, replacing the *nipa* huts. They attend mass during the *fiesta* in brilliant clothes.

Girls in the bars in Manila and Olongapo always say that their parents do not know what their life really is. 'Discovery by parents' is said to be one of the girls' greatest fears, along with sadism and the risk of catching a venereal disease. It is difficult to believe that when a girl is known as a 'sexy' in the *barrio*, the parents are ignorant of their daughter's work. Half-knowledge is perhaps the rule, where knowledge would jeopardise the income from Manila; the parent–child relationships; the status the families perceive themselves as having in the community; and, perhaps, relationships with respected members of the community who may have recruited the girls in the first place.

Locally, people's perception of what is happening to the young women of Samar and Leyte is hazy. Although some believe that the trade started soon after the Second World War, the general consensus is that it is recent. It seems that while there may always have been a market for girls from the area, it has perhaps only become extensive enough to be visible during the last few years. Now, it is as basic as feudalism to the economy of the region.

TWO INTERVIEWS

Sophie Dick conducted a number of interviews with people from a small fishing village in Leyte, trapped between the mountains and the sea, the only transport by boat. While the interviewer makes no claim that the accounts are representative they do provide further first-hand information about the lifestyle of many who 'go to Manila' and other places. It is not possible to deduce from the first story whether or not Marites made money from prostitution; Alex certainly does.

Marites

Marites was a working student at Roxas High School in Manila, and left after the fourth year to become a domestic helper and later a waitress in Tanay, Rizal. She then studied modelling at Karilagan. She was invited to join a group of seven models by their agent and manager, Mabel, who is now in Japan. Mabel is 19, and went to Manila to work when she was 14; she comes from the same *barrio* as Marites. Most of the girls lived in Mabel's apartment, though Marites was renting her own. Marites was the youngest when she started, at 16 years old.

At the beginning, she worked on lunch-time shows: 'high fashion' modelling. Later she progressed to morning and night-club modelling. For the night clubs, the girls modelled one see-through dress for every four ordinary ones. New girls were not required to wear see-through clothes. Mabel, however, is religious, and did not allow indecent modelling. Some groups were being invited for private striptease shows in houses and offices. The audience was mostly foreigners, and the group might be transported as far as Laguna or Baguio for the show.

Marites said that she had not heard of forced prostitution amongst her friends in the Philippines, although one 15-year-old connected with her group went to Japan with a Filipino 'white slaver' and came back after six months, having been horribly abused. Said Marites, 'She looks a wreck, she's got VD and she's addicted to cough syrup.' This girl has now returned to Japan after being thrown out of Mabel's apartment for stealing.

Most models come from Manila, according to Marites; the ago-go dancers were more often Visayan. She seems to have been proud to have been a model rather than a dancer, seeing it as more decent. In 1983, she married her childhood sweetheart from the *barrio*, who works as a waiter in a bar in Cubao, and has stopped work because she is pregnant. '*Nahiya ako* (I was ashamed),' she said, 'The customers despised us.'

Alex

Alex introduced himself as a callboy. His parents died ten years ago and he has been working in an expensive club in Cubao since he left school at 17. He has two married sisters in the *barrio* and eight other siblings in Manila. None of them knows what his work really is. He is now 21.

Alex is a waiter in a club where 20 male waiters and dancers work in one area, and 15 waitresses and female dancers work in another. For dancing naked with customers for three hours he gets 1000 pesos. He always drinks about five beers before this ordeal; his companions drug themselves.

The bar fine for men is 500 pesos. The girls get 30 pesos for dancing in bikinis, and the bar fine for women is 300 pesos. There are five rooms upstairs for sex. His clients are a mixture of foreigners, Filipino *bakla* and Filipina married women whose husbands, often, are abroad. Some of the waiters are *bakla*. The 20 waiters/dancers cover the working period of 6 p.m. to 3 a.m. in shifts, working in groups of five.

Alex had only once accepted a bar fine, with a middle-aged married Filipina. The work is 'a burden on his conscience', and he would like to study but actually spends all his money on his *barkada* (group of friends). He lives with the four other waiters from his shift as a bed-spacer in a house in Santa Ana, and this *barkada*, together with the other male and female employees, have become his 'family'. The girls are working students and study in the mornings. He was recruited by a married *bakla*, and then taken by a member of his present *barkada* to work in the bar.

MUSLIMS

There are comparatively few Muslim prostitutes but, when discovered by fellow Muslims, they are severely punished. Usually they are sentenced to a 'period of hard labour' for 'violating the laws of Islam'. At the beginning of 1985 a special team from the MNLF assigned to take care of 'wayward' Muslims seized seven girls from a bar in Cotabato city, 912 kilometres south-east of Manila, and took them to guerrilla camps in the mountains of Maguindanao province for rehabilitation. The Muslims, who 'publicly punish' women who wear tight jeans or sweaters, are known to impose extreme punishments on girls discovered working as prostitutes.

PORNOGRAPHIC FILMS

The bars and clubs in Manila operate within a 'sex for sale' atmosphere, uncontrolled by government. The Experimental Cinema of the Philippines (ECP) financed the 1982 international film festival through the showing of pornographic films all over the city. The ECP was the brainchild of Imelda Marcos.

Despite pleas from the Mayor of Manila and several women's groups, the 1985 festival went ahead as planned, starting on 14 February. Cardinal Jaime Sin, Archbishop of Manila, also complained to no avail. He criticised the then president's wife for presenting to Manila what he described as a 'river of filth and pornography'.

CHILD PROSTITUTION

Santa Monica Park in Manila is one centre of child prostitution. As twilight turns to dark, young girls and boys go off with strangers. Rooms nearby are let by the hour. This is one of the hardest vice rings to break for those concerned with the welfare of children, as it is controlled by some of the most ruthless men in the city. Child prostitution is springing up in many places in the Philippines, in fact anywhere with vague claims to being a 'tourist area'. Matabunkay, a seaside spot in Lian, Batangas, is a well known centre for Asian and European tourists where some seek sexual activity with children.

New levels of poverty push people into different ways of making money, and the sexual abuse of children in the Philippines is reaching alarming proportions, with many incidents undiscovered and unreported. By January 1985 the problem had become so worrying that police in Manila decided to impose a curfew forbidding minors – aged 18 and below – to roam the streets of the city at night. In the drive against child prostitution police were said to be starting to detain minors who could not explain why they were still on the streets after nine o'clock. But the 'campaign' appears to have been little more than a gesture. Child prostitutes are as freely available as ever.

Olongapo city, too, caters for all sexual preferences. The man on the corner of the street offers a 'woman'. The sailor refuses, but hesitates, and waits.

'Bit younger?' he enquires haltingly.

The man replies, 'Cost more. Take a few minutes.'

'How much?'
'Fifty dollars for a virgin.'
'How old?'
'Twelve years.'
The sailor nods.
'Wait here. Back in ten minutes.'
The sailor waits. The man returns. Both move away down a side street, away from the bright lights. As in Manila, child prostitution thrives in Olongapo.

Subic Naval Base became the focus of a national scandal in 1983 when a US Navy Admiral and the Olongapo city Mayor were caught trying to silence an Irish Catholic priest, Father Shay Cullen, a Columban. The issue was child prostitution. The furore was precipitated by the exploits of 40-year-old US Navy Petty Officer Daniel Dougherty – who had sexual relations with at least 12 young girls in Olongapo – when several of the girls came to seek medical attention for venereal disease from local Catholic social workers.

No sooner had the mayor's office heard that children were being treated at the clinic than it started to cover up the story. Mayor Richard Gordon took the girls into the city's custody and assigned them to a hospital ward with instructions to the staff that no one should talk to them. Just as quickly, Dougherty was moved out of the Philippines to Guam, ostensibly because he was due for routine transfer.

Meanwhile, the girls disregarded their hospital curfew and sought out Cullen who runs a nearby drug abuse centre. In his interview with them, the priest was able to piece together a picture of widespread child prostitution in the city. The interviews with five of the girls yielded a profile of their lives. They ranged from 9 to 14 years of age. All came from very poor families, some with no known male parent or none living with the family. Several girls had been raped by a local policeman and subsequently became prostitutes. The others had sold their virginity to American servicemen for US$25 to US$60. From then on they received $13 to $20 per 'visit'. The girls were infected with gonorrhoea, syphilis and *Herpes genitalis*.

Both Gordon and the base commander, Admiral Richard Dunleavy, asked Cullen not to release the story, arguing that publicity would make it difficult to apprehend Dougherty. Cullen made his interviews available to the press – and displayed photographs showing the girls' youth – when he learned that

Dougherty had already left the Philippines. At a press conference – in response to a magazine article – Gordon insisted that the girls were not prostitutes but rape victims and attacked Cullen for exposing the issue.

PAGSANJAN

The history of foreign paedophiles exploiting local boys in Pagsanjan goes back as far as the early sixties. One early story concerns General Hans Menzi of the newspaper *Bulletin Today* who used to pick up local teenage boys in his helicopter and take them to Manila. When he had finished with them he would return them to Pagsanjan and give them scholarships.

The filming of *Apocalypse Now* in the mid-seventies, just outside the town, was a turning point. Although the film crew were not paedophiles, many were gay, and the values of the community may well have been affected by the influx of glamorous foreign homosexuals. More obvious, however, was the effect of the overnight – and temporary – wealth that the filming brought to the town. A third factor was a charity sponsoring children in underdeveloped countries. World Vision puts First World people in touch with children in these countries, and the children then receive financial and other support. Many sponsors introduced by World Vision actually went to visit 'their' children in Pagsanjan, showering them with gifts, and even holidays in Australia. Some of the sponsors were paedophiles – World Vision has since tightened the procedures in its vetting system – but it has been claimed that at least six children were sponsored by paedophiles through World Vision.

Apart from the boys, Pagsanjan has only one tourist attraction: the river with its famous rapids and falls. Five hundred tourists arrive daily to experience the rapids, and the number increases to 5000 on Sundays. About 2000 boatmen take tourists up river. The price of an official individual ticket is 63 pesos (February 1985) but a boatman only receives 30 pesos after payments to the hotel for which he works and the Philippines Tourist Association, and *tong* on the river. Two boatmen can take two boatloads of two tourists each per day – if there are enough tourists. Outside the tourist industry there are no job opportunities in Pagsanjan. Pagsanjan is a rural town with much absentee landlordism, and no industry.

Pagsanjan has become internationally known – to paedophiles – through gay magazines in the West. *Spartacus* guide describes it as a world holiday centre for paedophiles, ranking it above Sri Lanka. The result has been that the town has become a centre of attraction for paedophiles. Some have built houses for the boys they 'love', and either live there themselves or send money – as much as US$100 each month – and visit regularly for long periods. Many of the men have business connections in the Philippines. Most are older and wealthier, their wealth making them invulnerable. During press outcries about paedophilia, for example, they have simply left and gone to Baguio city, or to their home country. When eight were deported in early 1985, two were back in Pagsanjan within two weeks, boasting of having paid bribes of only US$500.

Younger or poor paedophiles who may have commitments to individual boys, often rent houses in the town for holiday periods. Others stay in hotels or guest houses. Until the height of the anti-paedophile campaign in the town in 1984, all hotels except one were known to keep registers of available boys. The majority of the paedophiles are Australian, but Europeans are also common, notably Dutch, Swiss and German. There is a smaller group of Americans, and some Chinese who come from Manila for the weekend. There is one British man who teaches the boys football, and selects his protégés from the team.

Most of the new houses built for the boys are in one area, Maulawin, which is divided from the town plaza by a small river. Fourteen new concrete houses have been built in this once-poor *barrio*, and others are under construction. The Velasco family is the most numerous in the community, and the most powerful figure is 'Boy' Velasco. Velasco has police influence and is armed. His gang protects the paedophiles and pimps for them, sending collectors out to get Velasco's share from the boys after the night's work. Sometimes, when the favoured boys have grown too old to be attractive to their patrons, they will become pimps in order to maintain their status. These special and long-term protégés rule their families, since the family has become dependent on the boy for everything. These 'kept' boys, however, are the exception rather than the rule.

In 1984, it was estimated that of the 4000 boys in the eligible age group – that is, up to early adolescence – 3000 were, to some extent, involved in prostitution. This figure includes boys from Manila, Bicol and other areas who have been brought to Pagsanjan by foreign paedophiles, and left there. The rate per night in February 1985 was 200 pesos, the same as the rate for women in mid-level bars in Ermita, and much cheaper than in Olongapo – where the issue is perhaps more sensitive, and the American sailors have more money. If, in Pagsanjan, a relationship develops between a man and a boy, gifts are common: from Walkman cassette players to bicycles. Jeeps for family use and scholarships are not unknown, the 'few' receiving new houses. It becomes a matter of prestige for boys to have a rich and generous lover. Those who do not may be mocked by their companions in the *barrio*.

The pastor in Pagsanjan has noticed that the boys are never successful in later life. He commented that they have become too accustomed to drink and drugs – and a very easy life – to be able to make a success of anything. Even those boys given scholarships, or private tutors, do not take their studies seriously, and are in any case often absent on holiday in other resorts or even abroad.

Although they no longer keep registers of boy prostitutes, all hotels make a profit from the trade. Contrary to the law, there is no attempt by hotels to stop foreigners taking young boys to their rooms. One of the most notorious hotels is the Pagsanjan Falls Lodge. This was purchased by Jose D. Aspiras, former Minister of Tourism, through a dummy, Diaz, during the slump in tourism which followed the Aquino assassination.

The values of the whole town have been affected. Schools welcome prostitute scholars, and are often given large donations for graduation ceremonies, as are councillors at election time. The police records show no 'paedophile problem' at all: no complaints and certainly no prosecutions. This is despite the fact that foreigners often have drunken arguments and jealous fights in bars in the town plaza, opposite the church and municipal hall.

The following accounts are typical of what has happened in Pagsanjan. A local photographer was given a film to develop by one of the foreigners: of himself having sex with a local boy. He was apparently in a hurry to meet a deadline for a gay magazine, and was unable to wait for the usual commercial service available to the publication. The paedophile was evidently confident that this kind of behaviour was taken for granted in the town.

A kindergarten teacher noticed a 6-year-old pupil looking at his swollen and sore penis in the mirror. The child named a man who had been sucking it 'last night'. The teacher took the child home and told his parents, who appeared to be horrified and said that they would put a stop to it. The child failed to return to the kindergarten, and two months later the teacher was invited to the boy's birthday party – given by the paedophile.

The third incident was even more serious. It concerned a boy aged 7 who was confined to San Antonia de Padua Hospital, near Pagsanjan for seven days with rectal bleeding. A paedophile had failed to use a lubricant before penetration, and his anus had ruptured. The boy's mother went to the pastor, asking him for 3000 pesos if he could use the information to file a case on her behalf. She offered to set up the same situation again – the previous incident had, the pastor discovered, happened in the sitting-room – so that the police could catch the man *in flagrante*. The pastor refused to give her the money – she would anyway have been entitled to damages – and she is believed to have accepted 10 000 pesos from the paedophile as well as the cost of the hospital treatment, as a bribe to drop the case.

The Council for the Protection of Children was formed in 1981 to try to prevent boy prostitution in the town. Its main concern was the town's good name, but it completely failed to reach – let alone influence – those involved in the boy prostitution trade. It had no alternative to offer. The tourist trade was, however, affected. In addition to the Aquino assassination, the town received bad press coverage. The poorest people in the community suffered most. In a sense, the campaign has led to an increased polarisation of classes in the town. The poor see it as 'middle-class moralising' and no more. Their livelihoods are threatened by a declining tourist industry, however unpalatable the source of their incomes. It has even been suggested that the campaign represents the 'old' middle-class and rural aristocracy who are threatened by those now becoming wealthy through Pagsanjan's peculiar brand of tourism.

Attempts to tackle the problen have all been hindered by the lack of alternative sources of income for the town. The NPA offered to liquidate two particularly abusive semi-residents, but this was rejected on the basis that it would disturb the tourist trade, alienate the people and bring in the military. The church in Pagsanjan has decided to approach the issue from an economic and political angle. They, too, see prostitution in the town as a dramatic example of exploitation and dependency creation by First World countries. However, with the foreigners commending the boys and the town on their 'liberated morality' – and pouring cash into the hands of poor and needy people – Pagsanjan may well continue for some time as the centre of world attraction for paedophiles.

FURTHER 'LEGISLATION'

The question of child prostitution in the Philippines has been an important one for some time now. *Streets of Manila*, a 1981 French film, documented the existence of large numbers of child prostitutes, and the international media have returned to the problem several times – to no avail. Many children in Manila, and other towns and cities grow up virtually on their own in the streets and it is inevitable that significant numbers of them will have to turn to prostitution to support themselves.

Measures to combat the problem were again taken – on paper – towards the end of 1985 by the MMC headed by Imelda Marcos. Under an ordinance, taking effect from 1 December, jail sentences of between one and four years, plus fines for the rehabilitation of the minor, became possible for 'any person who shall avail of the services of a minor for prostitution and/or sexual exploitation'. It defined a minor as one below 18 years and also covered 'the satisfaction of lust by any act other than sexual intercourse', promoting or inducing prostitution, and even being found 'under suspicious circumstances' with a minor in a hotel room. Any foreigner found guilty would be deported only after serving any sentence passed.

The ordinance imposes the maximum penalty on minors' relatives or guardians found guilty of the offences, and lays down lighter penalties for owners of establishments where the offences take place as well as for people who fail to report cases they are aware of. However, with the high level of police corruption, the increasing number of paedophiles visiting the Philippines, and the abject poverty of so many families there is no reason to believe that this law will be more effective than any other.

GEORGE: A CHILD PROSTITUTE

The following is a true story.[1] But the name is not real. George, like many of his peers in the trade, is anonymous not because there is a wish to hide or protect him, but because many people hardly care anyway. As we have seen, more and more children condemned to a life of misery now roam the streets of Manila selling their flesh. Who sees their plight?

At the age of 14, young boys are supposed to be just beginning to feel the pulse of life. For George, this is not the case. In his juvenile life, he has already undergone so much trauma and so many troubles, enough to make anyone become weary of existence.

Born of a poor family in one of Metro Manila's slum communities, George was raised in hunger and want, within an environment of insecurity that promised no opportunities. The same environment contributed to the disintegration of traditional values and family life. George saw no future in the slums, and no escape for its inhabitants. He dropped out in his first year in high school and became one of the regular *'tambays'* of the neighbourhood. It was during this time that a friend of his who was a callboy began filling him up with stories about the trade. It did not take long for George to be convinced. The allure of money was strong. As he said, *'Siempre, gusto ko ring makahawak ng pera'* (I thought I could make use of some cash).

One morning, he surprised his parents with money. Asked where and how he got it, George gave the truth bluntly. There were no sermons nor lashings in reply, nothing except stoned silence from his father and mother. The money he gave them was the earnings he got from his initiation with a Frenchman, which marked his entry into prostitution. He was only 12 years old then.

George's male customers range from 25 to 60 years old and are of different nationalities. There are Germans, Japanese, British, Finns, Swedes and Americans. He also caters to female elderly matrons, which he prefers more than the males. *'Mas okay, ipipikit mo lang ang mga mata mo, parang si Alma Moreno na'* (I just close my eyes and imagine making love to Alma Moreno).

Every night, he sits in his usual hunting grounds which are either in Santa Monica or in the fastfoods near the plaza and waits for customers. 'You can tell a potential one by the way he looks at you,' says George. 'His eyes will never leave you. After a while, he will wink and then approach you. He asks your name, where you come from and other things so that you get to know each other. Occasionally, a customer will ask whether you're experienced or not. This type usually prefers those without experience, so that they can do whatever it is they plan to do and pay a small price for it.'

When connected with a pimp, the job of getting customers is easier. But since the boy has to hand over a cut from his earnings, say, 30 pesos out of 150, George prefers to operate independently and seldom gets the services of a pimp.

The next thing after getting to know each other, George continues, is going to a restaurant where the customer treats you. Usually, this is also the time when the bargaining takes place. Seller and customer bargain until they agree on a price. For George, it never goes lower than 200 pesos. The reason for this, according to him is, '*Binebenta ko na nga ang sarili ko kaya hindi ako tumatanggap ng mababa. Kawawa naman ako pag pumayag ako sa baratan!*' (I have sold my soul! Why should I sell it cheap?)

Then the ensuing scenario would be at the customer's hotel or motel room. Here the tragic ritual begins. They both take a bath, perfume themselves, start kissing. It usually takes about half an hour. Not long, since it does not take much time for a customer to get aroused, 'especially when they see me naked', George says, 'because they think I am sexy.'

Only half an hour, nevertheless, he still feels that it is the worst time in his life every time it happens. The sexual satisfaction is always one sided. Says George, '*Papaano ka mag-eenjoy, sapilitan, kungdi lang dahil sa pera hindi ko sisikmurain*' (You are forced – how could you enjoy it except for the money). 'The only consolation one gets is that if the customer is good and really likes you, he will buy you clothes. When you become friends, and he goes back to his country, he will surely send you a gift. If you happen to meet each other anywhere, he will also surely buy you something,' George remarks optimistically.

After hearing these things, one may wonder how George then views life. '*Malungkot, masaya*' (Happy and sad). 'Life is happy when you earn enough money to buy anything you want. Sad when you don't get customers or, as they call it, "*walang diskarte*". Bad when the police starts picking you up, commonly called '*bagansya*' (vagrancy), for no reason at all. If you don't have the money to give them, you go to jail for two weeks. The girls have an alternative and that is to spend a night with the policeman or barangay official.' Because George is not a girl, he has only two choices: either to make a run for it or get caught. The obvious and logical choice is of course the first. '*Binebenta ko na nga ang kaluluwa ko, pahuhuli pa ako. Para ano-magdusa lang!*' (I have tasted hell . . . but I won't suffer in prison!)

However, there are hazards in running from the police. If he remembers your looks, which is most likely, the policeman will watch out for you. Next time around, you're caught for sure. You had better be ready for the consequences, George reflects.

George escapes from the police most of the time. But he has been caught three times already. Fortunately, he has a brother (who like him turned to the trade) living with foster parents in France who sends the money to bail him out.

He vows to stop plying his trade soon because with the help of his brother in France, things are getting a little better for their family. When that time comes, it will be a relief for him, he said. *'Ayoko naman talaga sa trabaho ko, tingin ko sa sarili ko putik'* (I really do not like my work. I look down on myself as a scum).

Notes

1. This account is taken from Celine Salcedo, *The Human Society Monograph*, no. 71, 18 January 1985.

5 Persecution and Oppression

Under Marcos, the AFP grew in numerical strength, and brutality. They came to believe that their power was absolute. They considered themselves above the law. But the people in the *barrios* have not forgotten. Few communities escaped murder, torture, 'salvaging', looting, harassment or rape. Until the moment of his departure from Manila, troops loyal to the former president were shooting fellow Filipinos. Some gambled with their future, including high-ranking officers, and joined the opposition. Few have been called to account for the atrocities they committed. It is, however, important to record their behaviour. Many hold key positions in the country, and are already shaping the future direction of the Philippines. Significantly, in the days immediately following Aquino's claim to the presidency, the newly-promoted General Ramos 'regretted' that it was not possible to issue search warrants in respect of all the people whose houses and properties he wanted to investigate, perhaps not the best 'first step' in his suddenly-found new allegiance. After all, he was close to Marcos, part of his 'team' and must have known what was going on – for 20 years.

In August 1971 Marcos suspended the privilege of the writ of *habeas corpus*. The suspension of the writ was a crucial step in the establishment of one-man rule. A year later, martial law was declared and with it occurred a massive round-up of critics and protesters, about 30 000 in all. The 1973 constitution provided legal justification for one-man rule, and this was 'ratified' under conditions which did not make room for any dissent, much less allow any open expression of it.

The 1973 constitution vested in the former president not only executive but legislative powers. Basic freedoms of speech, the press, organisation and public assembly were curtailed through presidential decrees and general orders, most of which were still in effect until the day of Marcos's departure from office, though slightly modified and under different names. In 1985, over 2000 general orders, decrees and letters of instruction preserved the trappings of martial law. One of the most well-known and hated signs of both the arrogance and fear of the Marcos regime was the

Preventive Detention Action (PDA), formerly the Presidential Commitment Order (PCO), under which a person could be arrested and held without warrant and refused bail. The PDA could not be declared void by any court.

MILITARY GROWTH

Military force grew alongside executive and legislative powers, martial law seeing the development of the military as a partner of the president in the management of the country. Numbering below 100 000 in 1972, the AFP more than doubled between 1972 and 1975. In February 1986 it had a strength of nearly 300 000. This figure excluded some 200 000 members of the Integrated Civilian Home Defence Force (ICHDF) and 50 000 men who composed the other paramilitary units, intelligence groups and armed religious fanatics directly or indirectly supported by the military. Such might within the regular forces was made possible only through a corresponding increase in foreign military aid to the Philippines. Between 1970 and 1972 US military assistance to the Philippines amounted to US$55 million. During the first three years of martial law this more than doubled to US$118 million. For the 13-year period from 1973 to 1985, US military aid totalled US$660 million. This enabled the government to invest in more sophisticated military equipment. The AFP's procurement list for 1985, worth US$85 million, included night vision devices, anti-terrorist vans and microwave communications systems. The factors cited by the Marcos administration for the increase in AFP personnel centred mainly on the threat which various revolutionary forces posed to the regime, namely, the NPA, the Bangsa Moro Army (BMA) and the Moro National Liberation Front (MNLF).

It is probably less well known that the Australian government has also supported the AFP for many years. Australia's involvement in a military capacity began during the Second World War when Australian soldiers played a prominent role in the assault on the Visayan island of Leyte. This led, after the war, to study visits by AFP personnel to Australian military colleges, to joint land exercises between the two countries, and to the supply of defence equipment such as Nomad aircraft, and coastal patrol craft. The latest support has been in the form of high-frequency antennae for communications use, and reinforces a statement made in a WB–Australia document in 1982 indicating clearly that its projects in Northern Samar were primarily a support for the Philippine government's counter-insurgency programme. The Australian government has continued to take an interest in Philippine affairs. It gave A$18 million in aid to the Philippines in the financial year 1984/85. In an address to parliament on 25 November 1985 the foreign minister, Bill Hayden, once again identified communist insurgency as 'a serious threat'. He said that Australia had made a substantial commitment to the Philippines in terms of aid and that the country 'will continue to engage our active attention'. Hayden added: 'It is a member of our immediate region, of considerable interest to us for various strategic, foreign policy and economic reasons.'

AFP: STRENGTH AND ROLE

In 1985, a further 12 operational battalions were added to the 65 that existed in 1984. In May, the Army Reserve Command announced plans to form 68 provincial home defence battalions and eight companies. A battalion is made up of 600 to 1000 men, and a company of about 100. At least five companies form a battalion. The AFP – top-heavy with an excess of nearly 2000 officers at the beginning of 1986 – is composed of four military services: the army, navy, air force and constabulary. Of the four, the army is the largest.

Changes followed the declaration of martial law in 1972. One was the broadening of the functions of the National Intelligence Security Agency (NISA). From a minor agency gathering information for the president, it grew into a complex intelligence agency controlling all the intelligence networks of the four military services and the Regional Unified Commands (RUCs). NISA was under the Office of the President. Another development was the expansion of the Presidential Security Command (PSC). Before 1972, the PSC was a special unit under the Philippine Constabulary (PC) and mainly responsible for the security of the president and his family. During the period of martial law it grew into a force of more than 2000 men, a full-sized command operating nationwide, and also under the Office of the President.

In 1975, the Integrated National Police (INP) was fused with the PC. The move placed the INP under the command of the PC chief and took away from local officials an important source of political power. In July 1985, however, the INP was also placed under the Office of the President. A wider reorganisation of the AFP was taking place during the last days of the Marcos regime, with the likelihood that the PC would be attached to the army while a national police force was created. This being the case, the size of the army would have been further increased, with the police force under a new Ministry of the Interior.

In 1983 the RUCs were created. The regional units of the army, navy, air force and constabulary came under the jurisdiction of each RUC. RUC commanders reported directly to the chief of staff, bypassing the commanders of the four major services as well as the defence minister. This gave the chief of staff direct links with the units in the field, and it is worth noting that the geographical scope of the RUC is greater than any political institution below the national government.

A number of military officers, retired and on active duty, came to occupy high positions in government prior to February 1986, as well as in state corporations. Others are in private businesses. Few have lost their power or position.

After martial law, the military was given control over vital public utilities in transport and communications. Later on, military officers were assigned roles in various development programmes. In 1978, six out of 12 presidential officers for regional development were military officers. In 1981, three retired generals were national coordinators of the *Kilusang Kabuhayan sa Kaunlaran* (KKK) while another three generals were regional heads.

Under Marcos several government agencies were headed by active and retired officers. Wilfredo Nuqui was assistant director-general of the National Economic Development Authority, General Gaudencio Tobias was head of the National Housing Authority and General Vicente Evidente headed the Community Development and Services Deliveries under the Ministry of Human Settlements. The Philippine Coconut Authority had five military men in its roster of officers with Lieutenant-Colonel Felix Duenas as administrator. The Bureau of Customs and the Bureau of Posts were headed by Ramon Farolan and Roilo Golez, respectively. Both were reserve officers. In fact, Marcos made the Bureau of Posts an affiliate reserve unit of the Philippine Constabulary.

The names of high-ranking military officials could also be found on the lists of the board of directors of several government corporations. General Fabian Ver held a directorship in five state firms, and former navy officer Alejandro Melchor and Brigadier-General Pedro Dumol in four each. Retired and active officers who sat on the board of two government corporations were Antonio Venadas, Eustacio S. Baclig, Victorino Basco and Romulo M. Espaldon; while Air Force Commander Vicente Piccio, Judge Advocate General Hamilton Dimaya, Cesar Batlang, Amante Bueno, Ceferino Carreon, Jonas Victoria, Rafael Zagala, Ramon Casanova, Sinforoso Doque, Jose Miguel Paez and Ernesto Ogbinar, each sat on one.

At the time of his 'defection' to the Aquino camp Defence Minister Juan Ponce Enrile held a directorship in at least 11 state firms.

Retired officers could also be found in private corporations. Brigadier-General Francisco V. Gatmaitan was executive vice-president of the Manila Electric Company while Brigadier-General Mariano Ordonez sat on the board of the Allied Banking Corporation. Former navy officer V. L. Mamon was director of operations of the American President Lines, a multinational firm. The presence of military officers and men in the logging, security services and entertainment business is still common knowledge. High-ranking officers manage to hold investments abroad. Those in the lower ranks engage in notorious and high-paying activities such as gun-for-hire, protection rackets, gun running, narcotics trafficking, smuggling and illegal gambling. All make considerable sums of money.

For the ordinary soldier, however, very poor pay contributed to the low morale in the AFP, and continues to do so. Military personnel came to be feared, hated and despised under martial law, and afterwards. The AFP has always been riddled with graft and corruption: equipment used for personal business; and operational and intelligence funds misappropriated. Soldiers, for example, have traditionally been assigned to guard the *hacienda* (sugar plantation) of their commander's relatives. Favouritism and nepotism have been common. Letter of Instructions No. 776 gave the president the final say in the promotion of officers. Extension of service was also the president's prerogative. In December 1985 there were 33 'extendee' generals, most of whom were Ilocanos, occupying top posts. Marcos came from Ilocos.

With its need to muster maximum military strength, the government turned its attention to the youth. Presidential Decree No. 1706, more infamously known as the National Service Law

(NSL), allowed for the militarization of the school system. It enabled the military, through the Ministry of National Defence, to pursue military objectives – under the guise of conveniently labelled 'civilian' programmes – by brainwashing the school population into the acceptance of the regime's exploitation and oppression. Enrile was the Minister of Defence.

Sixty-one per cent of the AFP were deployed in Mindanao, where a quarter of the population resides, making it the most highly militarized area not only in the country but in the whole ASEAN region. Apart from Samar and Leyte, and as a result of the difficulties experienced by the people of Negros following the collapse of the sugar industry in 1985, Mindanao is the area of greatest poverty, and the scene of the most indiscriminate acts of repression and brutality.

Following martial law, the military and military-related groups were also used to facilitate the entry of commercial firms and plantations into rural areas where many farmers – as noted in Chapter 3 – lost their land to plantation developers engaged mainly in export crops, most of which are multinational, government or semi-government corporations. Many senior AFP personnel, as has been shown, had an interest in these enterprises, or acted on behalf of their 'cronies' in government. An instance of this, reflecting adversely on the UK, was the way in which the Commonwealth Development Corporation (CDC) – an organisation under the statutory authority of the Ministry for Overseas Development and in receipt of funds from the British Exchequer – continued to invest £6.4 million in a palm oil plantation in Mindanao, in the knowledge that a unit known as the 'Lost Command' had wantonly turned people off their farms and intimidated and murdered them, as land for the plantation was acquired. Colonel Carlos Lademora, the leader of the Lost Command, gathered around him some of the most unscrupulous men he could find, capable of extreme abuse and violence; mostly ex-criminals guilty of murder and rape. Their use as 'security guards' in the development of the Guthrie Plantation seems to have been no more than a matter for 'regret' in the eyes of the CDC.

EFFECTS OF MILITARIZATION

The effects of militarization in the country – both directly and through the paramilitary groups licensed by the army – were apparent in the extra-judicial killings that took place – locally known as 'salvaging' – and in the arbitrary arrest of suspected dissidents, the torture of political prisoners, prolonged detention and 'hamleting', that is, the forced evacuation of villagers. Abuses by the military became widespread, and most were well documented. Very rarely was an offender brought to justice, most cases were only investigated by human rights groups, and only a handful of military personnel have ever been prosecuted. In instances where soldiers were taken into custody they were usually not heard of again, but it is suspected that they were merely transferred to another unit elsewhere in the country. It is difficult to provide completely reliable estimates of the number of killings and atrocities that took place under the Marcos regime – and during the early part of martial law when the wholesale slaughter of Muslims occurred – but no fewer than 200 000 people undoubtedly died violently during the last 20 years. In 1985 no less than 5000 men, women and children were killed, this figure including soldiers and members of the paramilitary forces. During the height of the fighting in Mindanao – when the BMA and the MNLF were especially active – there were daily flights to the island of Mindanao. In the morning ammunition would be flown in, and on the return evening flight the aircraft would carry the bodies of dead soldiers.

The fight against the MNLF was especially concentrated immediately after the national elections for the *Batasang Pambansa* in May 1984. At least 3000 troops, using planes, helicopters and artillery were used to drive out a stronghold of about 500 Muslim rebels. One hundred soldiers were killed along with ten members of the MNLF. In that operation there were the first reports that the Philippine army was using chemical weapons, and the rebel victims and their families reported vomiting, dizziness and red patches on the skin. The MNLF – which receives training and equipment from Syria, Lebanon, Iran and Malaysia for its campaign to establish a separate Muslim or 'Moro' nation in Mindanao where most of the Philippines' Muslim minority is concentrated – has reported that the prolonged conflict with government troops in Mindanao forced 200 000 refugees to flee to Sabah in Malaysia. During an opposition rally near Malacañang Palace on 21 September 1984, the wife of an air force career officer – Mrs Lorna Yap – publicly testified that her husband had participated in napalm bombings against Muslim rebels sometime in 1974. The statement consequently led military officials to ask Lieutenant-Colonel Adelberto Yap to leave the Villamor Air

Base in Manila and vacate his government quarters 'in the interest of security'.

The accusation that napalm bombs and chemical weapons were being used was first made in September 1984 by Tarhata Lucman, a Muslim leader and former governor of Lanao del Sur province. Marcos and the armed forces chief, General Fabian Ver, immediately denied that the military had such weapons. Ver stated: 'We don't even have chemical weapons in our inventory so how can we use them?' However, the Defence Minister, Juan Ponce Enrile, later said that the military had napalm but that he was 'almost certain' it was not used in counter-insurgency operations. Enrile did not say where the napalm came from but, as indicated earlier, most of the Philippine's military equipment comes from the USA.

Muslim leaders quoted residents of Lanao del Sur as saying that there had been daily bombings in some parts of the province from May 1984 onwards, but that bombs dropped on 5 August smelled different. Many villagers fainted and suffered facial burns after the bombs hit.

The Ecumenical Movement for Justice and Peace said that its investigations showed that thousands had fled their homes because of intensified bombings, and that 300 people had died from the use of chemical weapons.

MILITARY ABUSES

Human rights violations involving the military and military-related units have been categorised into two groups: those resulting from general military policy relating to the counter-insurgency programme; and individual abuses by members of the military or paramilitary groups. In a report published in 1984 by a fact-finding mission on human rights and militarization in the Philippines, details were given of the military strategies which had been developed for bringing to an end the dissent of the people. The backbone of the plan was *Oplan Katatagan* (Operation Plan Stability) whose general aim was to 'win the hearts and minds of the people'. Implemented in 1983 it was enacted as Letter of Instruction 2-81 by virtue of Marcos's legislative prerogative given to him by the constitution's Amendment No. 6.

Under *Oplan Katatagan*, military field operations were divided into four strategic phases: *Clearing Operations* designed to destroy the political infrastructure of the local insurgency; *Holding Operations* involving the elimination of NPA cells and the establishment of a local defence network composed of the ICHDF; *Consolidation Operations* intended to deliver essential services and livelihood programmes to the people; and *Development Operations* where long-term community programmes were conducted in preparation for the withdrawal of the regular military units. Although civic operations – phases three and four – were given publicity by the government-controlled media in an effort to play down the programme's military operations, the emphasis was firmly on stages one and two: to 'solve the problem' of insurgency.

Abuses were condoned or encouraged as long as they achieved the desired result of eliminating the NPA from a particular area. During *Clearing Operations* the military conducted raids and 'zoning' operations in villages and communities suspected of supporting dissidents. These were usually undertaken at weekly intervals, often culminating in dialogues between local civilian and military officials. This was undoubtedly the most important phase where the military used a combination of psychological tactics and firepower to neutralise a community. During 'zoning' operations the people in the *barrios* were terrified, and completely at the mercy of the soldiers. The behaviour of the combat troops was markedly brutal. Cases of rape, manhandling and summary executions were common, especially in the remote areas where the villagers were 'trapped'. During their searches the soldiers looted freely, and destroyed property. During 1984 and 1985 the burning of houses and even whole villages was reported in many areas of Mindanao and Samar. As many as 6000 combat troops and support personnel were used in a 'zoning' operation which frequently involved the permanent or temporary relocation of civilians – 'hamleting' – in order to isolate anti-government forces and thus weaken the support they received from the community. This endeavour – to break the lines of communication between the members of the NPA and their supporters in the *barrios* – was at the centre of the *Clearing Operation*, and resulted in threats and harassment to villagers, and sometimes killings. After villages and communities had been evacuated the military declared the area a free-fire zone, and would kill people on sight. But the NPA was quick to disappear, and the success of the military in these operations was significantly limited. Most affected by the activities were the peasant farmers and their families. Their crops had to be abandoned, their homes were left unattended or destroyed, their animals ran wild or were taken by the soldiers, and they were forced to live in places where they had no further access to their land. If people were allowed to stay in their homes, they sometimes had to remove the outside walls, so that the military passing by could immediately see who was occupying the dwelling.

> The military commander said,
> Your town was like a beautiful lake;
> But rebels infested it like bad fish.
> The lake had to be drained of its water
> To catch them.
> Move further down;
> Leave your rebel-infested lands for
> guarded grounds.
> Strip your house,
> So rebels may not use it.
> Moving down
> We carried not a shingle
> Whither they consigned us.
> We do not know
> Nor do we know,
> When we will be back on our land again.
> For yesterday, men in droves were
> conscripted
> To labour for a new clearing—
> For a rubber plantation,
> To develop our 'rebel-infested' land.
> Now fear, now anger, override grief.
> Our long watchful vigil is only beginning.
>
> *Anonymous*

Holding operations were conducted to pre-empt influences within the community which were anti-government. Local leaders were installed who would report any activities within the *barrios*, or take action through the ICHDF or other paramilitary groups, and anyone suspected of having links with the 'NPA was likely to become the victim of extra-judicial killing or 'salvaging'.

The counter-insurgency thrust ran parallel to the 'hearts and minds' campaign run by the USA in Vietnam. Operation Phoenix, like *Oplan Katatagan*, placed importance on strengthening intelligence operations and involved the outright killing or detention of suspects, confirming ideas that *Oplan Katatagan* was masterminded and adapted for use in the Philippines by military advisers from the USA. The creation of paramilitary units based outside the community extended the capability of the military to monitor local activities. The fact that they were arming and handing over power to groups of men who would freely torture, kill, loot and terrorise people in the area was of little concern to the regional commander. The Philippine Constabulary (PC) which was originally a paramilitary force became – with the police – integrated with the AFP, leaving the ICHDF the largest paramilitary organisation in the country. In Zamboanga city there was a parallel force, engaged in similar activities but using a different name: Active Counter Terrorist Sector (ACTS). Their ruthlessness was only matched, within a major urban area, by the ICHDF in Davao city. The citizens of these major cities experienced death in their midst every day of the year. The military used the ICHDF and ACTS to engage in activities and abuse which the soldiers and their officers were loathe to do openly, for fear of censure and possibly prosecution. Many ICHDF members were notorious individuals and often former members of ultra-right religious fanatical groups.

ICHDF IN ACTION

Fifty-three year old Remedios Llena could only stare in shock and terror as she witnessed elements of the ICHDF and the PC rape and kill her 15-year-old daughter Virginia.

Remedios was working on their farm at around 4 p.m. on 23 December 1984 in Rubas, Jaro, Leyte, when she heard gunshots in the direction of their house. She rushed to the area and saw several men atop a hill strafing their *nipa* hut below. As she crouched behind the stump of a tree, she saw Virginia jump out of the house and slump onto the ground, trying to stop the flow of blood from a bullet wound on her arm.

The shooting stopped and a joint force of ICHDF and PC soldiers made their way downhill. From the group which approached her daughter, Remedios recognised four ICHDF members: Abraham Reyes alias Ambang Caigoy, Celso Daguman, Albino Arbas and Doring Morpe. She specifically remembered Reyes for he had once tried to grab the land she and her husband were tilling in another *barrio*.

Virginia was taken to a vegetable patch nearby where she was undressed and raped by Reyes, Daguman, Arbas and Morpe. Virginia shouted for help but Reyes stabbed her above the breast and below the navel, and shot her with a rifle.

Before leaving, the group looted the Llena residence and burned it, later, along with a neighbour's house. Virginia was buried the afternoon before Christmas Day, on 24 December at the Municipal Cemetery of Jaro.

An exhumation on 12 January 1985 confirmed the municipal autopsy report that she had died from severe haemorrhage due to multiple gunshot and stab wounds.

FANATICAL SECTS

In Mindanao, the military exploited to maximum use the pervasive folk religiosity in the region. They armed and trained religious cults and turned them into counter-insurgency units. Together with non-religious paramilitary groups, they were behind most of the killings which occurred daily, either prompted by the military or acting on their own initiative for a variety of reasons: 'religious', revenge, sadism or monetary gain. The following are the most prominent groups, still active but with the extent of military support unclear.

Ilaga (Rats)

This is considered the 'mother' group of the fanatical sects, and its members claim invincibility through rituals, the possession of *anting-anting* (amulets) – which they wear around their necks – and the rubbing of *lana* (oil) all over their bodies. They shave their heads. As modern animists – drawing on a mixture of animism, folk Christianity and even folk Islam – they prepare themselves for battle like the warriors of a jungle tribe. Members of *Ilaga* are forbidden sexual indulgence, or even entry into the homes of menstruating or pregnant women, before a military 'operation'. They have recourse to pig-Latin incantations before missions; forbid themselves meat on Fridays, and shrimps and squid on Tuesdays and Fridays; and – despite being sworn enemies of Muslim rebels – sometimes face Mecca for their pre-battle prayers. They must keep their feet dry during an 'attack'. To do otherwise is to ensure defeat.

The *Ilaga* gained fame because of their founder, Commander Toothpick, a man known in folk legend as having gained his battle prowess from an old mountain *ermitano* (hermit). The *ermitano* conferred an *anting-anting* on Toothpick, guaranteeing invincibility, on condition that he engaged in good deeds.

Indeed, before the *Ilaga* commission as ICHDFs, Toothpick and his men were regarded as protectors and folk heroes. Among Christian communities in Cotabato and Lanao, Muslim forces forcibly reclaiming land long sold to Christians found a formidable enemy in the disciplined forces of the *Ilaga* as, in battle formation, they moved in jump steps, right feet forward and singing 'Candida'. As members of the ICHDF their role and behaviour changed: soon they were murdering not only Muslim rebels but B'laan tribesmen and Christian settlers as well. Cotabato folk claim that Toothpick killed by PC troopers in 1983, had lost his invincibility because he had become a gun-for-hire. The tradition continues today with members of *Ilaga* involved in land-grabbing and extortion.

Philippines Missionary Benevolent Association (PMBA)
This group originated in Surigao and is led by Ruben Ecleo, the mayor of Dinagat island, and an ex-colonel. He claims to be a Divine Master, nothing less than Christ's reincarnation. Pig-Latin is also used by the PMBA, read from *libretas* for every emergency, threat or mission. Ecleo has convinced his followers that material possessions are obstacles to salvation, and there have been sufficient PMBA followers to sell whatever little they had to give to what must now be a very wealthy Divine Master in exchange for being given an identity as the chosen people of Pagadian, the Baganian Peninsula, Salug Valley, Lanao, Misamis Occidental and Zamboanga del Norte. Ecleo's armed bodyguards are known locally as the 'White-Eagles', and the group is said to be expanding its membership in the Visayan island of Samar.

Lost Command
Reference had already been made to this group in connection with their 'security guard' duties at the Guthrie Palm Oil Plantation in San Francisco, Agusan del Sur. The Lost Command first made the headlines in 1982 following its alleged involvement in the massacre of 45 men, women and children in the village of Las Navas, Northern Samar. Lademora's men once made up the Special Unit of the Armed Forces of the Philippines, organised in 1974 during the height of the Muslim conflict and disbanded some time later. As suggested earlier, the group continues to be active in a number of illegal acts: extortion, faked raffles and seeking a monopoly over the local gold-panning business. In 1984 Lademora was given a new assignment as regional commander of the ICHDF and many members of the Lost Command were integrated into the unit.

The Davao city cathedral bombing was allegedly carried out by the Lost Command and members of the PC based in Davao city. The bombing occurred on Easter Sunday, 19 April 1981, a few yards from the altar of St Peter's Cathedral. Two grenades were exploded within 30 minutes of each other. After the second explosion bursts of M-16 rifles were heard. Seventeen people were killed in the blasts, and over 200 injured.

4Ks or 4KKs

The *Kalihokan sa mga Kabos Alang sa Kagawasan ng Kalingkawasan* (Philippine Democratic Missionary Church) are found in the Aurora Hills and the Salug Valley of Zamboanga del Sur, in Sindagan, Zamboanga del Norte and in the south-western part of Misamis Occidental. Their founder and leader is Potenciano Marinduque, also known as 'Master P'. Another 4K master, 'Master Eve' is based in Dunmingag, Zamboanga del Sur. The 4Ks also claim invulnerability through rituals, the possession of *anting-anting* and the rubbing of oil. They are further said to be abstemious in the extreme – no smoking, drinking or gambling – but have shown themselves capable of the most brutal killings, and of arson. In Zamboanga del Sur, where 4Ks automatically joined the ICHDF, the initiation rite – in common with members of *Ilaga* – includes the killing of at least one person.

Tadtad

This group, whose name implies the dismemberment done to the bodies of its victims, that is, 'chop-chop' – and also known as the *Sagrado Corazon Senor* – is based in the Zamboanga–Bukidnon area and its members are found in clusters of communities along the Malindang mountains of western Mindanao. The group is 'hardcore anti-NPA' and, not only chops up its victims, but eats them. The death of an elected councillor in Bukidnon was attributed to *Tadtad* members. According to eyewitnesses, the man's headless body was chopped and cooked. This was said to be the group's 136th victim.

Rock Christ, White Rock and White Rock Jesus Christ

The *Rock Christ* group and its variants take their names from a certain large white rock on Mount Malindang which, it is claimed, bears imprints of the feet of Jesus. 'Rockers' wear white shorts for combat, and spread terror throughout the area with a well-documented list of killings, arson and massacres.

Philippine Liberation Organisation

The killing of a prominent newsman in Davao city in September 1984 was traced to this group. Allegedly made up of former members of the MNLF – now working with the military – it is headed by a man known only as 'Kapitan Inggo' and spread fear among the residents of Mandug, the community where the murdered newsman lived.

Others

Other fanatical groups in Mindanao include the *Patiks* of Bukidnon; *Bagong Jerusalem* (New Jerusalem); *Piniling Nasud* (Chosen People); *Patay-Buhi* (Die and Live); *Alpha Omega* (Beginning and End); *Katyann*; *Dos por Dos* (Two by Two); Things to Come Mission; Bolog Batallion; *Ontol Ligid*; *Moncadista*; *Kabisigs*; Church of Yahweh; Rida; *Katoliko Largo* (Catholic League); *Caballeros de Rizal* (Friends of Rizal); *Santa Lana*; and *Likus-likos*, a sub-group of the notorious *Ilaga*. In the north of the Philippines, in Luzon, such groups as the *Doce Pares* (Twelve Pairs) and the *PC'ing Yapak* (Barefoot Philippine Constabulary), based in Laguna, can be found.

DOCE PARES FIGURE IN RAPE MURDER

Elements of the *Doce Pares* gang, believed to be connected with the special operations of the military, killed Alfredo Matabuena, a farmer, and repeatedly raped his wife after they raided the couple's house in *barangay* Maracabac, Castilla, Sorsogon.

At about 7 p.m. on 16 May 1984, around six men approached the house of Matabuena. Two of the armed men entered the house while the rest remained outside. Matabuena was ordered to lie flat on the floor after which he was hit with the butts of their guns. They asked for money but Matabuena remained silent through the entire torture session. Finally, the men outside were ordered by the two men inside to take Matabuena away.

The two men put out the light before introducing themselves to their victims as 'good men belonging to the *Doce Pares*', and raping Elizabeth Matabuena, the 35-year-old wife of Alfredo. She tried to shout but one of the men bit her lips, causing these to bleed. They stopped for a while and went outside after Elizabeth begged them to bring her husband back. They returned without Alfredo, however, and raped her again.

One of the men later talked to her, and from several names of his kin that he mentioned, Elizabeth was able to identify her rapist. She claimed that it was Joaquin Janaban Jr, one of the *Doce Pares* leaders and a resident of the same *barangay*.

Not contented, he raped Elizabeth for the third time and left with his companion at around 10 p.m.

Elizabeth waited the whole night for her husband but he never came back. She looked for her husband next day at dawn and found him dead some 20 metres from the house. He had bruises on his nape and the portion of the neck below the chin had been pierced by a sharp object. Elizabeth herself was bleeding from the sexual assault of the two men . . . Her husband was buried the next day while Elizabeth was hospitalized.

Update, 30 June 1984

Many of the fanatical religious groups were set up and supported by the military, spreading fear and brutality in God's name. Catholic Church observers around Mindanao documented efforts by the military to promote such groups through 'seminars' patterned after religious revival sessions. According to one church official, military officers shouted hysterically that the communities and all forms of opposition were the work of the devil. They quoted the Bible and appealed to religious motivations in order to surrender to God in heaven and to President Marcos as his representative on earth. Entire communities were forced to attend the seminars, which began with prayer and were followed by hours of lectures by military officers. The seminar ended with all the participants standing and repeating an oath of surrender to God. 'The people know that these "religious and inspired" military officers had been personally involved in abuses and brutalities and in torturing hapless suspects during military operations', said a church official who was describing one seminar.

The religious sects say that they believe in Christian doctrine. The members of Nene Butak's group – part of an unnamed sect that claims a few thousand followers in Mindanao – clutched Thompson machine guns and old bolt-action Garand rifles as they set off in search of communist rebels. Prior to 1986 the military are said to have armed more than 200 paramilitary death squads in Mindanao with 17 000 weapons, in addition to the machetes which many groups use.

Butak's group supplements its studies of scripture with four books supposedly written by Moses but not included in the traditional Bible. These books include the titles *The Sixth and Seventh Books of Moses or Moses' Magical Spiritual Art* and *Mystery of the Long Lost Eighth, Ninth and Tenth Books of Moses, Together with the Legend that was of Moses and 44 Keys to Universal Power.* They have chapters on astrology, magical cures of the Hebrews, the healing powers of amulets and 'magic of the Israelites'. The books are printed in the USA.

The number of summary executions rose steadily throughout 1984 and 1985. Despite military attempts to discredit the NPA by associating them with the deaths of innocent people, there was no doubt that the bulk of the responsibility rested with the ICHDF, the fanatical groups, and the soldiers themselves. Most often, the names of ex-military officers appeared as the founders or leaders of the various sects.

In a special report on fanatacism in the Philippines, Sylvia Mayuga drew readers' attention to a study in the quarterly bulletin, *Pro Munda Vita*, published by the International Research and Information

Centre in Belgium called, 'Sects in Central America'. The article indicated that the proliferation of fanatical sects and cults in revolutionary situations such as the Philippines was too similar to the Latin American and the Vietnamese experiences to be mere coincidence. In May 1985, Marcos was quoted as telling the visiting CIA chief, William Casey, that these cults had proved useful in the counter-insurgency drive. Certainly within Latin American countries, there was an overriding political desire to break the influence of the Catholic church and the article recalls the words of President Roosevelt who, speaking in Patagonia, Argentina, said: 'I think that it will be a long and difficult task for the US to absorb these countries as long as they remain Catholic.'

A few years after these words were spoken, Rockefeller travelled through Latin America and came to a similar conclusion. When he later visited Central America he saw the development of some of the original BCC models, and returned to the USA saying that the *communides ecclesial de base* threatened eventually to become a major challenge to American interests, and that the need was to create similar organisations funded and directed by North America.

As Sylvia Mayuga points out, to that recommendation the Philippines owe the nationwide television shows called 'Club 700', the mysterious organisation called World Vision and a whole range of evangelical groups like Campus Crusade for Christ, all funded and run by Americans for what can only be American interests. Thus, it is easy to make the link with the systematic exploitation by the AFP of religious fanaticism in Mindanao where millions of hectares have been cultivated exclusively for American interests. Malaybalay, Bukidnon – where, for example, the *Tadtad* operates – is now firmly believed to be the home of an extensive American underground military installation.

ATROCITIES: PERSONAL ACCOUNTS

In the next chapter details of a number of other 'cases' – well-documented by human rights groups – will show further the extent of the persecution, oppression and killings faced by ordinary people in their everyday lives during the latter part of the Marcos era. It is easy, with the huge number of atrocities, to focus on 'statistics', and to stand some distance from the pain experienced by individuals and their families following the disappearance of their friends, neighbours and relatives; the discovery of their dismembered bodies; or their disfigurement after torture. Many people have had members of their family shot to death in front of them. I have listened – often physically nauseated by the details – to people who have suffered thus. Extracts from two such personal accounts are given below, the first by a woman whose husband had been killed some months previously; and the second by a doctor whose brother and his family had been murdered a few days before. In neither case were the murderers apprehended.

Evelyn Barcelona
This is the account of Evelyn Barcelona, aged 37 years.

We were living in a small place in the mountains about 120 kilometres from Cagayan de Oro city when my husband was killed by the military and some other men. [The men who first came to the house were later identified as members of the ICHDF, some of whom also belonged to a local fanatical sect, the name of which was not known. The 'seven soldiers' referred to later in Evelyn Barcelona's account would appear to have been regular members of the AFP.] I have six children, the oldest now 13 years, and the youngest was four months when Wilfredo was shot. My husband was a rice farmer, working about three hectares of land owned by my mother's sister. Because of the children I couldn't work, and the land provided us with scarcely enough to live on. We never had rice to sell.

My husband was abducted and killed on 16 August 1984. He was 41 years at the time of his death. The soldiers, ten of them, arrived at 5.30 in the morning to take him away, and the night before he was restless as he slept. People in the area were nervous. A Task Force, specially formed to round up alleged subversives, had been active in the area.

They came without warning and without a search warrant, ransacked the house but found no evidence. The military said that they were taking my husband away for investigation. I pleaded with them that I had small children and that one of them was sick.

At 10 o'clock I went to the barracks with food. My husband had had no breakfast. Because I was crying the soldiers at the gate took me to the commanding officer. He said that, because the military had been unable to find the NPA, Wilfredo had gone with some of his men as a guide.

At four o'clock in the afternoon seven soldiers brought my husband's body to the house. There was blood coming from his nose and mouth, his head was cracked and there were cuts in the back of his neck. He had a bullet wound in his chest, there were other bullet holes in his wrists and a knife had been plunged into his heart. The children were present when he arrived. Two of them kissed him. The soldiers said that, on the trip in the mountains, my husband had died during an encounter with the NPA. They seemed indifferent.

The military killed him. He was knifed in the heart to make sure he was really dead. Some witnessed what was done to him but were too scared to testify. One man saw my husband shot by some soldiers. They took him further up the mountain and just shot him. On the way from the house he was already being tortured.

When the soldiers had gone I fled with the family: eventually to an aunt in Cagayan de Oro. We left everything. Other soldiers came back later and destroyed the house. I'm too scared to go back.

I have been helped by an organisation since I came to Cagayan. They have complained to the military but to no avail, and we are still hoping to get permission to exhume the bodies to establish exactly how they died. Another man, a neighbour, was taken away and killed at the same time, also suspected of being a member of the NPA.

Life was very different when I was living in the mountains with Wilfredo. Three of my children go to elementary school. We all live with my aunt. I sell food: fried bananas. My grandmother also helps. The income is only 10 pesos a day. Not enough to live on.

The Bucag family

On 1 May 1984 in an election-related murder in Gingoog, Misamis Oriental, a family of three was brutally slain by members of *Tadtad*: Renato Bucag, 48 years; his wife, Melchora; and their 13-year-old son, Renee Boy. Renato Bucag's sister, a doctor, carried out her own autopsy on the three victims:

Eight armed men entered their home and fired their armalite rifles at them. The autopsy which I carried out revealed what else happened to them. Renato suffered 16 gunshot wounds in the torso aside from having stab wounds at the back. His neck was also slashed. Melchora had multiple gunshot wounds in the chest and stab wounds below the right breast and on both thighs. Her ears were slashed off. Renee Boy had an incision from the left ear to the mouth, cutting through the molars. He also suffered a stab wound which penetrated through his neck and wounds on both his thighs which measured up to eight and a half inches long.

Renato Bucag was chairman of the United Opposition whose members came from the Pilipino Democratic Party-Laban, Mindanao Alliance and Liberal Party. He also served as a city councillor for ten years. The price of public office – or suspicion of involvement with the NPA – was that family members were at risk. Children were often sprayed with bullets and many – like Renee Boy Bucag – died alongside their parents.

CESAR CLIMACO

Opposition politicians remained targets for assassination attempts while Marcos was in power. The elimination of the opposition was one of his main strategies. An acid-tongued foe of Marcos met his death on 14 November 1984, shot in the back of the head by a single bullet at close range during one of his regular morning inspections of the city. He was 68-year-old Cesar Climaco, the mayor of Zamboanga city, and a vigorous campaigner against crime and corruption as well as political graft. Always controversial – and one of the country's most colourful opposition figures – Climaco was elected in May 1984 to the *Batasang Pambansa*, the national assembly. He became especially vulnerable after his election, and took no additional precautions even though he knew that, in previous weeks, many of his colleagues in opposition in Mindanao had been murdered.

Two weeks before his death Climaco wrote to the AFP Acting Chief of Staff, Lieutenant-General Fidel Ramos, expressing fears of a possible murder plot against him, and of the rapidly deteriorating peace and order situation in the province. He was also apprehensive that Muslims who engaged marines in a shoot-out a few days previously would be accused of his assassination.

Said Climaco, citing the military conspiracy that resulted in Aquino's death, in his letter to Ramos dated 30 October: 'It is also very possible that a similar "military conspiracy" is now, either in the planning stage or is already in full implementation to eliminate the city administration which, in the hands of the opposition, is an embarrassing political situation that belies the vociferous claim of President Marcos that neither ballots nor bullets can bring down his Administration.'

Climaco was not asking for protection from the military, only that they take heed of the situation 'in the interest of the peace and tranquillity of the community'.

The mayor added in his letter that the military was spreading rumours that he was 'anti-Muslim' and that he had engineered the shoot-out against the marines. They were probably being disseminated to throw suspicion on Muslim groups, Climaco theorised.

It seemed that the Zamboanga mayor had predicted his own death, and even the events that would follow his assassination. Early in December, Climaco's relatives were invited by Southern Command Chief Major General Delfin C. Castro to Camp Navarro 'to view a videotape where members of the Alih clan, led by Rizal Alih, allegedly admitted that they (Alihs) killed Mayor Climaco last 14 November'.

Climaco's family, several of whom later received death threats, refused to accept the military's version. The slain mayor's son, Erwin, said: 'The Alihs were probably pressured, coerced, intimidated and tortured to admit a crime they never committed.'

I accompanied Climaco in his jeep on a tour of Zamboanga city shortly before his death. His driver had a rifle by his side, but in its plastic case. He could have been killed by political opponents; or as a result of a personal vendetta; or on the basis of a contract killing by underworld syndicates; or by a combination of all three. As elsewhere, business and politics were mixed in Zamboanga city.

As mayor, Climaco bombarded Marcos in Manila with telegrams, letters and reports on a range of issues, taunting him, challenging his authority or raising questions about very serious local issues. From the letters reproduced here Climaco can clearly be seen as a threat to government.

Climaco was buried, in accordance with his wishes, as cheaply as possible – the coffin cost 700 pesos – and in the clothes in which he died.

Six persons were charged with the murder: a year after his death. They were four members of the Alih family – Rizal, Nasim, Medial and Aisah – and two others named Kennedy Gonalez and one alias 'Alhabun', the latter not apprehended. The investigation took almost a year because of the reluctance of witnesses to come forward, and the fact that the identities of those charged were at variance with statements of the Climaco family, as already indicated, who did not believe that the Alihs were responsible. For some people it is perhaps comforting to learn that unlike the numerous murders which have taken place and remained unsolved in the Philippines, the Climaco case appeared to have been solved and the killers prosecuted. But then, is it not axiomatic also that truth is not enough, in an environment where truth must also be believed?

Cesar C. Climaco
City Mayor

Republic of the Philippines
Office of the City Mayor
City of Zamboanga
3 February 1984

President Ferdinand E. Marcos,
Malacañang, Manila.

Dear Mr President:
Are you still announcing to the World that your 100% KBL-Appointed Commission on Elections can be trusted?

In connection with the 27 January Plebiscite, the COMELEC Chairman is reported to have prematurely announced and proclaimed an Impressive

75 per cent to 80 per cent voters turnout, as was also reported in all of the KBL owned and controlled media.

What is suspicious, nay malicious, is that hardly has the plebiscite canvassing begun, and during the early evening hours of 27 January the Nation's numerous KBL and Administration owned Radio–TV networks . . . were busy echoing and parroting the reported prediction of a heavy voters' turnout, at 75 per cent to 80 per cent – a premature estimate obviously aimed at conditioning the minds of the Radio–TV audience, the Foreign Audience in particular, that the Philippine Electorate has 'resoundingly' supported your leadership by responding enthusiastically to your 'Go out and Vote Yes' campaign, thereby rejecting and deriding the POLL BOYCOTT Campaign of the Nation's Badly Fragmented Opposition.

Right here in Zamboanga City, the Guiwan Barangay Captain, who is reputed to be an 'On Today and Off Tomorrow' *BONA FIDE* KBL, in an early evening deceptive Broadcast, obviously echoing the KBL-appointed Comelec Chairman's prediction of 75 per cent to 80 per cent voters turnout, proudly went on the air bragging and proclaiming that in his Barangay, 80 per cent of the registered voters went to the Polls and voted 'Yes' – only to be humbled and shamed a few minutes later by City Councillor Abelardo A. Climaco, Jr who, after carefully going over the Plebiscite returns of Barangay Guiwan, at the Canvassing Hall, discovered that not more than 30 per cent of the Guiwan electorate went out that day to cast their votes . . . in Zamboanga City, out of a Total of 230 428 Registered Voters, *only 53 362 voted, or a measly 23 per cent*, with *177 066 Voters, or a whopping 77 per cent*, who COURAGEOUSLY DEFIED and DISOBEYED your Laws and Decrees which compel them to 'Go and Vote'!! Are you NOT DISTURBED, IRRITATED OR ANGERED by such a MASSIVE DEFIANCE??? Yes or No?

In the face of such a Massive Civil DISOBEDIENCE to your Solemn Decrees and Edicts, what shall we do?

If you BELIEVE in your claim that you are still in FULL COMMAND and in control of the Government, will it not be EMBARRASSING and a BIG SHAME for you and your KBL Hierarchy to find yourselves powerless to take the prescribed legal actions against all those 177 066 Voters of Zamboanga City who dared Challenge and Disobey your Mandates?

And if ill-advised by your Political Advisers, your KBL Administration decides to prosecute all those who advocated Boycott, as well as all those who failed to vote last 27 January; and if your KBL Administration is committed to do 'JUSTICE TO AQUINO AND JUSTICE TO ALL', may we know how soon will you start prosecuting all those who COURAGEOUSLY and PATRIOTICALLY defied your edicts?

We dare you, Mr President, to do your DUTY and PROSECUTE all those who BOYCOTTED the 27 January Plebiscite, not only in Zamboanga City but all over the Philippines, because if you do prosecute them, then the KBL will have reason to fill every room in Malacañang with additional and authentic medals and awards for your unprecedented COURAGE and BRAVERY in imposing your indomitable will upon the Great Majority of the Sovereign People!!!

But your COURAGE and INCLINATIONS for Justice will be Best

Tested and Demonstrated if the FIRST and FOREMOST to be prosecuted are your very own *in-laws* of the ARANETA CLAN – LUIS, Irene's father-in-law, and Father FRANCISCO, the Jesuit who solemnized Irene's marriage to Greggy! – these two ARANETA BROTHERS being among the leading and Outspoken and Patriotic Filipinos who courageously led the Massive Defiance to your Decrees and advocated a Total Boycott! Will you use the best KBL legal minds to have the ARANETA BROTHERS arrested?

Frankly, I have my doubts that you will prosecute any or both of the ARANETA BROTHERS – but if you do, you still have a chance to be a Good KBL President!

But if you FAIL to PROSECUTE these two ARANETA BROTHERS and all of the Great Majority of the Electorate who Refused to Vote last 27 January, then you will be unwittingly exposing your HOLLOWNESS as a Public Official and, above all, you will give yourself no other alternative (under the guise of RECONCILIATION and REPENTANCE, more of the latter) but to withdraw and repeal your unenforceable edict on COMPULSORY VOTING and forthwith, in TOTAL DISGRACE, Raise Up Both Hands, Throw in the Towel, Give Up, and bring down the Curtains of Power, with a Sad and Sour Note of GOOD BYE on your LIPS!!

THE END!!!

Yours very truly
(Signed) Cesar C. Climaco

Cesar C. Climaco
City Mayor

Republic of the Philippines
Office of the City Mayor
City of Zamboanga

15 December 1983

President Ferdinand E. Marcos,
Malacañang, Manila.

Dear Mr President:

This has reference to our Complaint Telegram to you dated 18 November 1983 relative to the sinking of the M/L Jawiya somewhere in the Sulu Archipelago sometime last month after having been fired upon by a Philippine Navy boat under the command of Lt Commander Joaquin Tan.

In connection thereto, we are furnishing you herewith a xeroxed copy of the letter dated 1 December 1983 of Mr Rojas Saliling, a resident of Campo Islam, this city, along with a xeroxed reproduction of the enclosure mentioned therein and its translation in English, which is a letter written by his daughter, N-ning Sali, on 24 November 1983.

In her above-mentioned letter, Ms N-Ning Sali claims that among the passengers who were on board the ill-fated vessel at the time of its sinking were children, some of whom were her relatives. According to Ms Sali, these were the following:

1. her aunt Amina and her four children, one of whom was only four years old;
2. her grandmother Amsura, her uncle Bing and one Nursida;

3. her uncle Ikih and one Layang and her four children;
4. her grandmother's son, named Pakka and her cousin, Samman, son of her uncle Hamdan; and
5. her grandmother Indah and her children, her Uncle Laja and one of his three daughters.

Ms Sali further claims that the dead bodies of her relatives, all of whom were killed by naval gunfire, have not been recovered to date.

Mr President, since the claim of Ms Sali strongly contradicts earlier statements made by Philippine Navy authorities to the effect that there were no students or teachers on board the ill-fated vessel on the basis of sworn statements given by alleged survivors, we feel that there is a compelling need to have the case re-opened in order that it can be subjected to thorough investigation, so that those responsible for such an act can be brought before the bar of justice.

The incident, as already stated in my aforesaid 18 November 1983 Telegram to you, has all the Criminal Characteristics of the Korean Airlines Plane destroyed by a Soviet Missile – hence, the need of a truly independent investigating Committee to elicit the truth and give justice where justice is due.

Very truly yours,
(Signed) Cesar C. Climaco

SALVAGING

The huge number of 'salvaging' cases during recent years must lead to the conclusion that the government opted to use abductions and political killings – apart from set patterns of detention, massacre and strafing – as a means of cowing the population into submission. The reign of terror experienced by some communities was parallel to occurrences in Guatemala, Argentina and other Latin American countries, in the face of the notorious death squads. It became increasingly difficult to account for all the people who were killed, and to identify those who were eventually found, their corpses mutilated beyond recognition. It became common for bodies to be fished out of the Pasig River, and the Agusan River.

I was in Himamaylan, Negros Occidental in Western Visayas shortly after the death of Elvie Degit, who was abducted on 14 January 1984, and was missing for two days. When the body of 16-year-old Elvie was discovered her left breast had been slashed off and the right arm and palm were heavily lacerated. Seventeen other wounds were found on her armpit, elbows, legs, feet, neck and back. Her body was found hanging upside down. Earlier, Elvie's father, Alberto, an active member of the BCC, had received death

Table 5.1   Disappearances, 1977–85

Year	Metro Manila	Luzon	Visayas	Mindanao	Total
1977	2	11	1	3	17
1978	1	3	4	2	10
1979	2	12	—	34	48
1980	2	17	—	—	19
1981	—	8	—	45	53
1982	—	16	2	24	42
1983	2	13	15	115	145
1984	7	34	24	93	158
1985	11	28	43	129	211
Total	27	142	89	445	703

Table 5.2   Recorded Extra-judicial Killings, 1977–85

Year	Metro Manila	Luzon	Visayas	Mindanao	Total
1977	—	24	21	6	51
1978	1	25	44	16	86
1979	—	56	38	102	196
1980	—	45	36	137	218
1981	—	65	28	228	321
1982	—	46	28	136	210
1983	1	62	41	265	369
1984	2	114	61	361	538
1985	8	53	74	260	395
Total	12	490	371	1511	2384

threats from members of the ICHDF that a member of his family would be killed. Alberto had been a witness to the salvaging of his neighbour by the same ICHDF men.

On 17 January 1981, Marcos lifted martial law – on paper – promising national reconciliation and the restoration of democracy. Although the number of political prisoners decreased after that, the total number of salvaging victims continued to grow. Five hundred and thirty-eight extra-judicial killings were documented in 1984, and 395 in 1985. In the region of Mindanao alone, the month of June 1985 saw a total of 13 people summarily executed by different military units, a month representative of many others – in Mindanao and elsewhere in the Philippines. The deaths in Mindanao in June were as follows:

Zamboanga del Norte
A 53-year-old resident farmer of Lowao, Godod and his 14-year-old son were salvaged by unidentified men believed to be members of the fanatical group, 4Ks.

Francisco and Rufo Landa were fishing in a river when their assailants attacked them with a *bolo*. Both sustained multiple stab wounds.

Zamboanga del Sur
The dead body of a 45-year-old resident of Labangan was found on 9 June at the Sibucao bridge in Dumalinao. Circumstances point to the ICHDF and military men as the perpetrators of the act.

Jovito Mamawi was on his way home when he was invited by friends to join a drinking spree with some ICHDF and military men. After the drinking session, Mamawi was brought by the military to their camp for unknown reasons. He was found dead the following day.

Five days earlier, a 26-year-old farmer was also killed in Dumalinao by unidentified men believed to be members of the ICHDF.

Pedro Tabamo was arrested on 2 June by a certain Sergeant Palumo, a military. He and his wife Adelaida were brought to the house of *barangay* captain Nicanor Fuentes for identification. Upon confirming Tabamo's identity, Sergeant Palumo left. Fuentes then revealed to the couple that Tabamo was on the military's liquidation list since he was a suspected NPA member. On 4 June Tabamo and his wife were roused from sleep by armed men who ordered him to come down from the house. Fearing that his family might be harmed, he complied. Tabamo was hog-tied and taken to a ricefield 400 metres away from the house. He was then stabbed 18 times and beheaded.

Davao city
The 25-year-old chairman of *Liga sa Kabataan sa Davao* (LIKADA) a military youth alliance, was salvaged on 27 June by military agents. Fernando Toralba Espiron was preparing for the celebration of the feast day of Mabini-Boulevard when he noticed two military operatives trailing him. He tried to run away but the men shot him in the legs forcing him to kneel down. His pursuers then fired two more bullets into his back. Espiron was dragged inside a cab. A witness claimed that the vehicle later headed for the Metrodiscom

headquarters. His corpse was found the next morning dumped under the Lizada bridge.

Misamis Occidental
The terrified family of a 38-year-old unionist could only stare in fear as he was shot point-blank with a .45 calibre pistol by four unidentified men on 19 June.

Herman Manco, a labourer of Red V Factory was resting with his family when four armed men barged into their house. Without further ado, the men shot him in the head and chest.

Misamis Oriental
A total of seven persons were salvaged in June 1985 by different military units in this province. Killed were Gerry Latoja, Bartolome Mendipol, Ricardo Dawa, Cristopher Humihon, Toto Umaynon, a certain Cado and Carlito Birador. Mendipol's corpse was found 20 metres away from the *barangay* elementary school. An exhumation revealed that he had been severely tortured as indicated by the loss of his teeth. Umaynon and Cado were also heavily tortured. Their arms were broken and their skulls were almost shattered. They also sustained multiple gunshot wounds. Birador was tortured during tactical interrogation in an attempt by the military to find out about his alleged involvement with the NPA. Unable to say anything, he was shot dead with an armalite rifle. His body was dumped inside a toilet hole.

The number of salvaging cases reported over the years testifies the extent to which the Marcos regime went in order to rid the society of suspected political dissenters and to abate the rising cries of protest. Victims of politically motivated summary executions were usually passed off as the casualties of 'encounters', or armed conflict between government troops and guerrillas of the NPA. Relatives knew that these allegations were false, often pointing to unmistakable marks of torture as proof of the fact that the victims were not killed in encounters.

From the scores of reports received by Task Force Detainees of the Philippines (TFDP), there seems to have been no standard procedure for eliminating those judged as threats to national security. Dr Remberto de la Paz, who shared his medical skills with all, was shot dead in his medical clinic in Catbalogan, Samar. Macli-ing Dulag, leader of the tribal opposition against the construction of the Chico River Dam was murdered when paratroopers quietly entered his village and strafed his home.

PREVENTIVE DETENTION ACTION

The Preventive Detention Act (PDA) was a presidential or executive warrant sanctioning the arbitrary arrest and detention of a person or persons suspected of having committed or about to commit what the Marcos regime considered to be crimes against the 'security and stability of the state'. It was one of the main weapons of political repression, applied mainly to quell democratic dissent in the country.

As with the regime's other instruments of repression such as the military and police, the use of the PDA was based on the assumption that 'crimes against the security and stability of the . . . regime' were necessarily crimes against the security and stability of the state. Thus, anyone who was critical of the Marcos regime – even if the criticisms were founded on just and legitimate grounds – was liable to be issued with a PDA.

The PDA came into existence with the issuance of Presidential Decree (PD) 1877 signed on 21 July 1983 but published only on 6 August 1983. It was one of about a thousand 'secret decrees' signed by Marcos who was empowered under the constitution's Amendment 6 to issue decrees and legislation 'whenever the regular National Assembly fails or is unable to act adequately on any matter for any reason that in his judgment, requires immediate action'.

PD 1877 affirmed the effectiveness of the erstwhile secret decrees 1834 and 1835, considered the most notorious of all the decrees created under Amendment 6. PD 1834 converted and penalised national security crimes such as rebellion and sedition into capital offences punishable by life imprisonment or death. PD 1835 left not a single utterance of criticism against the government to go unpunished. Its penalty included 'the forfeiture of his [the accused] rights as a citizen of the Philippines', including permanent disqualification from office, removal of the right to vote, confiscation of property and other cruel and unusual punishments.

The PDA covered persons alleged to have committed national security crimes. The decrees also increased all previous penalties provided in the national penal code.

Faced with a mounting protest over the 'chilling effects' of the two decrees, Marcos amended PDs 1834 and 1835 to PDs 1974 and 1975. The new decrees abolished the death penalty for crimes against public order and national security like subversion, reverting to a maximum of 12 years' imprisonment for such offences as originally provided in the Revised Penal Code.

Despite this major reversal however, the fate of individuals issued with PDAs still rested on Marcos's discretion.

PD 1877 required military authorities to apply for an arrest warrant from the civilian courts before arresting and detaining national security crime suspects. Such regard to due process, however, proved to be an ostensible ploy to project the PDA as less repressive than the Presidential Commitment Order (PCO).

The PCO was widely criticised for its gross disregard of the right to due process. Any arrest by virtue of the PCO could not be contested in court and only Marcos could grant the release of its victim. On the other hand the PDA did not change anything. In many instances, persons were already long arrested and detained before any PDA was produced. In such instances, the issuance of the PDA was made only to validate the fact of arrest and detention and secure the cases from further scrutiny especially by defence lawyers protesting violations against their clients' rights to due process.

The issue of preventive detention was rooted in the establishment of the US-backed Marcos regime as an instrument to suppress the Filipino people's nationalist and democratic aspirations. As such, preventive detention was an essential component of the government effort to block the advance of a people's movement determined to oust it.

The proclamation of martial law in September 1972, with Marcos invoking his emergency powers by raising the threat of rebellion as a disguise to control all government political and military machinery, provided the theoretical basis for the regime's resort to preventive detention as an instrument of political repression.

The president caused the suspension of the privilege of the writ of *habeas corpus*, and invested in himself and his armed forces preventive detention powers he had deemed necessary to combat the national security crimes. Preventive detention became official policy with the issuance of General Order (GO) No. 2 on 22 September 1972. GO No. 2 in turn gave birth to the Arrest, Search and Seizure Order (ASSO) which was to be the predecessor of the PCO and later the PDA. It was through ASSO that many of the

70 000 persons were arrested and detained for political reasons during the first five years of martial law.

GO No. 2 required that ASSOs were to be obtained through the judicial process. The courts never questioned the legality of the arrest order by the president or the then Secretary of National Defence or their use by military authorities. This was especially when 'summary information' or 'evaluated surveillance reports' were invoked as grounds for their issuance or use. The courts could never so question, anyway, since by virtue of GO No. 3 and 3-A they did not have any power 'to decide on matters relating to the validity, legality or constitutionality of decrees and orders promulgated or issued by the President or his duly designated representative'.

ASSO became officially part of the regime's arsenal of legislation only in 1978 when it was incorporated into PD 1498, otherwise known as the National Security Code.

On 17 January 1981, following pressures from its US backer (through the IMF–WB) to 'maintain a democratic façade' in order to secure its 'increasingly precarious position', the regime lifted martial law, through the issuance of Proclamation No. 2045.

As part of the 'normalisation' process ostensibly initiated thereafter, the regime abolished the dreaded ASSO. Proclamation No. 2045 stipulated, however, that while martial law had been lifted, the privilege of the writ of *habeas corpus* remained suspended in two regions of Mindanao and in all other places 'with respect to persons at present detained as well as others who may hereafter be detained for the crimes of insurrection, rebellion, subversion, conspiracy or proposal to commit such crimes as well as other crimes committed as incident thereto'.

Under Proclamation 2045, therefore, the policy of preventive detention remained as strong as ever. And while ASSO was indeed abolished, it was only replaced with the PCO.

In practice, PCOs were issued by the president simply upon the request of the defence minister, who in turn endorsed the reports of his subordinates. Neither the president nor the minister examined witnesses under oath despite the fact that the person covered by a PCO would continue to be detained 'indefinitely at the pleasure of the President'. The defence minister was, of course, Enrile.

On 20 April 1983, the Supreme Court sanctioned the broad powers of arrest and detention which President Marcos had claimed for himself, and declared itself powerless to review the exercise of those powers.

Reversing established doctrine, the Supreme Court held that the president's issuance of a PCO 'may not be declared void by the courts . . . on any ground'. The Supreme Court reasoned that in a situation of grave threat to national security, 'the duty of the judiciary to protect individual rights must yield to the [president], who takes absolute command [and] is answerable only to his conscience, the people and to God.'

This decision was widely condemned. Following the decision, prominent figures, including retired Supreme Court Justice Cecilia Munoz Palma, spearheaded a mass drive against the PCO. The Catholic Bishops' Conference of the Philippines prepared a message scheduled to be read in all Catholic churches all over the country on 7 August 1983, seeking the abolition of the PCO.

Averting this move, President Marcos announced on 5 August 1983 the abolition of the PCO and its replacement with an instrument which he said would afford greater protection to basic rights: the Preventive Detention Action.

ARREST AND DETENTION

The phenomenon of political detention cut across all social classes and spared no one who dared to defy the Marcos government. Be they active participants in the struggle for the restoration of democratic rights or mere bystanders in protest actions, they could easily become the next victims of arbitrary arrest, torture and preventive detention. In May 1985 there were 751 political prisoners in 108 Philippine military camps. This figure did not include people being held temporarily for interrogation, and those whose whereabouts remained unknown but who were thought to be in custody.

Political prisoners in the Philippines included:

(a) workers who fought for just wages and better living conditions;
(b) peasants and farm workers who fought for better conditions, for instance, in respect of land tenure and/or who were suspected of sympathising with or giving aid to guerrillas of the NPA or the MNLF;
(c) urban poor settlers who defended their right to have homes;
(d) students who expressed legitimate grievances against the

educational system or openly sympathised with the plight of the oppressed;

(e) religious and lay leaders who ministered to the needs of the poor and took up their struggle for justice;

(f) national minorities who defended their ancestral homelands against land-grabbers and the encroachment of government projects undertaken in the name of 'progress' and 'development';

(g) artists, writers, journalists, teachers, lawyers, doctors, nurses and intellectuals and professionals committed to the fight for human rights; and

(h) suspected members of groups branded as 'subversive' such as the Communist Party of the Philippines (CPP), the NPA or the MNLF.

Time and time again, government officials categorically denied that human rights violations were being committed. On 3 June 1977, speaking before members of the Foreign Correspondents Association of the Philippines, Marcos said that there were no political detainees in the Philippines. There were, in effect, more than 1000 prisoners being held at that time.

Table 5.3   Number of Arrests, 1977–85

Year	Metro Manila	Luzon	Visayas	Mindanao	Total
1977	414	345	214	378	1 351
1978	320	202	193	905	1 620
1979	265	183	111	1 402	1 961
1980	170	125	141	526	962
1981	52	304	255	766	1 377
1982	226	795	76	814	1 911
1983	185	152	108	1 643	2 088
1984	599	375	403	2 725	4 102
1985	737	132	227	3 729	4 825
Total	2 968	2 613	1 728	12 888	19 197

Not all persons arrested were placed in regular detention centres. There were cases where people were released after interrogation, mostly accompanied by some form of torture. The following were some of the different situations and circumstances which usually occurred during arrests:

(a) People arrested were mauled, interrogated and threatened at the place of arrest but were not taken to a camp, nor officially charged with any offence.

(b) Persons arrested were brought to military safehouses or other out-of-the-way places where they were systematically tortured while interrogated but were released without being taken to a detention centre in a military camp.

(c) Persons arrested were taken to a camp, tortured and then allegedly released but were never seen alive again.

(d) Persons arrested were taken to a camp and systematically tortured while interrogated and detained for long periods of time without any official charges being filed against them.

(e) Persons arrested were taken to a camp, tortured, interrogated, detained and officially charged with subversion, sedition and related crimes.

Many arrests were made during the night, or very early in the morning. In many cases, the arresting officers did not notify the detainee's relatives about the arrest or the whereabouts of the family members. Enquiries by the family were usually fruitless, or the military made promises to investigate which were never carried out. Tortures during interrogations sometimes culminated in the execution of affidavits under duress. Then, after months of detention, summary preliminary investigations (SPI) were conducted. As noted, sometimes detainees were released without having undergone an SPI. Trials and hearings even more rarely occurred.

PRISON CONDITIONS

With the exception of the Bicutan Rehabilitation Centre in Taguig – the government's showcase for 'compassionate rule' – prisons in the Philippines are unsavoury places. Political prisoners were especially badly treated. Sub-human conditions prevailed in the detention centres, characterised by unsanitary and inadequate food and water supply, poor ventilation, overcrowded cells and unavailable medical facilities. Sometimes roofs had no ceilings and the heat from galvanised iron became unbearable. Cells could be as small as 4 feet by 11 feet. Flies and larvae crawled in the toilet bowls inside the cells. Meals often consisted of corn grits and small dried fish. The daily food allowance for detainees was less than 10 pesos. On 26 February 1984, political prisoners at Camp Delgado rejected their supper: it contained live maggots.

Detention centres fell miserably short of the Standard Minimum Rules for the Treatment of Prisoners endorsed by UNESCO in 1975 and the Bureau of Prisoners Rules for the Treatment of Prisoners in 1959. Prison conditions did not improve and the Marcos regime maintained a policy of extirpation towards political dissenters.

TORTURE

Torture was part of the story of continuing political oppression in the Philippines. No one can speak about torture as well as the prisoners themselves, and there are now thousands of well-documented accounts of the ways in which prisoners were treated. Rarely did the government acknowledge even the mildest 'irregularity'. As we read in *Trends*, a TFDP report on political detention, salvaging and disappearances, the Philippine government subscribed to at least three international human rights covenants: the Universal Declaration of Human Rights, the International Covenant of Economic, Social and Cultural Rights, and the Covenant on Civil and Political Rights. Each provides for the protection of prisoners against any form of political abuse, psychological intimidation and degradation.

In 1974 Marcos made his now-famous remark on television: 'No one, but no one has been tortured.' He was quickly proved wrong by Amnesty International (AI), the Association of Major Religious Superiors (AMRSP), and the International Commission of Jurists based in Geneva. In 1977 Marcos conceded: 'There have been to our lasting regret, a number of violations of the rights of detainees.' He promised that future violations of human rights would not be tolerated.

AI again focused on torture and other forms of military abuse in September 1982. Marcos, who was then on a state visit to the USA, again denied any violation of human rights, and accused AI of being 'a tool of the communists'. After the imposition of martial law, no political prisoner who complained of torture – and there were many of them – or any citizen victimised by military harassment – and there were many more of them – reported receiving redress for any grievances.

In many cases, military officers directing torture were trained in US military schools as part of the annual package of military aid under the USA–RP Military Assistance Pact. About 250 officers and men go to the USA each year for advanced military training under the International Military Education and Training Scheme. In their book, *The Washington Connection and Third World Fascism*, Chomsky and Herman state: 'On the essentials – that is, creating a hospitable climate of investment and . . . allowing US occupation of major military base sites, Marcos has been entirely satisfactory, which is the main reason why his human rights violations will never be compellingly important.'

In 1979, when former US Attorney-General Ramsey Clark visited the Philippines he went to the AFP Intelligence Service headquarters in Camp Bago Bantay, Quezon city. The then commanding officer, Colonel Pedro Balbanero, was confronted with torture equipment found in the camp. The unabashed officer was quoted as saying that he had learned the techniques in Fort Bragg and other key military training schools in the USA. Some torture methods were similar to political torture forms employed in South Vietnam by American troops. As observed by Chomsky and Herman: 'The US global effort to maintain and enlarge the area with a favorable investment climate . . . necessitated regular resort to terror, directly (as in the case of Indochina) and more often indirectly through subsidy and support for repressive clients. Bloodshed and terror that contribute substantially to a favorable investment climate are "constructive" in the sense that they advance the end that clearly ranks highest in the priorities of Free World leaders.'

Father Pedro Lucero, detained in Camp Lucban, Catbalogan, Samar, was mauled, threatened and tortured by UZ operatives – the intelligence agents of the Eastern Command. In an interview with the Visayas Secretariat of Social Action and the Visayas Ecumenical Movement for Justice and Peace, he said: 'I was handcuffed . . . Then they began banging the door . . . They poured water all over my body for 30 minutes . . . The military interrogators stripped me naked. They hit me about the head, breast and belly . . . amid loud and boisterous laughter.' He said he was also forced to eat fish and chicken bones, and that he was 'sexually abused'.

Peter Villasenor was arrested by elements of the Marine Battalion No. 4 in June 1982. He was heavily tortured. Bullets were inserted between his fingers and his hands were then squeezed. His fingers were seared with lighted cigarettes, his fingertips pricked with thumbtacks and his earlobes punctured with staple wire. His torturers flicked his genitals with a stretched rubber band, burned his sexual organ with lighted cigarettes and inserted a piece of coconut midrib plucked from a hard broom into the urethra.

The body of Sixto Carlos Jr was stretched on a wide surface like a flat iron sheet. His hands were hog-tied and his feet buckled to the sheet. A hook was fastened to the rope around his numb hands. Each time Sixto refused to answer a question, his interrogators pulled the hook higher and higher, stretching his body. His arms and legs became more and more painful as the interrogation continued. Hot water was poured over his body. His testicles were repeatedly struck with a small wooden hammer. Former political science professor and chairman of the *Samahan ng Demokratikong Kabataan*, Sixto was arrested for his active participation in political activities. The 'stretching exercise' he went through originated in the Middle Ages and is one of a range of practices revived, modified or newly invented in the Philippines in order to 'torture evidence into existence'.

Crude and sophisticated methods of torture were reported by the thousands of men and women who became victims of the AFP. These included:

(a) applying lighted cigarettes to various parts of the body, including the ears and the genital area;
(b) the stripping, sexual abuse and sometimes raping of female detainees;
(c) submerging the face of the victim into a faeces-contaminated toilet bowl (sometimes known as the 'wet submarine');
(d) pressing a hot iron against the soles of the feet;
(e) pouring gallons of water on the victim's face, thereby blocking the mouth and the nostrils, and creating the sensation of drowning and suffocation;
(f) giving electric shocks to various parts of the body, especially the finger tips and the genitalia;
(g) hitting both ears simultaneously from behind (known as 'the telephone');
(h) keeping the detainees from sleeping through continuous interrogation; and
(i) beating with fists, gun butts and rubber hoses.

All these methods of torture remained in use throughout 1984 and 1985, and new ones were being developed, for example, the application of hot pepper to the eyes, mouth and genitals, and slashing off fingertips. There are 'psy war' tricks as well, for instance, Russian roulette, whereby a single bullet, usually a blank, was loaded into the cylinder of a revolver. The torturer then spun the cylinder and pulled the trigger the moment it stopped. The detainee came near to losing his wits, wondering whether the gun would fire or not. In between those who survived the torture and those who died in the process, were the detainees who suffered psychologically because of severe torture. Some will never recover.

This chapter concludes with two personal accounts of imprisonment and torture. The first concerns Erlene Dangoy, 16 years of age, who was arrested in 1985 by police and paratroopers, then raped and subjected to other sexual abuses by her captors. The second account is by Karl Gaspar, and is taken from a collection of his prison reflections called *How Long?* edited by Helen Graham and Breda Noonan.

Erlene Dangoy

I am Erlene Dangoy, 16 years old, a woman female detainee here at the PC/INP Jail, Davao Metrodiscom. . . .

I was arrested by police and ICHDFs, 11 a.m. last 19 March at Kilometre 13, Panacan on suspicion that I killed Erlinda Batulan of Panacan Relocation. After taking me to the Sasa Police Station, I was brought to the Office of Commander Coral for investigation. When I told them that I knew nothing of their accusation, they kicked me hard. The police tortured me – they applied electric shocks to my fingers, inserted bullets between them and crushed my hands and forced me to eat newspapers. I collapsed when they hit my nape with the butt of a .38 calibre pistol. When I recovered, one ICHDF named Jun Orogo made a move to stab me with a knife. I screamed and suddenly, urine and blood flowed out from me. For the second time, I lost consciousness.

That night the military brought me to a dimly lighted room. They removed my dress and my underwear and forced me to dance nude. In protest, I cried, screamed and squatted on the floor. I was terribly ashamed. Then they forced me up, kicked me and grabbed my hair. Weeping, I was forced to obey their perverse orders when they threatened that I would be secretly killed and buried.

20 March. Military men came and interrogated me again to see if I knew anything about the 'movement' and if I really did kill Erlinda Batulan. They kicked me again when I could not tell them anything. 'Tell the truth and we will help you,' the men said. But what did I know about their allegations? One policeman interrupted me. 'You bitch! You still lie even if your lips are already bleeding.' I pleaded again, 'I really don't know anything, sir. Have pity on me. Please stop hurting me, I cannot bear it any longer. I do not know anything.' They responded by slapping me.

That night, a military man whom I could not recognise pulled me up and pointed his gun at me. Two other men waited in the room where he led me. They laughed as I entered. One of them grabbed and undressed me. As they muffled my screams, two of the men began squeezing and touching my body. I could not do anything to stop them because they held my hands. Then they forced me to dance to the music they had prepared in their cassette recorder. Displeased, they took some hot pepper which they rubbed all over my body. The men laughed as they saw me flinching in pain.

21 March.   I was forced to sign a piece of paper. I did not want to sign at first but they again inflicted pain too much for me to bear.

23 March.   I was brought to the site where they said the killing of Batulan took place. They wanted me to pinpoint who my companions were in the alleged killing but I had nothing to tell.

24 March.   I collapsed because of hunger. Since my arrest they had not given me a grain of rice because they said I was hard-headed. They accused me of being an NPA and a criminal. In the evening, the military abused me again. I screamed and cried.

25 March.   My mother and Father Jack visited me. I did not tell them about what had happened to me. I just wept. When they were gone, I was summoned by the commander who then threatened to kill me should I tell my parents or relatives about the torture. I was transferred that same day to the barracks, at the Davao PC/INP Metrodiscom.

At around 5 p.m. they led me to what they call the Guard House Post No. 1 located near the road. One of the guards cautioned me not to sleep near the bars since men were situated there. I slept so soundly that night – I was too tired and hungry. I was startled at past midnight when I felt someone kiss my cheek and take hold of my hands. When I opened my eyes I saw a uniformed man whose namecloth bore the name Capuyan. I tried hard to break loose from his grasp but he boxed my stomach and legs and pressed my hands. Right there and then, I lost consciousness.

When I regained my senses, I was shocked to see my hands tied and my mouth gagged. My legs and body were in pain. I saw blood! When I looked down I saw my breasts bared and my panties torn. At that moment, I feared that the worst had happened to me. Capuyan warned: 'If you tell this to the other guards and to your parents, I will kill you.' He untied me and left.

27 March.   At dawn, the beast Capuyan came back to my cell and raped me again. I felt like a dead person – my body was too weak to fight, too tired, too painful. I wanted to shout, but not a sound came from my lips.

28 March.   Capuyan who was on duty as guard early that morning, raped me for the third time. Two guards arrived and touched my body. They squeezed my breasts . . . Capuyan came back to my cell and threatened to kill me and my parents if I said a word to my mother or to his officer.

29 March.   They transferred me to the women's cell. My mother visited me there. I did not confide my condition because I feared for her own safety. I did not have the appetite to eat, I was crying and sulking. I was worried that these men would get used to abusing women. Then I thought, well, I should expose what the military men did to me even if it means death. Then, other women will learn that such cruelty exists.

10 April. I shared my experience with women companions in the cell . . . I narrated everything to them. They advised me to write to people outside so I could hire a lawyer and be examined by a doctor. The following day, I wrote to women lawyers and to TFDP for help.

In less than a week, Attorney Pocot came and asked me about my condition. Attorney Tupaz, a woman lawyer, also came and heard my case. Prior to these visits, I would tremble every time I saw soldiers. . . .

When the rape and all the abuses done to me were exposed, a certain Ferrer brought me to the commanding officer who investigated me on my accusations. I told him everything. As I shouted, 'Shameless! Heartless!' he slapped me. He threatened to kill me should I be released. I told him it didn't matter any more because I would pursue my case just the same.

After several days, I was brought to a military doctor by a policewoman, supposedly for a medical examination. I suspected that they were also sexually abusing me because they were touching those parts of my body that need not be touched.

They imprisoned the rapist Capuyan. I was happy to know he was jailed . . . , but I was worried about the sincerity of it all. I was afraid they were only doing this for pretences.

At the end of the month, Capuyan's mother came and tried to convince me to drop the case. I grew all the more angry. The commanding officer also asked me to drop the case since I'd be released just the same. I only laughed at him.

I was released 16 July with the help of Attorney Pocot and TFDP . . . I know I tried hard to free myself from fear and shame not for my own sake but for all the victims of this kind of oppression. We should not let fear pull us down.

I hope that those who have read this will take the initiative to help dismantle a cruel, oppressive system. As women we should not be overpowered by these events. Let us all unite.

(*Update*, vol. 1, no. 2, 15 October–14 November 1985)

Karl Gaspar

Karl Gaspar, 'a lay theologican and church worker, a poet, artist, dramatist, musician and long-term human rights activist', disappeared on 26 March 1983. After two weeks of persistent denial of any knowledge of his whereabouts, the military finally announced that they had arrested him.

As soon as the military allowed contact between Karl and his family he began to write his reflections on events as they unfolded, thus beginning the phenomenal two-year correspondence which he maintained until his release in 1985. Karl wrote, on 8 March 1984:

As old detainees are released, new ones take their place. Two weeks ago, four new detainees, all young boys with an average age of 18 years, were padlocked here. Their case is now in court, and they are charged with murder, sedition and subversion. One look at the boys and the charges seem ludicrous. They look so fragile and innocent, one cannot associate them with guns. The alleged leader of the group, Jimmy, wears a rosary around his neck and says that he is involved in the rosary crusade in his parish. They had been tortured mercilessly before they were brought here. A week after their arrest they appeared in court with their lawyers who demanded that they be transferred here for safety.

Yesterday – Ash Wednesday – our Lent was off to a gloomy start. Just when we thought that the military's practice of *hulbot*, forcefully taking the detainees out for interrogation or to act as guides for military operations, or even to be 'salvaged', had ceased because of our hunger strike, it happened again! The four, Jimmy, Lito, Jun and his brother, Boy, were taken out and taken to another building in the compound. There they were blindfolded and interrogated and forced to confess. They were hit all over their fragile bodies by their interrogators. Jimmy received the heaviest beating. His head was covered with a plastic bag throughout the interrogation and torture, and he almost suffocated. The torture lasted from 1.00 p.m. until dusk, and when it was over they crept into our cells. They were pale and looked very frightened. Jimmy, haggard and forlorn, walked like a zombie down the aisle to their cell. One could feel the sense of outrage among the other prisoners whose collective heart reached out to these four victims of military abuse.

Just this morning the news report announced the death of another young man at the hands of the police. The night before, he was picked up, interrogated and tortured. In the morning he was released to an older sister who had been looking for him. She rushed him to the hospital where he died of internal haemorrhage.

So what else is new? The savagery of this fascist regime continues to devour innocent victims. There is outrage and an ever deepening anger among those who are within the circle of victims. The wrath born of direct witnessing of such gross violations of human rights becomes part of the swelling dissent now escalating throughout the country. But placed against the backdrop of world events – the Iran–Iraq war, the Lebanon tragedies, the carnage in Central America, the current moves of the *apparatchik* in Moscow to send feelers to the other old man in Washington who is seeking re-election, etc. – local events pale in their 'newsworthiness'. But from the perspective of our cells, these are the events that matter much more, happening as they do right under our noses.

How long, Lord, before those in captivity are set free? How long before the night gives way to the new dawn so eagerly awaited but which seems to take forever to break out on the horizon? How many more bruised and dead bodies before the madness ends? How much more anger will explode across the wide plains of our bleeding land before a conflagration threatens to engulf us in a catastrophe?'

Karl Gaspar was released in 1985. The other political prisoners detained by the military had to wait a further year for freedom, or even longer.

6 1985: The Child, the Priest and the Crowd

For some people in the Philippines 1985 was probably neither worse nor better than 1984, 1983, 1982 or 1981 . . . A few made a great deal of money – mainly through exploitation and unfair practice; very many others suffered harassment, arrest, fear – and death. All sectors of the community were affected: children, adults, church workers and priests. Expectations and aspirations changed overnight. Families mourned. Communities grieved. Life goes on for those whose families were disrupted, for those whose families were torn apart. But things can never be the same again. The reality of poverty may strike forcibly and permanently following the death of the breadwinner; a child may be psychologically damaged by a harrowing experience; parents may never recover from the death of their child; and a community may become fragmented – and deteriorate – after the assassination of a charismatic leader. These events occurred each day in the Philippines throughout 1985: the result of greed, corruption and indifference. The likelihood of real change in 1986 or 1987 seems remote.

The following incidents, among many others, show how children were regularly wounded – and slaughtered – in the Philippines, in 1985 as in previous years:

On 29 January 1985, soldiers belonging to the 29th IB strafed the house of Arsenio Odvina. A bullet grazed Arsenio's shoulder before hitting three-year-old Arnel in the stomach. *The child died the following day.*

On 31 January 1985, *13-year-old Robinson Cabon was shot dead* in Sapang Dalaga, Misamis Occidental, by a member of the ICHDF, Luciano Puyod.

On 11 February 1985, in Roxas, Zamboanga del Norte, *six-year-old Nericel Bulat-ag was shot dead* by soldiers of the 44th IB and unidentified paratroopers in a raid in which the child's uncle and a neighbour were wounded.

On 20 February 1985, soldiers of the 34th IB Bravo Company under Sergeant Isidro Tarayao entered the *barrio* of Canyupay in

Borongan, Eastern Samar and shot dead Arnelia Odang and her husband Simplicio. *Their seven-year-old daughter, Armila, her knee shattered with bullets, was lifted from her chair to the ground by two soldiers and left to die.*

On 9 March 1985, Joaquin Adilan and his son Santos were killed on the island of Masbete, Bicol, by a group of drunken soldiers led by Sergeant Elpidio Daligdig. Joaquin was ploughing the field at the time he was approached by the group. After mauling and kicking him, the soldiers shot the man in the back. Police Fireman Walter Tagalog, ICHDF member Cresencio Andeza and *six others later went to the Adilan residence and stabbed 16-year-old Santos to death.*

On 4 May 1985, *a six-year-old girl was wounded* together with six other people in Santiago, San Luis, Surigao del Sur when 20 soldiers of the 23rd IB riddled their home with bullets.

On 14 May 1985, *13-year-old Marife Regalado was wounded* by a gunman who shot dead her father in front of her. This occurred at Binuangan, Maco, Davao del Norte.

On 15 June 1985, ICHDF *paratroopers* in Tuluman, North Cotabato, *massacred Celestino Carino, his wife Viana, and their four children.*

On 19 June 1985, a combined team of the 9th IB, police and the ICHDF, strafed the home of Diday Estole, *killing the woman and her four-year-old son.* This happened in Unidos, Plaridel, Misamis Occidental.

On 1 July 1985, at 1 a.m. in Carmen, Surigao del Norte, 16-year-old Benecio Pocot, a rattan cutter, was picked up by two members of the PC and a member of the ICHDF. *Benecio's bullet-ridden body was found nearby four hours later.*

THE CHILD

The violent deaths of many children in the Philippines have been sketchily documented. They fell where they were shot – or were cut to pieces – and were buried soon afterwards, sometimes with a minimum of ceremony. Death by violence must, at any time, be like no other experience. For a child, the degree of terror can never be fully understood.

The story of an 8-year-old girl from the Manobo tribe, Imelda

Tawide, had all the aspects of this terror – although I believe Imelda to be still alive. It is a story that affected me personally: I have seen the hardship of the Manobos, and experienced their gentleness and hospitality. And Imelda lived with her family in Kalilid, the base from which I set off for the mass wedding described in the first chapter.

Imelda and her family were forced into hiding in the province of Agusan del Sur in order to escape death at the hands of the ICHDF, a group organised in this instance by PANAMIN (Presidential Assistance to Tribal Minorities). The girl was a star witness when three members of another Manobo family were massacred by the ICHDF. She further survived another attack resulting in the death of her two older brothers.

Imelda's ordeal began on 3 May 1985, after the child had witnessed some frightening incidents. She, her mother, an older brother, and a younger sister were in the house of Mauricio Calderon in Kalilid, San Luis, when two members of the ICHDF arrived. They were identified as brothers Lorenzo and Pungo Paminsalan. The two men roused the sleeping Calderon and shot him in the chest before he could stand up. The man's 16-year-old son, Balodoy, tried to escape but had three bullets fired into his back. Calderon's other son, Manuel, 13 years of age, was also killed. The three bodies were dumped in a nearby well.

Imelda, her mother, brother and sister were separated when they scampered for safety. Imelda's brother and sister hid in a nearby house; her mother at the Philippine Packing Corporation; and Imelda at the house of Datu (tribal chief) Mantambungan – who happened to be the father of the two members of the ICHDF. Imelda was not allowed to leave. In the afternoon her two elder brothers, Garing and Kiyambaw, were brought to Mantambungan's house and later ordered to look for their mother in the forest. Imelda's brothers refused to go to the forest. Mantambungan and his sons told Imelda and her brothers that there had been an ambush, resulting in the death of Calderon and Imelda's mother fleeing to the forest. The next day, 4 May, the two members of the ICHDF told Imelda, Garing and Kiyambaw to go to a nearby house. Their mother might be there, the men said.

On the way, a group of ICHDFs met the Tawides and strafed the two boys with M-16 rifles. Garing, 14 years, and Kiyambaw, 13 years, were stripped naked and dumped in a shallow grave at the side of the road. Imelda escaped.

Imelda recalled that when the ICHDFs began firing, her brother Kiyambaw told her to run. 'I ran as fast as I could. As I went far I could only hear Kiyambaw's fading voice *"Dagan, Imelda, dagan"* [Run, Imelda, run],' said Imelda. The ICHDFs caught up with Imelda in a house where she had sought refuge. She was taken to Calderon's house, and was told by the wife of one of the ICHDFs that Maki, another son of Mantambungan, had a plot to kill her. Imelda recalled: 'At dusk on 7 May one of the ICHDFs ordered me to fetch water from a creek several metres away from the house. On my way I remembered the plan to kill me. I sensed death awaiting me at the creek. I was terrified. I left the water container at the side of the road and ran towards the forest.'

After spending two nights in the jungle, Imelda reached a logging road on the morning of 9 May. She rode on a logging dumptruck bound for San Luis, and went to a family friend. This friend took Imelda to her mother who had succeeded in getting her younger daughter and son to join her in the office of the Philippine Packing Corporation. The Tawides then went to Kalilid and sought protection from the religious community. They were subsequently helped to go into hiding in order to escape the attention of Mantambungan and his men.

Imelda is now only 9 years old. She has seen a man and his two sons shot in front of her; she witnessed the slaughter of two of her brothers; she knows what it is like to be hunted; and she has lived like an animal in the forest – on her own. She knows that, even now, there are men who wish to kill her. Imelda is a child of the Philippines. Imelda is a child of our time.

THE PRIESTHOOD: A CONSTANT RISK

Many priests have died in the Philippines, most of them quietly after a lifetime of service to the people of the country. A number have been killed in accidents, or in unexplained incidents. Some have been murdered. Father Cesar Legazpi died in a motor cycle accident near Davao shortly before the arrival of two members of the British parliament – Alf Dubs and Colin Moynihan – on a visit in 1983 to Mindanao on behalf of the Parliamentary Human Rights Group. Their particular concern was the continuing abuse of human rights on the palm oil plantations at San Francisco and Lorento, both in

Agusan del Sur. Father Legazpi had been very involved in the discussions within the community about the Loreto project and was associated with those people who had written to the CDC asking them not to continue financing it. Dubs and Moynihan had hoped that the priest would assist them in their investigations, but his death prevented consultation with many who could have helped to establish a more precise account of events. Questions surrounding the 'crash' involving Father Legazpi and his motor cycle were never satisfactorily answered. Despite strong opposition, the two-man delegation subsequently recommended the further implementation of the project.

Father Rudy Romano is still missing. He disappeared in Cebu on 11 July 1985 and has not been seen since. He was abducted. Witnesses expressed no doubt that the men who took the priest away – in a white Ford Cortina bearing government plates RP402 – were *sekreta* (intelligence agents). Father Romano was vice-president for the Visayas of the militant *Bagong Alyansang Makabayan*, and a prominent anti-government member of the clergy. His companion on the morning of his disappearance, Rolan Ybañez, also a member of the Coalition Against People's Persecution, was kidnapped two hours after Father Romano. He, too, is still missing.

THE PRIEST, FATHER FAVALI

The priest whose story is told in greater detail here, is Father Tullio Favali, PIME. As I remember him, he was a quiet, gentle – yet determined – man who enjoyed conversation and an ease in relationships. He was murdered on 11 April 1985.

Favali was born in Italy in Sustinente, a town in the Mantova province, on 10 December 1946. He was ordained a priest on 6 June 1980 as a member of PIME, an international missionary society that was founded in Italy in 1850. PIME, in translation from the Latin means 'Pontifical Institute for Foreign Missions'.

The priest was assigned to the Philippines and arrived in November 1983. After a period of study at a language school – in order to learn the Ilongo dialect – he was asked to serve as an assistant parish priest in Tulunan Parish in the Diocese of Kidapawan, North Cotabato. This was in June 1984. In February 1985 Favali was appointed parish priest in Tulunan where he worked with Father Peter Geremia, PIME, who had been in Tulunan since 1980.

On 11 April, in *barangay* La Esperanza, Tulunan, at Crossing 125 on the highway, a group of local ICHDF members were seen talking and drinking. Among their number were the Manero brothers – Bucay, Edilberto and Elpidio – all heavily armed. The Manero brothers joined the ICHDF because of their membership of *Ilaga*, and are notorious in the district. Among the Maneros, Norberto Manero Jr – usually referred to as Kumander Bucay – is the best known. Feared for his wanton killings and cannibalism, he has been decorated several times for his contribution to the anti-insurgency campaign. The last occasion was on 5 February 1984, during the Senior ICHDF Commanders' Conference. The award was signed by Colonel Ernesto Calupig.

Norberto Manero Sr is proud of the fact that he shot his own son, Noel, also a member of the ICHDF, in the head on 15 January 1984 when the latter refused to stop molesting his mother. Manero Sr says that the murder is proof of the way in which he disciplines his children. Noel Manero was buried inside the Manero house in La Esperanza. To this day the family dines on top of his grave. They use his tomb as a dining table.

Around noontime on the day of Favali's murder, placards were displayed by the group on which was written 'Grand Showing: Kumander Bucay vs NPA'. Below the heading were two columns of names, on one side names of members of the ICHDF and, on the other, those of local residents suspected of being members of the NPA. The wording on the notices was clearly visible from the *carinderia* or eating places on the highway. When a local resident, Rufino Robles, approached the group and asked 'Why is my name on the list?', Edilberto Manero drew his gun and shot at him. The surprised man was able to deflect the bullet, and was slightly wounded in the hand. He ran for cover, scampering for safety to the house of Dominador Gomez, who had himself earlier that day been shot by Edilberto in one of those incidents, fairly common in Tulunan, which happen for no grave reason or provocation, but which result in injury and death. Sensing that others might be injured or killed, Robles sent an urgent note for help to the priests in the *kumbento* (priests' house).

Favali had just returned from a *fiesta* in the *barrio* of San Vincente when the note reached him. The note was actually addressed to Father Geremia, a priest who had always been vocal against abuses in the community, but was read by Favali. He sped off immediately on his motor cycle to respond to the call for help, heading straight for the house of Gomez to see the wounded man. Unknown to him

Edilberto Manero had been earlier marching up and down the road shouting 'Today, I will kill a priest', while his companions had warned the occupants of the Gomez house not to leave, or else they would be shot.

Favali was still placating the victims when he noticed that Bucay Manero and his men had pushed his motor cycle to the centre of the highway, let out the petrol from the tank and set it on fire, amidst cheering and shooting in the air. 'What have you done to my motor cycle?' Favali asked Bucay and the men who stood watching. Edilberto answered him with another question: 'Father, do you want your head blown off?' Favali was seen raising his hands, apparently trying to calm the man down, but even before he could say anything, Edilberto aimed his Browning automatic rifle at the priest and shot him repeatedly.

Favali was first hit on one side of his stomach and, as he spun around, he was shot again and again at the back of his head. His skull was blown off, and his brains scattered around. The priest fell to the ground on his stomach and even as he lay there – in a pool of blood and brains – witnesses say they saw Edilberto kick Favali's body, turn it face upwards and shoot it again and again. After that, he stomped on the priest's body until his brother Bucay restrained him by saying that the priest was already dead.

The ICHDFs then gathered around and Bucay took a portion of the priest's brain and scattered it all around. His men followed suit and, it is reported, some of them even ate bits of the brain. 'Tomorrow we are going to be in the headlines because we killed a priest,' one man shouted. Later, fragments of brain still clinging to their clothes, they left to resume their drinking, loudly singing a Visayan song popular in the area, 'Baliling', a name which Bucay would later give his brother Edilberto in commemoration of the priest's killing. The shooting happened at 5 p.m. For more than two hours the group continued their wild celebration, while people watched in horror from nearby houses and eating places. Passengers in passing vehicles were aghast. Bucay and his men went around boasting and threatening others. There were at least 17 in the group.

Meanwhile, the other priest in the parish, Geremia, was coming along the same road on his motor cycle from another *barrio*, completely unaware of what had happened. He noticed large groups of people along the road; many kept on shouting at him to stop and turn back. However, nobody told him what had happened. Eventually he reached the *kumbento* by taking side roads, and learned that his colleague had gone out in response to a call for help. Geremia went to the police station, requesting an escort. The police were reluctant to accompany him. Eventually two policemen agreed to ride with him. By that time it was dark. When they arrived at Crossing 125 most of the houses had been vacated. Favali's body was lying on the road where he had been shot. Geremia approached quietly and anointed it. The policeman warned him to take cover. He was worried about Geremia's safety. Later, the body was taken to the *funeraria* (funeral parlour) in Mlang where the mortician who cleaned it lost count of the number of bullets he removed. Ten days later Geremia wrote in his diary about the horror of what he had seen: 'I saw Tullio on the ground with his brains scattered around, his mouth eating dirt, his blood like a dark carpet.'

MEMORIAL MASS FOR FATHER TULLIO FAVALI, PIME

Immaculate Heart of Mary Parish Church, Quezon City, 11 May 1985

Homily given by Msgr Orlando Quevedo, OMI, Bishop of Kidapawan

For one brief year, he was part of our salvation history in the Diocese of Kidapawan. Only the Lord knows how many blessings he brought to the people of Tulunan. He brought a ready and tranquil smile into our midst, so often punctuated by the grieving of widows, the wail of children made fatherless by ambuscades, salvagings, and liquidations. His quiet, unassuming, and unhurried ways reminded all of us that the miracle of God's kingdom will only happen at God's own time and in God's own ways.

But this I firmly believe – that God sent him as a priceless gift to the Church of Kidapawan in the midst of testing and tribulation.

Because the Church educates and evangelises, because the Church raises the faith consciousness of people, because she organises the poor farmers and workers towards self-reliance, mutual support, and concerted action to improve themselves and to defend their rights, her activities are often blocked, her leaders harassed and threatened.

The killing of Father Tullio cannot be understood apart from this situation. For his role as a priest, leader, and teacher, he was suspected as a communist and treated as an enemy to be destroyed. Father Tullio's mission continues among the people of Tulunan. It continues as long as there is anyone who needs the healing grace of God. It continues through time and space whenever and wherever someone responds to the plea of the poor for the liberating love of God. And the memory of Father Tullio will remain, even as his death marked his total solidarity with the poor of God in Tulunan parish.

As a stranger he came among us. Briefly we walked with him, broke the bread of God with him. And then in a flash he departed as a friend – friend who gave up his life for all. There is no greater self-offering than this, no greater love.

NATION'S LAMENT FOR A SLAIN MISSIONARY

Homily given by Jaime L. Cardinal Sin, Archbishop of Manila at the Immaculate Heart of Mary Parish Church, Quezon City on 11 May 1985

The mounting frequency of these assaults on human life where Filipinos kill Filipinos is fast becoming our own version of Argentina's dirty war, and of Nazi Germany's holocaust. If we continue in unabated violence, our generation shall soon achieve the grisly record of having slain more fellow Filipinos than were killed in our wars against foreign invaders.

O my people! What explanations can we give our children to lessen their disillusionment as they come to know that the guns that shattered the body of Father Tullio were wielded by Filipinos whose bizarre laughter made a mockery of his death and whose uniforms proclaimed them to be protectors of our homes?

Father Tullio Favali came to us believing in our readiness to accept a gospel of peace and love. In the huts and byways of rural Cotabato, he found Filipinos who could not be bought, Filipinos who would not kill brother Filipinos, citizens of a land they were proud of and whose austere lives were rich with the things of the spirit: of kindness, of gentility, of friendship, of reverence for God. No wonder that he fell in love with our people. No wonder that when he heard his Filipino friends cry out in distress, he unhesitatingly rushed to their side – and sealed his life of service by his death.

And once again, above the harsh staccato bursts of gunfire, once again we hear the now familiar refrain: 'The Filipino is worth living for . . . and he is worth dying for!'

For my dear brothers and sisters in Christ who are in government, in the military, in the hills and mountains – listen, listen to the cry of our people. It is a cry for peace for the children of Luzon, peace for the children of the Visayas, peace for the children of Mindanao – peace, peace, peace for all our people!

Shortly after Favali's murder, Edilberto Manero wrote a letter 'from somewhere in the mountain' addressed to the 'people of Tulunan'. The letter was written in block letters, and copies were found in different parts of the town. It was signed 'Cmndr Baliling'. The text was as follows (original spelling):

We killed 'Tulio' the parish priest of Tulunan for the reason that we love Filipino people. We back 70s when rebellion uprises, when we defend and fight against the MNLF or the outlaws. After 10 years of struggle just to defend our beloved countrymen the Italian priest like Pedro (Peter) Tulio, Michael came to our place to poisoned and spoils the minds of our pityful people in remote areas by letting to be believe the communist principles and to destroy the democracy of our Filipino people . . . So we the concerned citizen don't want to be governed by the communist we put justice to our hands because we cannot resist what Italian priest run over to the people of Tulunan.

So in behalf of democracy we came to fight the CPP, NPA and PKP regardless of what they are we do or die for the good our people. Our mission to fight the CPP, NPA, PKP and to kill the imported Satan priests who arc against the Phil. government.
Foreigner priest is not (Ilonggo)
Ang pumatay nang dahil sa inyo/Edil.

It was to heal the wounds of conflict – among the Muslims, the B'laan tribesmen and the Christians – that the Italian missionaries were sent to Tulunan in 1980. It was thought that, being foreigners, priests would be met with less suspicion by non-Christian communities – and perhaps even Christian communities – than an Ilongo priest would. Writing in *Panorama* on 16 June 1985, Sheila Coronel gives evidence of this continuing suspicion – to say the least – of the Italian missionaries. She quotes the words of two powerful men in the area, Vincente Almirante and General Cesar Tapia, RUC 12 commander.

Almirante, a prosperous Ilongo farmer, is also the commander of some 600 ICHDFs stationed in the town of Tulunan. Dark and heavy-set, this man who considers himself a devout Catholic, speaks in a voice the loudness of which betrays the owner's confidence in the unassailability of his logic: '*Ang sa akin lang, mapatay mo yang pari sa liblib, okay lang. Sabi ng iba ang diperensiya, pinatay sa* public place . . . *Ang mga paring ito kasi, galing sa* Italy and in Italy, there are many communists. *Alam ko ang* upbringing *ng mga paring ito, komunist sila. Si Pope John Paul, galing sa* Poland and Poland is a communist country.' (In my opinion, had they killed the priest in a secluded place, it would have been all right. The problem is, as some people here say, they killed him in a public place . . . You know these priests, they're from Italy and in Italy, there are many communists. I know their upbringing is communist. Even Pope John Paul comes from Poland and Poland is a communist country.)

Living in Tulunan this is the strange reasoning that – perhaps over centuries, certainly over decades – has made sufficient sense to some people to make them kill and injure. The military and the ICHDF have been brainwashed into stopping, at any cost, what they see as the 'Red tide'.

Tapia explains that it does not take a great deal to kill a priest: 'I have been talking to a lot of my friends. I'm a member of the charismatic movement in Manila and in Iligan. Our impression of the religious is, from the time they shed off their habits and wore street clothes, sometimes worse than what we are wearing, they lost that aura of holiness. *Ang tingin ng tao* they are just ordinary agitators if they shout in the streets. So it's not so difficult to muster enough bravado now to kill a priest. *Hindi bali sana kung naka-*habit, *kagaya noong araw* when I was a boy, *malayo pa nakikita mo yung* priest, immediately he looks like a saint to you but now, *kung minsan naka-tsinelas lang sila, naka-T-shirt, nakamaong.'*

Coronel then poses the question: Who would have thought that there would be such a deadly conncction between a priest's wardrobe and his murder?

But the question, as Coronel suggests, is much deeper. As elsewhere throughout the Philippines, relations between the church and the military have been tense. Any suspicion of a lay leader's involvement with the *rebelde* was likely to lead to arrest, torture and even death. Good Friday and Easter Sunday 1982 in Tulunan were occasions when the people tried to show their real feelings: of support for Geremia, and hatred of the military. The incidents – although not without violence – were without deaths. They could easily have become massacres. Says Orlando Quevedo, Bishop of Kidapawan: 'The growth of the NPA has been attributed by government and military officials to the activities of the church in terms of education and evangelisation. The fact that many bccame aware of their rights and became vocal about abuses gave more reason for the local government and military officials to say that the church is contributing to the growth of the NPA. I imagine that . . . the fact that they are often frustrated in their attempt to discover who the NPAs are makes the church the most visible culprit.'

When Favali was killed, Kumander Bucay was obviously in command of the entire ICHDF team of La Esperanza. A long list of killings has been attributed to the group of Bucay and his wife, Leonarda Lacson Diesto Manero, alias Kumander Inday. These include:

(a) On 29 May 1977, a B'laan pastor, Fernando Guymon, along with his wife and children, was murdered. And on 29 November 1977, Leopoldo Ojacastro, a vital witness to the Guymon massacre, was killed.
(b) Bishop Reginald Arliss and the clergy of the then Prelature of Marbel in letter dated 11 October 1979, quoted sworn statements giving details of massacres and cannibalism, among which '. . . the two Mamalumpong brothers were slaughtered, sliced into

pieces, their internal organs taken out and cooked to be eaten, by Kumanders Bucay and Inday and their followers . . .'

Bucay is also regarded by military authorities as their 'folk hero'. He has often been directly linked with the military on official missions and is treated with great respect by local authorities. Father Tullio Favali died at the hands of the ICHDF, at the hands of the Manero brothers. There is no expectation that the murderers will be brought to justice. His death, however, does represent one more step for the people in the fight against the reign of unlimited terror in which they are forced to live.

As I said earlier, I believe that the child, Imelda Tawide, lives. She had an experience of death at eight years of age. Her brothers were killed as she watched. The memory will never be erased. Tullio Favali did die, a savage, brutal killing, extraordinary even in the Philippines. Many people were affected: his family, his religious community, his workers in the parish, his congregation – and the church in the Philippines.

THE CROWD

Significant and painful as the death of an individual is, the continuing massacres in the country served, even more, to underline the harshness of the Marcos regime. For a considerable time massacres occurred in the Philippines. Whole communities – men, women and children – were slaughtered. Nobody knows how many thousands of Muslims were butchered by government forces and their paramilitary groups in the early 1970s.

Massacres – the killing of groups of people – were, outside the Muslim community, still a new phenomenon in 1983. At that time there were perhaps two a year. By the middle of 1984 they were part of the standard operational procedures of the military, tying in with the movement away from increasing the number of political prisoners and towards 'salvaging'.

The massacres continued throughout 1984 and 1985. On 20 September 1985, 7000 people were gathered outside the town hall in Escalante, situated just 98 kilometres north of Bacolod city in Negros Occidental. They were demonstrating as part of a three-day *Welgang Bayan* (People's Strike) to protest against 'hunger, extreme poverty, and increasing militarization' throughout the island of Negros.

Demonstrators began gathering in front of the municipal hall about 9 a.m. on the second day of the rally. No permit for the gathering had been issued, according to the police. At 1.30 p.m. Escalante Mayor Braulio Lumayno and senior PC Commander Captain Modesto Sanson ordered the crowd to disperse.

Two of four firetrucks being used by the military, all loaded with armed soldiers, were stationed in front of the municipal hall and – at about 1.30 p.m. – they moved just beyond the protestors along the highway going south. One stopped at arms-length distance from the demonstrators. Without warning, it suddenly hosed them down with water. Many said that the water had been chemically treated. Inch by inch it closed on the ranks of protestors until it ran out of water. The other firetruck also began hosing down the crowd but the water pressure was not enough to disperse the people and it, too, soon ran out of water. The protestors clapped.

Immediately, the military began throwing teargas cannisters at the crowd. When Jovelyn Jaravelo threw one back to the empty town plaza about 100 metres away from the municipal building, soldiers near the firetrucks opened fire, killing Jaravelo. At this moment a machine gun was spotted – mounted on top of the municipal building. When it opened fire, many dropped to the ground or fled for cover. Twenty-seven people died. More than 30 were wounded. It was the worst attack since 1978 on anti-dictatorship street militants.

At first nobody would go near the municipal hall where the dead bodies and belongings of the demonstrators were piled up near the flagpole. A number of bodies were still moving, a priest recalled, as they were heaped by the soldiers one upon another like the carcases of slaughtered cattle.

The military defended their action. 'Under the circumstances, the soldiers had no choice,' said General de Guzman. In Manila, Ramos said that the military acted in self-defence. For the *welgistas*, however, it was maintained that they did nothing to provoke the soldiers. Soon after the shooting, Dr Pedro Hinolan, who runs a private clinic in Escalante, was quoted as saying: 'All the 12 victims we treated could not have been standing. They were all lying. The men who shot them were at an elevated position.'

An interview with a young fisherman was reported in *Veritas*, dated 6 October 1985. He had a bullet wound in his shoulder and was being treated in hospital: 'I hope the good Lord will make me well again. Now, more than ever, I must continue to fight. Why should I be afraid? We did not attack the military. We were unarmed. Besides, how could we have attacked them when we were sprawled on the ground with our arms linked to one another?'

Local radio commentators – controlled by the regime – attempted to brainwash the community: 'Communist priests and *welgistas* were behind the anarchy and violence,' one said.

Overnight, Escalante became well known to Filipinos. On the eve of the election – after feelings had been running high for some time – Enrile ordered an official inquiry into the massacre, recommending multiple murder charges against Lumayho, Sanson, and several members of the PC. The announcement was made in the same week that the armed forces chief, General Fabian Ver and 25 others were acquitted by the Supreme Court of the Aquino assassination.

For the people of Escalante, 1985 was a bad year. As Patricia Adversario wrote: '. . . the passers-by find their eyes drawn from the machine-gun atop the tower to a row of 27 paper coffins lining the road in front of the rural bank. The coffins stand there, mute but eloquent symbols of the martyrdom that people are willing to go through. Long after the coffins have disappeared, it is to be hoped, the legacy the martyrs left us will be remembered.'

7 Resistance and Revolution

The propaganda put out by the Marcos government through the official press, and by those supporting American financial and political interests in the Far East, about the irritation rather than the threat of the NPA was very far from the truth. In effect, the revolution began many years ago and Filipinos continue to engage in what they describe as a 'protracted war'. As discussed in Chapter 8, the 1986 election brought about cosmetic change only, and the release of political prisoners. The Philippines revolution has yet to occur.

With more than two-fifths of the population still directly or indirectly supporting the underground movement; with the people continuing to be organised at a pace reflecting the depth of their suffering and discontent; and with 60 000 men and women actively participating in advancing the people's war, it is only a question of time before the launch of the strategic offensive. Activists smiled in 1985, when I suggested 'within two years'. Undoubtedly, as a first response to the change of presidency, a number of guerrillas will come down from the hills. With no prospect of economic or social change, however, they will as quickly return. The revolution has merely been delayed. Significantly, in one of the first statements Ramos made after his move to the Aquino camp he declared his intention to 'crush' the guerrilla movement.

Filipinos are patient, quietly determined but in no doubt about the eventual outcome, as shown by the way in which they have approached their task since the beginnings of the NPA in 1969, systematically planning and organising. The war is seen in three phases as the balance of power is tipped in favour of the NPA: the strategic defensive, strategic stalemate and strategic offensive.

With guerrilla fronts now operating effectively in nearly every province the war is entering a most critical stage: the final sub-stage of the first phase. Strategic stalemate cannot last long before the culmination in the third phase.

The present advanced sub-stage is characterised by the presence of bigger and more organised mass bases in the *barrios*, advanced military tactics, favourable terrain for engaging the AFP, good communication, adequate means of transportation and almost sufficient NPA strength. Parts of Mindanao especially – where the government has poured in additional troops – are now highly organised with 'Red areas' under the full control of the NPA. Similar 'Red areas' are to be found, for example, in Negros and parts of northern Luzon. Travelling with guerrillas in these occupied territories feels 'very safe', much safer than in many of the heavily-militarized zones.

The NPA, an obscure ragtag guerrilla band in 1969, has steadily established itself as a formidable armed force, well organised in its fight against the US–Marcos dictatorship and, now, in its resolve to rid the Philippines of American imperialism. The final sub-stage necessitates the accumulation of more and more arms. M-16s are common; M-1 Garands and M-203s – Armalites with grenade launchers – are prized. Hence the numerous ambushes which have demoralised the army and built up the NPA arsenal. Some members of the AFP have always engaged in trading arms and passing information, perhaps making their own deaths less likely in the face of an attack. In the confusion following the departure of Marcos, quantities of arms were freely available, and the NPA took full advantage of this.

Contrary to government statements – before and after the election – the NPA is a popular movement: 'Nice people to have around' one villager told me. Most Red fighters are farmers, operating on the principle of surrounding towns and cities from the countryside, with armed city partisans – sparrow units – working from within the most heavily populated areas.

Mindanao, for a long while the government's Achilles' heel, is divided into four underground divisions: Eastern, Western, Southern and North Central. Company-sized formations of 65 to 100 fighters rapidly increased in 1985 to battalion size, 500 to 800 men, for instance, in Eastern Mindanao. In the NPA standing army most combatants are 18 to 20 years old, with commanders about seven years older. There are still comparatively few women.

In contrast, however, the armed city partisans, well organised in Davao city, for example, have a high percentage of girls, 15 to 20 years of age. Their primary task is in organising and information gathering, with guerrilla work a second strand. They also deal with informers, carry out sabotage and obtain arms, for example, from local security guards. People soon learn to be silent after an incident. It is easy to become the next victim.

The following NPA account shows the way a sparrow unit approaches its task:

For the past two days Ka Ben and Ka Dan had kept the notorious policeman under surveillance as he moved about in Camalig, Albay. Now they closed in on him. Boarding the jeepney where the target was seated beside the driver, they took up their positions, with Ka Ben right behind him. Conscious of his many crimes against the masses, the enemy alertly kept an eye on the passengers through the rear-view mirror and released the safety lock of his M-16 rifle. Ka Ben pretended to ignore him, while actually waiting for his chance. The moment the enemy was distracted Ka Ben drew his pistol in a flash and fired, grabbing the M-16 at the same time. Ka Dan, acting quickly, finished him off.

Operations such as this were carried out in cities and urban centres every day prior to the election. This partisan work mainly involved the confiscation of arms for NPA units in the countryside and the liquidation of notorious enemies – regular military troops, policemen, ICHDF members, informers and others who had incurred blood debts or otherwise harmed the ordinary people. This will continue, and may increase as old scores are settled. Former Marcos supporters are now very much at risk.

Partisans have always attacked government officials who actively engaged in counter-revolution. Although usually protected by their personal 'army' they were eventually caught off-guard. Mayor Pablo Lucero of Calbayog city in western Samar, for example, was killed while playing tennis. Captain Orlando Caalim, a policeman from Abucay, a town in Bataan province, 50 kilometres west of Iloilo city, was shot in the back of the neck, shortly after boarding a jeepney to go home. On 2 January 1985, the mayor of Zaragoza municipality, Nueva Ecija province, 95 kilometres north of Manila – Rogelia Lagmay – was killed with three of his escorts as he walked up the stairs of the municipal building. It was to have been his first day in office since an anti-graft court cleared him of misappropriating 29 000 pesos worth of government supplies. On 3 February 1985, Jaime Gabunada, a 'gambling boss', and four of his associates were shot in Cagayan de Oro city in Mindanao. Twelve gunmen entered Gabunada's house as he drove his jeep into the compound, heavily fortified with electrified barbed wire. The attackers carried high-powered arms including an M-79 grenade launcher. On 31 March 1985, Mayor Federico Cua was shot by three men who walked up to him as he was talking with a group of people in front of his house in Javier, Leyte, 593 kilometres south-east of Manila.

By means of these partisan operations the NPA demonstrated to the military that they were not even safe within the cities. Detachments have now, more than ever, to be of a sufficient size and military installations have to be guarded. The leaders of the sparrow units are ruthless and dedicated, adjusting quickly to changing situations in the post-Marcos period. Usually they are selected from regular guerrilla units. Apart from military experience, they are also required to gain experience in mass work by joining an armed propaganda unit for a time. They also undergo a training programme, learning how to draw and fire a gun quickly, how to approach a target, and how to confiscate an enemy's weapon. They also receive training in karate and other technical skills.

As opposed to the NPA in the hills, partisans have operated in white areas, so secrecy and prudence have been important. This is the key to maintaining the initiative and the element of surprise. Partisans cannot act in a set pattern which could be easily recognised by the enemy. Their appearance, dress, actions and mannerisms are those of ordinary people, but with an elaborate system of codes and signals. The establishment of a support network is important. People in the white areas take care of their financial needs, provide quarters, places from which operations are launched and fallback positions. In some cases supporters also help the partisans by playing tricks on the enemy, diverting their attention and confusing them.

Now that the people's war has entered the advanced sub-stage of the strategic defensive, partisan work has assumed added significance. This entails a shift in the focus of partisan operations in the light of local conditions. For example, instead of simply confiscating weapons, partisan activities during a certain period might concentrate on crippling an enemy organisation – especially its intelligence units – sabotaging communication lines and military installations, or liquidating key military and other personnel. Former Marcos supporters have endeavoured to regroup in many areas.

The guerrillas – whether urban or rural – have never engaged in wanton killing, having a strict code of conduct. While informers were shot on the spot – and, as has been shown, many were killed each month – corrupt local officials or those who destructively supported the regime were always given three warnings before arrangements were made for their execution. Currently there is post-Marcos 'work' to be completed.

After ambushes in the rural areas the NPA would bind the wounds of the military, provided they had surrendered and handed over their weapons. There were – and are – inevitably, internal disagreements about whether such men should be allowed to live and fight again. Well-trained medical units have always been part of the team when ambushes were carried out.

Members of the NPA do not like living the lives they do, they do not welcome the harsh conditions in the forest, sleeping in hammocks made of rice sacks slung between trees, and the constant exposure to hunger, thirst and disease. But they know their cause is just. Their focus is sharper now that their major enemy has left the country: it is even more people-centred. They also have fun between their rigorous training sessions: singing to guitar accompaniment, telling jokes and composing songs to keep up morale. They have eight points of discipline: (a) pay fairly for what you buy; (b) pay for what you have damaged and return what you have borrowed; (c) do not destroy property; (d) do not destroy crops; (e) do not swear at people; (f) do not take liberties with women; (g) do not ill-treat captives; and (h) do not take a 'single thread' from the masses.

Often, however, they have been desperate for medicines. Weak with fatigue they succumb to common ailments. Bouts of malaria sometimes affect whole units, and at these times the support of people in the *barrios* – in providing urgent medical supplies – has been essential for survival. Little wonder, therefore, that it is this link between the people in the *barrios* and the men and women in the hills that the army has been especially eager to break.

There are many snakes in the hills, making sleeping in the open hazardous. One commander described how, on waking one morning with his men, they discovered a python asleep nearby. It had eaten their dog. The python provided a meal for the men who found the dog crushed inside. Elsewhere, I have known a python swallow a dozen chickens, and there are reports that – on two occasions – young babies have been devoured.

Cristina's husband went to the hills in November 1984. A year later she went to her parish priest, telling him that she was going to join her husband. He suggested that the plan should be discussed with the family. This Cristina did – with her children and her parents. Her decision remained the same. They all agreed that, without a revolution, there was no future for the younger generation. Cristina wanted a future for her children whether she was with them or not. Violence, in Cristina's opinion, is justified where there is oppression; where all other means of bringing about change have been tried without success; and when a call to arms represents the collective will of the people. Justification on all three counts became more than ever apparent during 1985. As Cristina says, the institutional violence of the Marcos regime – propped up by lies, deceit, violence, and America – was the ultimate in oppression. Aquino's election gave hope, but little else. No actions of the present administration can bring about radical change. As Cristina said after the election: 'The collective will of the people has yet to be expressed.'

Young children have sometimes joined their parents in the hills, and with increasing frequency as the 'Red areas' became safe. One family I stayed with had a two-year-old visitor, Maria, waiting to be collected by a friend of a friend. She was to join her parents in the mountains. Two days later, she left, her future a mixture of certainty and uncertainty.

And young people have been involved in the struggle. Tales of bravery abound and children of all ages – 'Red fireflies' they are called – communicate with amazing speed at the approach of strangers, banging stones or bamboo sticks as part of their signalling system. There is tragedy, too. Fourteen-year-old Antonio was carrying medicines for a wounded member of the NPA. Suddenly the military arrived, and he paused to rest at the house of an elderly neighbour. The soldiers entered the house and the neighbour – uninvolved as it happened – was harassed and beaten about the head on discovery of the package containing the medicines. Antonio was grieved to witness the brutality, and told the military commander that he was responsible for the packet. He was shot on the spot. Antonio is a child of our time.

Despite the extraordinary conditions of life in the NPA, marriage is an option for the *armado*. Having served the movement for at least two years, courtship may be initiated, after receiving permission from the *armado's* collective. When a year of courtship has been completed the respective collectives of the man and woman announce their engagement. This stage is a period for developing the basis of marriage in very different and difficult circumstances – love for the masses and love for each other. Also during this stage the two collectives meet to evaluate the couple's capacity for the 'discipline and honour' of marriage.

Towards the end of their engagement the couple elects a marriage collective composed of their choice of sponsors and a solemnizer. This collective exists solely for the particular marriage and functions like a marriage-encounter therapy group scrutinizing the merits and demerits of the couple. This collective – which, of course, includes the couple – sets the wedding date if there is consensus that the couple is ready.

The wedding is usually held in a supportive *barrio*. The ceremony begins with a reading on the theme of marriage selected by the marriage collective. It is followed by speeches delivered by the sponsors on the importance of proletarian love – how the couple's love for each other must be contextualized in their love for the people. Each *ninong* and *ninang* – 'godfather' and 'godmother' – addresses the audience and then the couple.

Then a representative from the people in the *barrio* greets the couple, and the man and woman give their response, explaining their reasons for getting married.

There is an official text for the marriage pledge which, in essence, is a commitment to serve the people. The oath is taken with the couple's hands placed on M-16s. The Red flag is draped on the shoulders of the newly-weds to symbolize their union within the Communist Party. In closing, the 'Internationale' is sung. The celebrations, in the manner of the Igorots, last well into the night with singing, dancing and drinking. The NPA, recognising the conditions of poverty in the *barrios*, discourages lavish celebrations, but most often – in typical Filipino tradition – the people themselves want to make the most of the occasion.

Although the movement frowns on broken marriages, divorce may take place with the formation of a divorce collective. This body, just like the marriage collective, exists only for that particular divorce and must receive the consent of both parties. If one of the parties objects to the proceedings, a moratorium is declared on the marriage, that is, the marriage is considered binding but not operative. There are five grounds for divorce: (a) arrest and the prolonged imprisonment of one party; (b) treachery against the movement; (c) mental derangement; (d) physical incapacity; and (e) hindrance – when one party prevents the other person's performance of political objectives.

There are over 20 000 Red fighters – NPA regulars – nationwide, of which about half have high-powered weapons. About 9000 guerrillas are in Mindanao. These men, in turn, are heavily dependent on the 'mass base' from which they receive their support: food, medicine and information especially. Working with those who support the movement is reminiscent of the French resistance in the Second World War. There is always information to be passed, for example, about troop movements; plans to be made, for instance, about maintaining supplies; and individual problems to be solved, for example, when a wounded guerrilla needs medical attention. Towards the end of 1985, Joy recounted the events of her week as we talked in a squatter hut in a small city. She lived with the guerrillas in the hills: organising and educating, and occasionally taking arms. In a recent ambush she had killed two soldiers, and was still upset by the experience. Her present mission was different: finding a doctor in the city who could be trusted, and would remove a bullet from the thigh of one of her own men back at the camp. As Joy moved down from the hills and through areas where the military presence was heavy, she changed everything about her: clothes, hairstyle, make-up, identity, and role, resuming – in essence – the persona of two years previously. Two things, however, did not change: her watchfulness and her determination. She remained constantly on guard, mindful of every knock at the door, of everybody who looked at her, of every detail of the conversation. Joy had been well trained. Her determination showed in the way in which, within 48 hours, she had located a 'friendly' doctor and made precise arrangements for a rendezvous with the wounded guerrilla together with the transport of medicines and supplies to carry out the operation. Joy disappeared as quickly as she came, shedding her urban role as she slipped away to the safety and danger of the hills.

REBEL PRIESTS

There are a number of priests who have joined the guerrilla groups – probably 12 or so – and fight with them in the hills. Most have become leaders, but choose to keep a low profile. Two who have been unable to do so are Father Frank Navarro, 38 years old, who leads the main regular guerrilla units of the NPA's Southern Front in Mindanao; and Father Conrado Balweg, 42 years old, a legendary figure operating in northern Luzon in the Cordillera mountains.

Navarro was initially one of the Filipino priests caught up in the theology of liberation, a movement which – as in South America – brought the church closer to the poor and oppressed. In 1983, protesting about a warrant issued against him and two other priests, Navarro left his parish in Surigao del Sur and simply climbed the mountain to join the NPA. From his mountain hideout he reflected:

A priest is a priest forever. I consider my involvement in the revolution a supplementary ministry in an exceptional situation . . . I know violence is against the teachings of the church, but this revolutionary violence is a product of institutionalised violence by the state and our desire to defend ourselves.' Navarro reiterates his belief in God and acknowledges that others in the NPA do not believe: 'We respect each other. Different beliefs do not hamper our cause because we do not often discuss religion. Our main concern is to serve the people and to discuss solutions to their problems.

After one raid, Navarro and his companions slipped out of the forest and found a car. They thought of using it to get away but there was no key. A boy approached Navarro: 'Father, here is the key.' When asked how he knew he was a priest the boy replied: 'Father, I'm from your parish in Tagum.' Navarro neither smokes nor drinks. Unlike Balweg, he is not married.

One of the most wanted men in the country, Conrado Balweg has had a price of 200 000 pesos on his head. A striking figure, determined yet full of humour, he realises that his death may be by the bullet. Shortly after I left him, 51 of his men were reportedly killed when 3000 soldiers swept through the area supported by helicopter gunships. This was later found not to be correct; it was a further example of military propaganda. Indeed, from March 1984 to April 1985 Balweg's men suffered no casualties, and killed 46 soldiers, six military informers and captured 76 firearms in 29 encounters.

Crossing the mighty Chico River and climbing the mountains beyond the rice terraces – in order to meet Balweg – was physically demanding, a long way even from the small town of Bontoc. The last part of the journey was made during the hours of darkness, the armed escorts indicating stage by stage on their two-way radios that a visitor was on his way. The atmosphere in the guerrilla camp was relaxed, yet the watchfulness of Balweg's men was never in doubt. They remained constantly on guard. At night beacons were occasionally lit on neighbouring peaks – and as quickly extinguished. In most instances the communication systems of the guerrillas are more effective than those of the military. The dress of the freedom fighters is varied: pieces of army uniforms, American fatigue trousers and flak jackets, and Chinese blue caps with sewn-on red stars. Many wear denim jeans.

Balweg says that joining the revolutionary movement was not a sudden decision but a gradual process. Coming from a very religious family – his people are Tingguians – he describes his father as a 'man of peace, a pacifist, ever conscious of relationships within the community'. He was brought up 'obsessed with the idea of peace' with endless novenas, rosary meetings and prayer rallies. He first encountered violence at school, blaming the anti-minority prejudices of the Ilocanos. Balweg tells his own story:

My Ilocano classmates were always picking on us Tingguians. They would slash the backs of our shirts with razor blades, often slicing the skin. When we complained to the Ilocano teachers they just made fun of us. Some of us Tingguians were near the top of the class, but none of us ever received honours. This created great dissatisfaction among the Tingguians. Maybe, I thought, it was because there were no educated professionals among us. I began to think that perhaps the way to regain dignity for our tribe was to become a priest, since the Ilocanos had a great respect for priests. In 1971 I received the sacrament of Holy Orders and became a missionary of the Society of the Divine Word (SVD). My first assignment was in the parish of Luba, Tubo, Abra. This was a Tingguian area. I had always seen priesthood as an honourable way for the minorities to rise above discrimination and chauvinism. At last I could put my beliefs into practice, focusing on spirituality and the theology of Incarnation . . . At that time I had not yet read anything at all on Marxism. I had not even met a Marxist. I learned, however, that there were those who had already labelled me 'communist', perhaps because of my emphasis on service to the PDO – the poor, the deprived and the oppressed.

1973 was an important year. I became involved with the land-grabbing activities of the Cellophil Resource Corporation. One day 40 soldiers arrived in town. They went straight to the church to pray. They said they were Malacañang Palace guards. The next day a helicopter landed in the plaza. The men who got off spread out a large map. They said that Imelda Marcos had ordered a cadastral survey. They pointed to the mountains. Why is there a *kaingin* up there? Who built those houses on our mountain? they demanded.

Things developed quickly after that. Our bishop, a German called Odilo Estpeuller, took a pro-Cellophil stance against the people living in the forests. During an assembly of SVD priests of the Abra-Cagayan province, we found that he had accepted 400 000 pesos in exchange for campaigning for Cellophil from the pulpit and from the church-owned radio station in Abra.

My parish became the centre of resistance against Cellophil. We did research and documentation. We found out that they had been granted the biggest forest concession in the Philippines. It included most of Abra. The name-calling started. Twelve German priests – we called them the 'dirty dozen' – wrote a position paper denouncing four priests in the Tingguian areas as 'communists'. The government and the military picked up their line. But I was not a communist. I had still never met one.

I became interested, however, and was soon to make contact with the underground. By 1976 the NPA had been wiped out in our area, the north

Abra. It was in Mindanao that I had my first tentative contact. I was attending a conference on tribal Filipinos in Tagum, Davao. I was told of the NPA activity in the area by some priests assigned there. They spoke highly of the NPA and suggested introducing me. I was surprised to find that the people they were talking about were church workers. They were not really NPA, but rather sympathisers. They were most supportive to me in the anti-Cellophil campaign, helping me to systematize my apostolate and make our organisations more issue-oriented.

I read *Philippine Society and Revolution* by Amado Guerrero in late 1978. It was the first Marxist text I had ever read. I was able to place my personal experiences of discrimination and exploitation in the context of Philippine history. My idea of spirituality began to be developed further. I began to see that the essence of spirituality was justice, justice for the masses suffering economic exploitation, political exploitation, educational and cultural exploitation. I began to question the role of the church as an institution. Never in the history of the Philippine church had the institution taken the side of the basic masses.

By 1979 the military decided it was time to put a stop to our organising. My liquidation was ordered. Bishop Estpeuller knew about this, and he figured that my death would inflame the Cellophil issue even more. He told me to go away, and I decided to take indefinite leave of absence. In June that year I joined the 'revo'. I thought I would be dead in six months. But I was happy. We had always been taught in the church to be ready for death at any instant. When I was ordained it was stressed that the essence of priesthood is the offering of one's life with absolutely no conditions. Here in the revolution you can demonstrate every day that you are ready to offer your life for the masses . . . What is important is the relationship between man and God. I have difficulty with the concept of a personal God with whom I have an individualistic one-to-one relationship. I can believe in the Supreme Being who created man as a social animal. The relationship between man and God cannot exclude the rest of society, the people of God . . . We have to build a new system, a new church, that will respond to the needs of the Philippine people. I use the masses. I commune with the communities. Christ made a total offering of himself to the people even to death. Whether I am here or not the masses will still fight. I have never had a grudge against the church even though I was condemned by the institution. People now regard me as a person and not as a priest. This revolution is a revolution of the people. The main force is the peasants themselves. I am just an ally. Political liberation is as important as spiritual salvation.

When I went on indefinite leave from the SVD and joined my friends in the mountains I expected to undergo extensive military training. The political work turned out to be more important. Bearing arms gave us the freedom to help the masses organise themselves, to help them fight for their rights and to establish the political power that rightly belongs to them. There came a time when I had to use my weapons. Four months after I arrived we had our first encounter with the military. It is one thing to carry a weapon but when you are facing people who are also armed it is something else. You realise that the gun is not just for decoration. It wasn't easy. I know that the soldiers I faced also came from the basic masses. They were doing the dirty work for Marcos and his cronies. The experience made me lose sleep for a month. I would see the casualties, and all the blood. It was the same for all of us. The killing was always a bad shock. But we know that we are at a point in our history when we must fight so that freedom will triumph. It is a matter of accepting the reality of violence. In the beginning the form of violence was that of nature over man. One could suddenly die of diarrhoea or appendicitis. Then man learned to control nature. But then a new form of violence emerged, and violence was used by man over man in the pursuit of class interests. When one class dominates another, contradiction and struggle become inevitable, and violence erupts. So it is a matter of which violence you practice, the unjust violence of the ruling class or the just violence of the revolution. Revolution remains the only option in the present Philippine society.

Killings are only part of our work. I must emphasise the political aspects. We hold meetings in the *barrios*, contacting a relative or friend to ensure that there will be no difficulties. Nowadays, because of the popularity of the NPA and its cause, we usually go straight to the *barrio* official. Here in Kalinga or in Abra it is most often the peace pact holder [see later]. We introduce ourselves and ask permission to hold a mass meeting.

The first topic usually discussed is security; for example, what to do when the *kaaway*, the soldiers, show up; what to answer if interrogated; or what to do if the *barrio* is harassed. Then the educational process begins. It starts with a social investigation. The masses investigate their own situation. They identify their needs and problems, and consider whether their problems are caused by internal or external factors. We sit down for a whole day or several days, depending on the amount of data that can be gathered on the community's economic, political, cultural and health aspects. When people in Cordillera speak of rights it is their rights to ancestral lands.

BODONG

Balweg is interested in the peace pact as an institution. He himself holds three peace pacts for his tribe. Peace pacts were developed by tribes in Kalinga and in Abra to limit tribal wars and head-hunting that were caused by territorial disputes. One tribe took another tribe's land, so they fought. Gradually the *bodong* or peace pact evolved as a way of maintaining peace among the tribes. The terms would be debated and then there would be a feast. The peace pact holder was responsible for enforcing the *bodong*. If two tribes have a peace pact and a member of one tribe comes to the other's territory, there is an obligation to protect the stranger against harm.

The *bodong* system plays a part in the political development of the tribes. They band together to defend themselves against outside forces. The Cellophil land-grab was a classic example.

The rallying cause in Luzon, however, remains the Chico River

Basin dam project. The government planned to build four dams that would displace 100 000 Bontocs and Kalingas. They would have lost their rice terraces, their forests and their burial grounds. To members of these tribes their land is their very life. Losing their land means losing their lives.

The tribes resisted the building of these dams. Before this, the *bodong* was strictly a bilateral treaty. A tribe would have *bodong*s with many tribes on a one-to-one basis. The NPA helped the tribes in the struggle against the construction of the dams, particularly by introducing the idea of a multilateral *bodong*. The government hurled the full force of the military and PANAMIN against those who resisted the building of the dams. On 24 April 1980 one of the leaders of the struggle, the Kalinga *pangat* Macli-ing Dulag was brutally murdered by Lieutenant Adalem and his soldiers, uniting the tribes even more. The dam project was stopped.

SUCCESSES

In 1984 the NPA seized a huge quantity of firearms, and killed nearly 700 military and paramilitary men in about 250 offensives in 35 provinces. On average, there were five tactical offences each week. Among the major offensives were the following:

(a) Ambush on the 111th Philippine Constabulary Company in Rizal, Cagayan, 5 January (15 high-powered firearms seized).

(b) Raids on ICHDF and police units in *barrios* of Daalican, Zamboanga del Norte, 17 January (27 rifles seized).

(c) Simultaneous raids on a police station and a detachment of the Philippine Constabulary, Butuan city, Agusan del Norte, 17 January (20 rifles seized).

(d) Raid on a detachment in a logging camp in Sugay, Agusan del Norte, 15 March (20 rifles seized).

(e) Raid on a detachment of the 36th Infantry Battalion in Rosario, Tubay, Agusan del Norte, 16 March (30 rifles seized).

(f) Ambush on an AFP convoy in Banawe, Ifugao, 21 May (21 rifles seized).

(g) Execution of INP Brigadier-General Tomas Karingal in Quezon city, Metro Manila, 24 May.

(h) Raid on a detachment of the 42nd Infantry Battalion in Dungawan Central, Guinayangan, Quezon, 24 November (29 rifles seized).

Table 7.1　Firearms captured, 1985

M-16	426	BAR	12
M-1 Garand	98	M-60	43
Carbine	101	Unspecified rifles	419
M-79	6	Sidearms	512
M-203	37	Shotguns	37
M-14	20		

Again, in 1985, guerrilla warfare spread and intensified. The NPA acquired more and stronger weapons, recruited more fighters and formed larger units. There was considerable deepening of the support of the people, and an unusually high number of senior army officers, including several commanding officers, were killed.

The NPA has lacked external assistance in its fight against the AFP, and has never been in a position to fight a full-scale war. It is, of course, possible that the current hands-off attitude of the Chinese and the Russians to the insurgency will change if the NPA looks to have a clear chance of success, or as Ramos intensifies his anti-insurgency campaign. However, though the NPA aims to secure coastal areas with a view to importing arms, geographical isolation will always make it difficult for large quantities of arms to be shipped. Although both the CPP and the NPA prefer to be without pressures from the Chinese, Soviets and Vietnamese, and some of their 'guidance', the price of independence can be high. It may no longer be considered worthwhile.

Even without outside support, the struggle continues to intensify. War – according to the leaders of the National Democratic Front (NDF) – like revolution, is both a science and an art. In combining theory and practice, in regarding the implementation of their cause as both a science and an art and in emphasising skill in leadership, frequent reference is made to the basic document of the CPP: *Specific Characteristics of Our People's War* by Amado Guerrero. Guided by this text the war has moved from the early sub-stage to the advanced sub-stage of the strategic defensive, and now moves into strategic stalemate. Encirclement of the cities from the countryside – encouraging thrusts by urban guerrillas and in the rural areas – confused the AFP and weakened their position during the latter days of the old administration, thereby laying the foundations for a people's war on a nationwide scale.

While armed struggle is seen as the primary means of bringing about a lasting and only solution to the problems of the Philippine people, it does not negate, but is in fact complemented by, the parliamentary struggle as secondary means. The NDF is concerned with organising people: farmers, fishermen and workers. It has, as members, strong and active organisations, for example, *Kabataang Makabayan* (KM) or Patriotic Youth, *Katipunan ng mga Gurong Makabayan* (KAGUMA) or Federation of Patriotic Teachers, *Makabayang Samahan Pankalusugan* (MASAPA) or Patriotic Association of Health Workers, and Christians for National Liberation (CNL). There is, too, educational work, and mobilising people within the parliamentary context. But, as one powerful – and charming – leader said to me: 'Primarily it is better to walk silently with a big stick.'

The development of the NPA campaign is markedly different from that of the people's war in China which advanced, wave upon wave, from a number of extensive bases and liberated areas which were immediately established in the early sub-stage of the strategic defensive. In the Philippines emphasis was placed on the establishment of guerrilla zones and guerrilla fronts nationwide, avoiding the premature establishment of base areas and even guerrilla bases. The NPA has grown as a long process of developing, expanding and intensifying guerrilla warfare in both urban and rural areas, adapting to the archipelagic and mountainous character of semi-feudal and semi-colonial Philippines ruled by a single power with a unified machinery of reaction. For some time the NPA has been concerned with the transitional development of guerrilla warfare towards regular mobile warfare, and of guerrilla fronts towards guerrilla bases. At the same time, efforts were directed towards the advancement of the mass movement by the intensification and the launching of urban protests and uprisings. During 1985 these were at their height. Their first success was manifested in the overthrow of the Marcos government.

Opposition to Marcos brought together all shades of political opinion. The next goal is the attainment of national freedom and a real people's democracy, not yet established. The Aquino election was but a stepping stone in the struggle, part of the historical development of the Philippines leading to the ultimate success of the revolutionary movement.

Senior members of the NDF agree that the outcome – in terms of the final political direction – is uncertain. There is a fair assessment of the future in the NDF literature:

In essence, the people's democratic revolution is a bourgeois democratic revolution and not a proletarian revolution. It is a democratic revolution against imperialism, feudalism and bureaucratic capitalism and not a proletariat revolution to supplant capitalism with socialism . . .

Because the democratic revolution is essentially a bourgeois democratic revolution and not a proletarian revolution – even if it is under the leadership of the proletariat – it follows that what it will establish will not be a proletarian government but a democratic coalition government of all anti-imperialist and anti-feudal forces. While it would not be a proletarian state, it would not be a bourgeois state either, since it will be ruled jointly by the democratic classes and strata.

The class basis of the democratic coalition government would be the revolutionary alliance of all revolutionary classes in Philippine society. It means that the people's democratic revolution is the unified action of the working class, the peasantry, the urban petty bourgeoisie and the national bourgeoisie and other anti-imperialist and anti-feudal forces, in waging revolutionary struggle and in organising state power. To solve the existing basic problems and the fundamental contradictions in our society, what is needed is the full, not just formal, participation of all four revolutionary classes in the establishment and wielding of democratic political power. The exclusion of any of these classes will result in the revolution's failure.

What will be the direction of the democratic coalition government of the people's democracy that will be established? Depending on the class composition of the revolutionary coalition, it could lead towards socialism or towards capitalism. It all depends upon which class force will effectively lead the democratic coalition and the entire people.

NATIONAL DEMOCRATIC FRONT

One of the driving forces in the fight against Marcos was the NDF, the 'illegal' umbrella organisation led by the CPP which coordinated the activities of different cause-oriented leftist bodies. In its programme, the NDF rightly asserted that 'the overwhelming majority of our people have awakened and are demanding an end to the hated dictatorship', and that principles and bases of popular unity had been understood and accepted by almost all. Certainly, within the broad front of the NDF, the political achievement equalled and, indeed, exceeded the military one. Points of unification now include an end to foreign domination; genuine freedom for the people; unhampered economic development that serves the interests of the people; the reduction of military power; and justice for all. The NDF also seeks 'untiringly to unite, develop and coordinate all possible parties, groups and individuals . . . for greater participation in the ongoing people's war . . . until total, nationwide victory is won and a new republic with a democratic coalition government is established.' That government has yet to be established.

Published in 1985, the new text contains a 12-point general programme and the specific programme for immediate implementation. It was based on the 1982 draft and on the comments, criticisms and suggestions from various forces, organisations, groups and individuals within the NDF or allied to it.

The general programme covering the entire process of the national–democratic revolution gives strategic guidance and direction for the implementation of the specific programme. The programme has been expanded to 12 points from the original ten and also clarifies the policies of the NDF on major questions facing the nation.

The specific programme, on the other hand, contains the immediate tasks for implementing the general programme and responding to the needs of the present situation. Sets of issues with ten items each fall under the categories of political, military, economic, social welfare, culture and education, and foreign relations.

The 12 points of the NDF general programme are as follows:

1. Unite the Filipino people to overthrow the tyrannical rule of US imperialism and the local reactionaries.
2. Wage a people's war to win total, nationwide victory.
3. Establish a democratic coalition government and a people's democratic republic.
4. Integrate the revolutionary armed forces into a single national revolutionary army.
5. Uphold and promote the free exercise of the people's basic democratic rights.
6. Terminate all unequal relations with the United States and other foreign entities.
7. Complete the process of genuine land reform, raise rural production through cooperation, and modernise agriculture.
8. Carry out national industrialisation as the leading factor in economic development.
9. Guarantee the right to employment, raise the people's living standards and expand social services the soonest after establishing democratic state power.
10. Promote a patriotic, scientific and popular culture and ensure free public education.

11. Respect and foster the self-determination of the Moro and Cordillera people and all ethnic minorities.
12. Adopt and practise a revolutionary, independent and peace-loving foreign policy.

The NDF programme was first published in April 1973 upon the establishment of the Preparatory Commission for the NDF. This was revised and released with elaborations in 1977 and republished in 1980. It was further revised in 1982 before publication in 1985.

Members of the NDF compare events in the Philippines with what has happened in Iran, Vietnam, Nicaragua and El Salvador. Addressing a meeting of Philippine diplomats on 6 December 1985, Foreign Minister Pacifico Castro rejected this. He said that the Vietnam War was a struggle for national liberation while Iran had an Islamic revolution against dynastic monarchs. Nicaragua, he stated, had no democratic tradition, and El Salvador had been ruled by military dictators until the elections in 1984.

In combination, it is these four points with which the opposition identifies. The NDF portrays its struggle as one for 'national liberation'; certainly the authoritarian rule of Marcos had all the hallmarks of a 'dynastic monarch'; 'democratic tradition' in the Philippines is weak; and – under the direction of Marcos – 'military dictators' had almost unlimited power. It would be foolish to assume that, because a few actors have been changed, the revolutionary process has been halted.

8 Certainty and Uncertainty

There has been both certainty and uncertainty in the Philippines for some considerable time: notably, during the election period, during the Marcos regime and, of course, earlier than that. The certainties range from the corrupt, cruel and oppressive nature of the Marcos administration; to the increasing poverty and unrest of the people; to the continuing strength of the institutional church, sadly disappointing in its overall effectiveness; to the determination of the USA to maintain its defence and economic interests at any cost. The uncertainties have included information about possible successors to Marcos – from within his own party or from the opposition; the question of the re-imposition of martial law; the manner in which the army would react when Marcos died, quit or was overthrown; the timing of the revolution; the extent of direct US military involvement in the face of a threat to their bases.

It has always been clear, however, as Renato Constantino says in *The Post-Marcos Era: An Appraisal*, that: 'the post-Marcos era will be characterized by the same policies and programs and they will be implemented by the same breed of technocrats but behind a façade of democracy. In this sense, the post-Marcos era will be essentially the same as the Marcos one, only with a new set of actors and with just enough cosmetic changes to barely accommodate present popular dissent and beguile a majority of the citizenry.'

The presidential – and vice-presidential – election was originally scheduled for early in 1987. Throughout 1985, however, there were rumours that the date would be brought forward and in November of that year a 'snap' election was announced. After a number of changes, 7 February was decided as the date.

ELECTION: CONSTITUTIONAL VALIDITY

The 1986 presidential election was of dubious legality from the start and narrowly escaped being declared unconstitutional by the Philippine Supreme Court. The Marcos-inspired constitution only allowed for a mid-term or snap election in the event of the president's 'permanent disability, death, removal from office or resignation'. None of these four contingencies had occurred. The constitution further stipulated that in the event of a vacancy in the presidency, the speaker of the National Assembly would be acting president while the election took place. Marcos overcame this provision by filing a post-dated resignation which would have only taken effect in the event of his losing the election. In this way no vacancy occurred, and the speaker was not called upon to take over as acting president.

It is not surprising that 11 motions were quickly filed with the Supreme Court, contesting the constitutional validity of the special election bill passed by the National Assembly. Five justices of the Supreme Court declared the bill – and, therefore, the election – to be unconstitutional and invalid. Seven justices were more cautious, and refrained from going that far. In practice – prompted by Marcos – the court majority decided the issue before it was one on which it could rule. This was not the same as giving the election a clean bill of constitutional health.

THE CAMPAIGN

When he first announced the election the president declared categorically that the issue was *Marcos*. Although the discussions on both sides wandered far afield during subsequent weeks they always returned to the main theme: Marcos. 'Policies' were always a secondary consideration. In fact, neither side seemed to have any. On 16 December 1985, Aquino told reporters after a rally that she had no specific plan of government. 'The only thing I can really offer the Filipino people is my sincerity', the *New York Times* quoted her as saying. There was no clear presentation of economic arguments by Marcos or Aquino, the latter unnerved by her need to make constant adjustments to her words and position in the light of American 'advice', uncertainty and string-pulling. Under the cover of 'fair elections' the USA had to keep their options open just a little. There was a slight chance that the Marcos machinery could have covered the fraudulence at the polls. At one point, in their desperation, the USA even put pressure on Aquino to form a coalition with Marcos. As it became clear, however, that a Marcos victory was not possible, the USA gave their unqualified support to Aquino, and put into top gear the plan which – from about May 1985 – they had hoped would work.

In the first rounds of the campaign Marcos and his propaganda machine had the upper hand, and the opposition was fragmented. The president kept his opponent off-balance by a series of accusations, and these included references to her dead husband. Gradually the campaign became more acrimonious, with killings on both sides.

Accusations were made day by day. Benigno Aquino was accused of having helped found the new Communist Party of the Philippines and the NPA; Marcos pushed hard at 'Cory's inexperience'. Aquino loudly admitted that she was 'inexperienced – inexperienced in lying, cheating, stealing, and assassinating my political opponents'. Days before the *New York Times* and the *Washington Post* alleged that Marcos's claims to being a war hero were fraudulent, and that he had collaborated with the Japanese, Aquino was questioning the president's 17 wartime medals and his war record. The extensive property ownership of Marcos, his family and his cronies was again raised, with evidence pouring in to support the accusations. Marcos retaliated, weakly trying to regain Washington's undiluted confidence by playing on Reagan's strong anti-communist predilections and – building on his earlier references to Benigno Aquino – by painting his opponents as communist-dominated.

MARCOS'S HEALTH

Marcos's poor health became more and more the focus of attention, each election appearance underlining his deteriorating physical condition. He was often bandaged when he appeared on stage, had frequent nose-bleeds, stumbled on many occasions and was even carried to and from the platform by his aides. Twice he wet himself as he made speeches, and many times retired to a portable medical cubicle which travelled everywhere with him, others entertaining the crowds meanwhile. The frequent jibe of the opposition was: 'How can Marcos control the nation when he cannot control his bladder?' Although there has never been any official confirmation, it is widely accepted that the symptoms which Marcos has displayed indicate that he suffers from a condition known as *systemic lupus erythematosus*.

Lupus, as it is called, slowly wastes away the body's immune system. It is treatable, but not curable. It results in muscle and joint pains, fevers, chest pains, headaches, depression, and inflammation of the kidneys. Marcos became a pale shadow of his former dynamic and energetic self – and for the first decade and a half of his presidency he did display tremendous energy – often suffering from exhaustion, visible ageing and, relative to his former eloquence, occasional incoherence. Lupus, by itself, could account for all these symptoms. The fact that it was well known that he was seen by doctors from the USA, that the presidential palace imported its own kidney dialysis machine in the early 80s, and that Marcos was being treated with cortisone, confirmed the rumours. Marcos's illness was undoubtedly one factor which – towards the end of 1985 – accelerated US moves to orchestrate the shift of power.

CHRONICLE OF EVENTS

Before further analysis of the last days of the Marcos regime and speculation about the future, a summary of events, and particularly the events during the early part of 1986, might be helpful. The following are the principal landmarks in the 20-year presidency of Ferdinand Marcos:

9 November 1965. Senate President Marcos, who switched from the ruling Liberal Party to bear the Nationalist Party standard in the presidential election, defeats incumbent Diosdado Macapagal.

1968. Embryonic New People's Army starts rural communist insurgency with just a few hundred militants.

1969. Marcos re-elected for second – and theoretically final – four-year term.

21 August 1971. Marcos suspends *habeas corpus*, saying that the country is menaced by communist insurrection.

21 September 1972. Marcos declares martial law, blaming public disorders caused by both right and left. Political foes are among thousands of dissidents arrested, notably arch-rival Senator Benigno Aquino.

January 1973. New constitution introduced, extending presidential term indefinitely and naming Marcos prime minister as well.

December 1976. Libya helps Marcos reach a ceasefire pact with Mindanao Muslim rebels, but the truce breaks down in late 1977.

7 April 1978. First election under martial law for newly-created Legislative Assembly.

May 1980. Benigno Aquino freed from jail to have medical treatment in the United States.

January 1981. Marcos lifts martial law, having first passed legislation ensuring that he keeps all-embracing executive powers.

May 1983. American bases pact extended, giving United States forces further tenure at Subic Bay and Clark Air Base.

21 August 1983. Benigno Aquino gunned down at Manila International Airport on return from self-exile, bringing about a political crisis aggravated by further economic deterioration. Marcos denies involvement but close aide General Fabian Ver and other senior military officials are charged with conspiracy to murder.

May 1984. National Assembly elections. Opposition candidates make startling gains and claim that they would have achieved more but for poll-rigging by the government.

3 November 1985. Marcos declares that he will hold a special presidential election, and 7 February 1986 is eventually determined as the date. Pressured by Washington which is concerned about the power vacuum and the growing communist threat, Marcos intends to placate domestic critics and demonstrate to the United States that he still enjoys popular support.

2 December 1985. The year-long trial of the armed forces chief Ver, a long time ally of Marcos, and 25 other defendants accused of the 1983 Aquino assassination ends in the acquittal of all defendants.

3 December 1985. Corazon Aquino declares her presidential candidacy. Initially the opposition is fragmented, and Salvador Laurel also declares his candidacy. Eventually, however, he agrees to become Aquino's vice-presidential running mate and the opposition forms a united front against Marcos.

18 January 1986. Manila's Catholic Archbishop Jaime Sin accuses Marcos and his party of spreading propaganda about his presidential rival, and intimidating voters. Cardinal Sin further says that any government winning by such 'evil tactics' has no moral authority to govern.

5 February 1986. Two days before the presidential election Aquino addresses the largest political rally in the history of the Philippines, an estimated one million people gathering in Rizal Park, Manila. A citizens' watchdog group, NAMFREL, announces it will post poll-watchers to report ballot results early in an attempt to prevent fraud in the vote counting.

7 February 1986 NAMFREL workers and foreign election observers, especially from the United States state that they have witnessed many instances of fraud, vote tampering, violence and intimidation by Marcos officials and supporters.

8 February 1986. Aquino shows a significant lead in NAMFREL's tally of precinct results. The government vote-counting proceeds much more slowly, and shows Marcos leading.

15 February 1986. The National Assembly, in which Marcos's ruling party holds two-thirds of the seats, finishes the official vote count and declares Marcos the winner by 1.5 million votes.

16 February 1986. Aquino announces a campaign of non-violent civil disobedience aimed at pressurising Marcos to resign.

22 February 1986. Defence Minister Juan Ponce Enrile and Lieutenant General Fidel Ramos, Ver's deputy, saying that they and opposition leaders were about to be arrested, resign from the Marcos government and take refuge in military camps in suburban Manila. They demand Marcos's resignation and his relinquishing of power to Aquino.

23 February 1986. Marcos continues to declare himself elected, says that he remains in charge and threatens to use force to crush the revolt.

24 February 1986. Air force officers in seven helicopters defect and land inside the camp. Church-backed Radio Veritas says Marcos and his family have left the country. He later appears on television to deny that he has fled, and declares a state of emergency. Rebel soldiers storm the state-owned Channel-4 television station and exchange fire with pro-Marcos troops, Aquino supporters immediately announcing that she has set up a new government. Ramos reports fighting with pro-Marcos forces at Villamor Air Base near Manila airport, while Marcos again declares that he is still in effective control of the Philippines. Continuing to support Marcos, Ver says he is ready to 'annihilate' the rebel forces. Entrenched in Malacañang Palace, surrounded by tanks, armoured cars and his remaining loyal forces, Marcos orders a dusk-to-dawn curfew which is promptly ignored by tens of thousands of Aquino supporters who converge on both Malacañang and the army camp. The embattled president urges his supporters to bring their guns to defend his palace.

25 February 1986. Loyalist troops guarding the palace fire at crowds of jeering demonstrators after firecrackers are set off among Aquino supporters. Several people are hit. Four people are shot dead in a gun battle as Aquino is interviewed by rebel-controlled television. Aquino is sworn in as President of the Philippines by a Supreme Court judge, with Laurel as her vice-president. She names him also as her prime minister, Enrile as defence minister and Ramos as military chief. Ramos is promoted to full general. Marcos takes the oath of office at Malacañang for his fourth term. A televised broadcast of the palace ceremony is cut off. At least eight more people are reported killed in a gun battle at a Manila police station. Marcos and his family arrive at Clark Air Base in four helicopters – one 'loaded with cargo' – and the group flies into exile at 11.50 p.m.

VER TOLD NOT TO ATTACK

Here is an edited version of a critical dialogue that occurred between President Ferdinand Marcos and his military chief, General Fabian Ver, a day before they fled the presidential palace. The dialogue took place as thousands of people were preventing ground troops from reaching military defectors holed up in Manila's Camp Crame.

Ver: Sir, we just came to assure you that we are in full control of the situation and that we are ready to destroy them and annihilate them at your command. We have placed our troops in position but they are engaged in a very, very massive disinformation campaign . . . we just wanted to show you that we are strong and organised and ready to neutralise any force.

(Mr Marcos was asked by a reporter if he would accept the death of civilians in dealing with the situation.)

Marcos: All I would like to ask is that the civilians stay in their houses because . . .

Ver (interrupting): The air force is ready to mount an air attack. We request the civilians to leave the vicinity of Camp Crame immediately, Mr President. That's why I came here for your orders so we can immediately strike them.

Marcos: Ah . . .

Ver (interrupting): We have to immobilise the helicopters they've got. We have two fighter planes flying now to strike at any time, sir.

Marcos: My order is not to attack.

Ver: We are left with no option to do so.

Marcos: Yes, but . . .

Ver (interrupting): Our negotiations and our prior dialogues have not succeeded.

Marcos: I understand General Ramos is issuing orders like a chief of staff. All I can say is we may have to reach a point where we will have to use heavy weapons, but you utilise small weapons, hand or shoulder weapons, in the meantime.

Ver: Can we give the commanders, sir, the option to decide what is best under the situation?

Marcos: If they are overrun, if there is any attempt to take . . .

Ver (interrupting): Our attack forces are being delayed. I understand you gave them orders to wait.

Marcos: I told them to wait because . . .

Ver: They are massing civilians near our troops and we cannot keep on withdrawing. You asked us to withdraw yesterday . . .

Marcos (interrupting): My order is to disperse without shooting them.

Ver: We cannot withdraw all the time.

Marcos: No, no, no. Hold on, you disperse the crowds without shooting them. You may use any other weapon.

Ver: We will carry out your order, sir.

South China Morning Post, 29 February 1986

US INTERVENTION

It is no secret that the 7 February elections took place as a result of strong pressure from the Reagan administration and the US Congress, making it yet one more incident of US intervention in the affairs of the Filipino people – but probably the most important – since the turn of the century.

Beginning with an administration demand for a large increase in military aid to the Marcos dictatorship, moving on to Pentagon pressure on the AFP to 'reform', and ending with a big influx of US military advisers into the country, the escalation of US intervention then carried over directly into the Philippine political processes. Through both CIA Chief Casey, who visited in the spring of 1985, and Reagan's personal emissary Laxalt, the US administration pressed the Philippine dictator to hold elections. Throughout 1985 there was growing uncertainty about the security of their bases.

US pressure into the holding of a snap election was the culmination of its determination to maintain military interests in the region. With the 'arrogance of power' typical of American office-holders, a Republican from Texas, Senator W. P. Gramm – echoing the views of Reagan himself – said, a month prior to the elections: 'There is no good alternative to Clark and Subic bases and they are here to stay.' This was reported in *Bulletin Today* on 12 January 1986. Gramm's remarks were made as if the US owned the Philippines and the wish of the Filipino people, in 1986 or in the future, did not count.

Yet, the Bases Agreement dated 14 March 1947 was invalid, illegal and immoral from the very start. Filipinos rejected the first Philippine Independence Act, the Hare–Hawes–Cutting Bill, in 1933 because it provided for US bases which were 'inconsistent with true independence and violated national dignity'. Thus, the US Congress was forced to enact the Tydings–McDuffic Law which stated that there would be no bases and this was enshrined in the constitution in 1935 so that any changes had to be approved by the people. Nevertheless, when independence neared, the bases became part of the package. As US State Secretary Stettinus wrote to President Truman in 1945: '. . . the question of Philippine independence is conditioned on satisfactory arrangements for bases'. Since the Bases Agreement violated the Tydings–McDuffic Law and the Philippine constitution, it should have been presented to the people for their approval.

Filipinos have long since seen the bases as a mark of servitude, and an impairment to their sovereignty. They recognise that they are not instruments of defence, but of attack. Neither the USSR nor China is the enemy of the Philippines.

Thus, having given the Marcos dictatorship more support than any preceding US administration, Reagan came forward to sponsor free elections in the Philippines. Nobody believes that Reagan was suddenly concerned with Philippine freedom. Maintenance of the bases and continued US domination of the economy – not democracy – were the Reagan administration's objectives. Washington was worried that Marcos was losing his ability to protect its interests. From the point of view of those in the USA wishing to preserve a dominant influence in Philippine affairs, it was felt that an early election would serve either to refurbish Marcos's credibility or to open the way to efforts to prepare a suitable alternative.

Under the banner of free elections – a goal to which nobody would object – Reagan managed to get bi-partisan support in Congress for his escalating intervention. This backing had been more difficult to obtain when he simply gave Marcos uncritical support. One of the most ironic results of Reagan's policy was that it gave Marcos the opportunity to pose as a defender of Philippine political life from outside interference. Like Reagan's championing of free elections, this was mere hypocrisy. Marcos had enriched himself over the years at the US taxpayers' expense; he had decreed preferential treatment for US investors: he had given the Pentagon everything it wanted in his country, including the right to store nuclear weapons on Philippine soil and to use its bases there as springboards and supply points for the projection of US offensive power.

THE COUP

There seems little doubt that the USA staged the 'coup' in February 1986. The CIA began its work in May 1985, giving its support to the Reformed Armed Forces Movement (RAM). Many RAM supporters were trained in the USA. I spent time with army officers in Mindanao in September of that year. The occasion was a 'disco' given by the AFP for the local community. Three or four thousand people were present, with the officers acting as hosts. They were 'off duty' although they had their weapons at hand and the plaza was surrounded by members of the local ICHDF, armed men placed every few yards on the outside of the crowd. The NPA were in the region, and the army camp had been attacked before. As the evening moved towards the morning, the officers became progressively drunk and their curiosity increased about the sole foreigner at the gathering. I was linked with the CIA. The officers asked questions. I asked questions. At that time a division was already noticeable between those who were thinking seriously about the reform movement – mainly graduates of the Philippine Military Academy – and others committed to Marcos and the extremes of his administration.

Everything was precision-timed from the moment that the final outcome was accepted, and the USA saw a need to dump a dying Marcos: making a deal with him in collaboration with Aquino and her followers; Cardinal Sin's earlier diplomacy with leading figures in the plot (only a few months earlier he had been publicly embracing Marcos); and Reagan's special envoy Philip Habib's role as overseer-in-chief of the transfer of titular authority. He left just before the most important announcements were made in order to look after the USA's other interests in Latin America. Most significantly, it was a spokesman from the US embassy in Manila who told journalists to go to Camp Aguinaldo – where Enrile and Ramos made their first statement – four hours before the defectors spoke to the media. The USA needed, with some urgency, to establish Aquino's authority in what was becoming an unstable situation. Above all, they had to get the weight of the army behind the new administration and Ramos and Enrile had, of course, been picked because they were probably the only two Marcos supporters who could change the allegiance of the soldiers in a matter of hours. In some ways, the shift of power *was* an army coup, but with a popular figurehead loved by the people in the presidential seat. The full story of the plot and the Enrile–Ramos change of loyalty must eventually be known: why the USA picked them; how they were contacted; the risks they ran as individuals in their decision to change sides; the risk taken by the USA in backing them; the extent of Sin's involvement; what advice the USA gave to Aquino; and how Marcos played out his role as the 'bad' man – naturally as part of the right-of-passage agreement for his family, friends and close associates, and all their possessions. The former president had served the USA quite well, but was now expendable. His successor could serve them better.

As part of her election pledge, Aquino said that she would bring Marcos to justice. The *New York Times* dated 17 December 1985 reported her as saying that she would arrest her opponent for her husband's murder if she succeeded him as president. 'I will file charges against him', she said. Later she modified this statement, the *New York Times* said, adding: 'Maybe it doesn't even have to be me'. On 26 February 1986 Aquino announced that she would not seek the extradition of the former persident. Perhaps this was all part of the deal for 'assistance' to be given 'to an old friend and ally', the words used by US presidential spokesman, Larry Speakes a day earlier to describe Marcos.

Asked on 6 March 1986 about crates of money taken by Marcos

to the USA, Reagan said that he was unaware of this and had always believed the man to be a millionaire in his own right. The 22 crates transported with Marcos to Hawaii contained jewellery, artwork and documents relating to business dealings, as well as Philippine pesos. '. . . the information that I have always had,' continued Reagan, 'was that while his salary was extremely modest as president of his country and obviously could not ever have made him wealthy . . . he was a millionaire before he took office in 1965. And so there is probably some wealth that is his legitimately by way of investments over all these 20 years.'

Asked if he had knowledge of 'extensive looting by Marcos of tremendous amounts of wealth from the Philippines . . . that he tried to sneak out of the country with him' Reagan replied, 'No'. The following day, 7 March, it was reported in the *New York Times* that Marcos personally received most of the US$80 million payment for awarding Westinghouse the contract to build the first nuclear power plant in the Philippines. The principal demand for the plant, as noted in Chapter 3, came from the USA, to ensure adequate energy supplies for their bases.

Questioned about the personal effects of the Marcos family and those who accompanied them – 90 in number – presidential spokesman Speakes said in Washington: 'We assisted with bringing out a number of items that they needed.' The statement was made shortly after the arrival in Hawaii of a C-141 transport aircraft.

Australia's Qantas airline was asked to carry tonnes of gold bullion out of Manila a few days before Marcos's downfall. Worth about US$7 million, the gold was to have been sent to Sydney, and then probably shipped elsewhere. The attempts of a Filipino intermediary to persuade the Perth mint to purify the gold bullion were unsuccessful.

SUDDEN DEPARTURE

A half-eaten meal lay on a banqueting·table, a scrawled note lay on the presidential desk, there were some bills for flowers, and a pile of bullets and guns lay on the floor.

Everything pointed to someone leaving in a hurry – and that's what deposed Ferdinand Marcos did on Tuesday night.

The ailing and unloved 68-year-old Philippines president, his wife Imelda . . . close relatives and his armed forces chief General Fabian Ver were whisked out of Manila by US helicopters leaving behind an eerily silent palace of treasures.

Servants left behind prayed in the chapel. Some had tears streaming down their faces as they chanted over and over again: 'God have mercy on us.'

The peace was soon broken by thousands of Filipinos who stormed Mr Marcos's Malacañang Palace, shouting: 'We have won, we are free.' By midnight, an estimated 20 000 people had surged through the palace's wrought iron gates – some seeking revenge against the man who had ruled them for 20 years, others just curious to see the opulence of it all.

Before the crowd arrived, reporters wandered freely through the ornate rooms of the Spanish-colonial palace in central Manila where, only hours before, Mr Marcos was sworn in for a fourth term and vowed he would never resign. Downstairs, tables were overturned and paper littered the floor. In a huge ornate reception room with mirrors on every wall and chandeliers hanging from the ceiling, the half-eaten dinner – it looked like a curry in an aluminium foil container of the type supplied by fast food restaurants – lay on a long table.

Maps with voting figures showing how Mr Marcos had fared in the disputed 7 February presidential election that led to his downfall were on display in an ante-room. Rifles, a machine gun and bandoliers of bullets lay nearby. Reuters correspondent John Parker found himself alone in Mr Marcos's study. He sat in the ex-president's chair and put his feet up on the leather inlaid desk scattered with the last scribbled notes of the old regime – including one noting the names of military men written by Mr Marcos himself . . . Among the notes on the presidential desk was a copy of a statement by White House spokesman Mr Larry Speakes dated 24 February with the carelessly underlined passage: 'Regrettably there are now reports of an attempt to resolve the situation by force which will surely result in bloodshed.' Also on the desk was an appointment card dated 22 February for a meeting with President Reagan's diplomatic trouble-shooter Mr Philip Habib.

Another reporter found himself in the palace medical room. 'There was this huge machine with flashing lights and wires. It looked like something out of a Frankenstein film set,' he said. Mr Marcos's bedroom contained oxygen tanks, a reminder of his failing health. On his bed was a combat helmet. There was also a video tape entitled *Hitler: A Career*. Some documents had been torn up and thrown down the toilet.

In Imelda Marcos's bedroom, a carved wooden crown hung over a giant bed. There was also a painting of the president's wife – a former beauty queen – as a young woman. She was depicted half-naked . . .

Youths lounged in the presidential chair in the state room, others burnt documents outside. People rampaged through the administrative section of the palace ripping down pictures of Mr Marcos and his wife, tipping over tables and chairs and forcing open locked doors and ransacking desks. The crowd later stormed the main palace building, hauling down chandeliers, plundering sitting rooms and making off with shoes, towels and radios. Some amused themselves by flushing the presidential lavatories . . .

Hongkong Standard, 27 February 1986

Had Marcos won with credible elections the USA would have been equally satisfied. Many feel that this would have been the preferred outcome. Nothing has been settled by the election of Aquino. The USA intends to spend about US$1.3 billion to improve the bases, and they had no wish to make that kind of investment in the face of uncertainty about the future. For the moment, the present 'deal' is the best they could have hoped for.

Aquino, 53 years of age, was a reluctant candidate but became a determined campaigner who rallied millions of Filipinos in a drive to put an end to the Marcos regime. She became well known only after her husband was assassinated in 1983. As a daughter of the wealthy Cojuangco family of Tarlac province, which has sprawling sugar plantations, Aquino is the first cousin of Eduardo Cojuangco, a close business associate of Marcos and believed to be one of the wealthiest men in the Philippines, controlling a coconut monopoly granted him under the Marcos administration.

The US government has been very clever. Their officials criticised the Marcos regime for human rights violations and graft and corruption, but played on the fact that Filipinos desperately wanted an election to rid themselves of Marcos and to give democracy a chance to establish itself. They hid the fact that – in most respects – they were as responsible as Marcos himself for the plight of the Filipinos and, in contrast to the wishes of the people to be sovereign, they intended to keep the country as a neo-colony. The Marcos government became so evil that Filipinos were willing to pay almost any price to get rid of it, and its leader. The USA knew this for certain by December 1985, and took advantage of it.

In the excitement of anticipated change, Filipinos set aside their own recent history, and its control by the USA. For instance, the US government knew that martial law would be declared one year before it was; and they approved it for the oft-quoted range of economic and defence reasons. One was, according to W. Scott Thompson in his book, *Unequal Partners*, because Marcos would continue to improve the position of foreign investment; and another that military bases and a familiar government in the Philippines were more important than the preservation of democratic institutions (*US Senate Committee Staff Report*, 18 February 1973).

And what happened during the year of martial law? As Bello, Kinley and Elinson reported in 1982 in *Development Debacle: the World Bank in the Philippines*, the USA pushed policies on Marcos that kept wages down and poverty up; stopped labour from organising, striking and picketing; favoured foreign rather than domestic investment; imposed external loans that they knew the

Philippines did not need or would use improperly; and allowed the widespread corruption and abuse that – at the point of an intolerable level of embarrassment – they felt obliged to criticise.

US 'human rights' policies in developing countries must not be confused with the publicly stated rhetoric of upholding human values. Specific results may vary from insignificant change to the occasional release of political prisoners or less press censorship but, historically, the outcome is rarely relevant. As James Petras rightly says: '. . . the central issue to be taken into account in evaluating the "human rights" policy has to do with *its success or failure in reconstituting the capacity of the United States to intervene in the Third World.* Given rising mass movements, especially in Latin America, and given increasing interventionist orientation of US policy throughout the first part of the decade, growing confrontation may be expected. US interests in preserving, or no more than marginally changing, repressive state apparatuses, and Washington's wholehearted support of "free market" economic policies in the Third World are inevitably in conflict with the mass pressure for dismantling repressive regimes, nationalising multinational property, and redistributing income and wealth. As the Third World changes from being a passive "human rights" victim to being an active protagonist of revolution the US shifts from being a critic of repression to a promoter of intervention.'

THE FUTURE

In *El Filibusterisimo*, Rizal predicted a revolution in which all the suffering and oppressed elements of Philippine society would be involved. That was in 1891. The election of Corazon Aquino is not the manifestation of that revolution. The press was wrong in its banner headlines about 'rebellion' and 'revolution' in the Philippines. The removal of Marcos was but a further stage in the process. Aquino's is not a 'revolutionary government'. Indeed, the election may be regarded as having delayed the revolution. The release of nearly 500 political prisoners was, of course, to be welcomed. Despite the re-establishment of *habeas corpus*, what guarantee do they have of continued freedom in the face of new levels of US anxiety as the time draws near to negotiate a further deal to ensure the future of their bases, especially as top men in the present Philippine administration were responsible for their imprisonment and – in some instances – subsequent torture? The waves of discontent from all sides yet to be faced by the Aquino administration may surpass those experienced by her predecessor. As early as March 1986 the storm clouds were gathering. The euphoria surrounding the new president will last for a while. Aquino is generally popular, especially with the media – both in the Philippines and worldwide; she is in marked contrast to Marcos; her promises are more convincing; and she has public charm. Further US money will perpetuate the illusion of economic recovery. A number of new programmes will be announced, with greater sincerity and greater integrity than could be seen in those launched by Imelda Marcos. There will be popular moves: attempts to recover some of the money stolen by Marcos, his family and members of his administration. The legal battles could take years. Lawyers will grow fat. The cash gain to people in the *barrios* will be nil.

The proclamation and establishment of a 'revolutionary government' appealed to the people, and the Marcos machinery had to be dismantled. But, again, was the change largely cosmetic? Aquino has constantly asked Filipinos to be patient. The first formal test of their patience will be seen at the time of the local elections, postponed from May 1986 until the following year. Aquino has promised new elections to the National Assembly, too, about that time. The number of election-related killings will be important to record. There were 900 connected with the elections to the National Assembly in May 1984, and 110 in the six weeks leading to the presidential election.

Land reform is a priority in the Philippines, as it has been for centuries. No cosmetic change of leadership, however, can hope to make serious inroads into vested interests, as much a way of life for powerful Aquino supporters as it was for Marcos's own followers. Any gradualist approach to land reform will take generations to complete. It will be some time before the farmers realise this. Meanwhile, the multinationals increase the areas of their plantations, and land-owners take steps to secure their positions.

THE CHURCH

The institutional church has a key role to play. Many bishops displayed surprising acceptance of the Marcos presidency, condemning those who sought to break – or even to examine – the barriers of the established church. The mainstream of priests and nuns still do little more than encourage the mass of the people to accept their lot, and to pray about their poverty and the sickness and death of their children. A commitment to social action is not universal. They do, of course, engage most successfully in charitable works and minor projects. At best, however this only gives temporary relief from suffering. Not even priests and nuns can experience this suffering, as close as many of them are to their parishioners. They do not have to weep over the deaths of their natural children; they will never starve; money will always be found by their congregations to keep them in reasonable health, and to pay for their operations. I am not condemning them. I admire their faith, their selflessness, their courage and the way in which they deny themselves so much for the sake of their fellow men.

But the longer the church continues on this path, the greater the suffering that Filipinos have yet to undergo. There are however, other forces in the church to be taken into account: those following the theology of liberation. Latin American liberation theology is one of the most important and positive developments in the post Vatican-II church. It is perceived as a threat to many economic and political interests in the Philippines in much the same way as it has been viewed in Central and South America. Underlining certain essential elements of the Gospel which speak of man's obligation to come to the aid of the poor and to employ the resources of government for the sake of society's weakest citizens and not its strongest, it challenges the church to be more attentive to its own complicity in the perpetuation of unjust and oppressive systems. Politically conservative Catholics must continue to be confronted with this social and philosophical issue.

Liberation theology takes as its starting point a situation of injustice, of dehumanising socio-economic inequality, and of violence institutionalised in political or economic power structures, all of which is frighteningly apparent in the Philippines. Its departure point is the experience of a situation that contradicts Gospel demands, and of the 'mystique' of liberation based on faith in Christ as a liberator. There are controlling voices from within the church that speak of the incompatibility of Christianity and communism. Theirs is a language which sounds more ideological than pastoral.

Writing on the question of a theology of reconciliation between Christianity and communism, Father Rene Davis, who teaches in Havana's diocesan seminary of San Carlos, makes three fundamental points. First, he notes, Christianity as a faith and as the living out of a faith is not an ideology. The Christian faith ought to influence social, political, economic and cultural life. If it fails to do so, it becomes an alienating distortion. It seeks neither to offer a concrete model of society nor a political strategy for this model.

Secondly, Davis suggests that to oppose Christianity and communism in general terms is to fail to distinguish the values of communism from its errors and to close the door to any reconciliation. The Christian faith is not, and ought not to be, seen as in contradiction to communism. Neither should communism be seen as contradicting Christian faith. Only its distortions and the socio-political repercussions of these are in opposition to the faith.

As his third point, Davis focuses on what he considers to be the 'red problem' for the church by posing two questions: 'If the faith is catholic, that is to say, universal, must it not take on all human reality, helping to purify the reality of error and sinfulness?' and 'If the faith is catholic, must it not be concerned that the Gospel reach everyone?'

THE PEOPLE'S CHOICE

Religion is not going to disappear, but it must cleanse itself of those distortions to which it has traditionally been prone. Neither is communism going to disappear. To the extent that it is inspired by a desire for equality among people, a desire for equality rooted in every human being, it will have to become more democratic if it wishes to achieve a better balance between freedom and equality, which is another requirement of human beings, essential for their dignity. Filipinos are a dignified people. Their future lies in the mutual accommodation of their deep-seated religious tradition and their need and demand for greater equality and the redistribution of income. Ultimately there will be a violent revolution in the Philippines and the violence will be tempered by the degree to which this accommodation has taken place.

The theology of liberation, and its expression, is, therefore one strong hope for the Philippine people. In my opinion, 1991 is a year to be reckoned with: the centenary of Rizal's prophetic message – the words of an intellectual – and an appropriate time to withdraw from defence commitments and from further engagement in unfair and unequal economic practice with the USA. A five-year period should allow sufficient time for the debilitating effects of present and future US domination to be put into perspective and absorbed by the people; and for a permanently legitimate opposition to present its case.

The similarities with the Philippines a hundred years ago are now quite clear. In Chapter 2 an analysis was made of the various contributions to the revolutionary movement. On the one hand were the intelligentsia who failed to see the restlessness of the masses, and who were too cautious to recognise their ability to respond to adequate appeals. The reformists of the time were essentially conservative, for they demanded no more than making their country a province of Spain. The Aquino administration will move slightly further away but seeks desperately to accommodate the USA. On the other hand, the 19th-century revolutionaries led by Bonifacio – a man of the people from Tondo – stood for armed confrontation with the colonizing power, believing that only force could produce freedom and independence. The emergence – or not – of a modern-day Bonifacio may be the deciding factor in the struggle of the people between now and 1991.

9 Postscript

Eight months after Aquino's election the political scene remained as precarious as ever. Socially, there was continuing unrest among the people as more families slid into the extremes of poverty; and, economically, the country showed no sign of recovery. On the surface, Aquino retained much of the popularity enjoyed at the time of her election, the media reporting her crowd-drawing appearances with all the orchestration that accompanied parallel publicity during the Marcos regime. Certainly there was an increase in the number of tourists visiting the Philippine Islands during the summer of 1986 and, in most towns and cities, the levels of tension experienced by people in the street were reduced. The Philippines stands poised for the next move in the complex political game being played by Aquino, Enrile, Ramos, the AFP, the NPA and the USA.

Meanwhile, there were more beggars on the streets, prostitution flourished and each day people died violently or were injured – civilians, rebels and soldiers. Typhoon Peggy struck Luzon in July 1986. More than 120 people were killed and 35000 made homeless. Armed conflicts continued throughout the country: on 26 June 1986, four soldiers and a civilian guide died in Malolos, north of Manila, following an NPA ambush; on 1 July, 13 soldiers were killed when a convoy was attacked; on 9 July, 12 people were injured when a grenade was thrown in Basilan; on 10 July, at least 11 people were injured in a further grenade attack in Zamboanga city; on 11 July, 18 men were shot to death by the military when 300 members of the PMBA, armed with only hunting knives and *amulets* rampaged through the villages of San Antonio, Jasaan, Misamis Oriental, believing that their *amulets* made them invulnerable to bullets; and on 11 and 12 July, 16 NPA guerrillas and five soldiers were killed in two days of fighting in Prosperidad, 50 miles from Butuan city. Sixteen other soldiers were injured. The clash followed a dawn attack by an NPA force of 300. Pursuing troops were killed when their truck hit land-mines planted by the rebels along a dirt road.

Ramos and Enrile can only envisage a military solution to the 'subversive problem', and the government's peace talks with the NPA came to a halt in August 1986 when Enrile revoked safe conduct passes for the rebels' negotiating team.

The Muslims, particularly, have been involved in numerous

kidnappings during the post-Marcos period – of nuns, priests, foreign missionaries and foreign businessmen – with the re-issue of warnings by the US embassy in Manila that it is unwise for Americans to travel in Mindanao.

Contrary to world press statements, there were still political prisoners in the Philippines: 337 at the end of June 1986. Those who were detained were said by the present administration to be criminals and, therefore, technically, not political prisoners. The onus has been placed on TFDP to prove that those in custody have not committed criminal acts. Only then will consideration be given to releasing them. In most instances, the 'criminal' label is not accurate. The military has an investment in keeping locked up for as long as possible anyone likely to be critical of the army and the new government, or who is in a position to supply detailed information about individual atrocities by military personnel during the Marcos era. However, as TFDP has experienced, witnesses to the truth outside the prison setting are all too rarely willing to testify on behalf of those held captive. The killings have not stopped. Old scores have to be settled by Marcos supporters. The Philippines is still a country in which it is better to be silent, rather than run the risk of being silenced.

Marcos himself has played a part in attempting to destabilise the government, funded – it is presumed – from the millions of US dollars he is known to have diverted to personal use during his last two years in power. This was estimated on 15 July 1986 by the Philippine Commission on Audit to be not less than US$67 million. The Marcos cause has not died within the country, with weekly rallies in Manila drawing crowds of 5000 supporters. On 9 July, Aquino placed a ban on rallies and demonstrations which, in her words, 'furthered the rebel cause'. Many supporters are those who have suffered financially and lost positions of power following their former leader's departure. After a rally on 6 July in a Manila park, Arturo Tolentino, the running-mate of Marcos in the February election, had himself sworn in as vice-president and said that he would act as president until Marcos returned home. Hundreds of Marcos loyalists, together with six generals and 400 soldiers, occupied the Manila Hotel. With all the ingredients of a comic opera, the attempt to install a new government fizzled out when Defence Minister Enrile refused to change sides again. Forty-eight hours later the mini-revolt collapsed. Within a government known to be divided, Enrile appears to be the man to watch. In large areas of the country, the military are the government, not Aquino.

THE DECIDING FACTOR: UNITED STATES INVOLVEMENT

The USA has kept a close eye on developments in the Philippines since the February election, sending a succession of high-ranking officials to the country. Philip Habib, trouble-shooter at the time of the crisis, returned, followed by the former ambassador to the Philippines and now assistant secretary of state, Michael Armacost. Defence Secretary Caspar Weinberger, Admiral William Crowe, who heads the US joint chiefs of staff, and State Secretary George Schultz, also visited.

Reagan himself telephoned Aquino from Hawaii and talked with Vice-President and Foreign Minister Laurel in Indonesia. On the other hand, Reagan has continued to pamper Marcos, in exile in Honolulu, and even attempted to persuade the Aquino government to provide the deposed dictator with a passport.

Within the US government officials have been emphasising the following themes: (i) the USA admires the way the Marcos regime was peacefully toppled, and claims the election to be a success of US policy; (ii) the USA is prepared to help the new government achieve economic recovery along the lines prescribed by the IMF and the WB; (iii) a substantial portion of the aid should be used in military expenditure and other necessities relating to the 'counter-insurgency programme'; (iv) the settling of accounts concerning misdeeds of the previous administration should not be allowed to create instability that can hamper recovery; (v) the Aquino government should not prevent Marcos and his family from moving to a third country; and (vi) elections should be held as soon as possible.

US officials were apprehensive about the present mix within the Aquino government. They constantly pressed her to uphold their interests, while at the same time strengthening the conservative camp with a view to later confronting or replacing the more liberal bloc within the government. In addition to strong support for the army, the USA has courted business and financial officials who now control the Finance Ministry and Central Bank, grouped in such organisations as the local American Chamber of Commerce and the Employers' Confederation of the Philippines. The USA has given encouragement to the leadership of the Trade Union Congress of the Philippines which has been waging a slander campaign against the militant workers' movement, and to those conservative leaders and institutions of the Catholic church which condemn armed struggle.

Enrile, Ramos and the USA know that they cannot simply defy the liberal bloc without bringing about a burst of indignation from the people. Yet, they have to change some of Aquino's views – or get rid of her – before she is definitely persuaded to set forth on a nationalist path. The USA has to consider events carefully. People Power is still very much in the minds of Filipinos, and could easily be tipped in favour of armed revolution.

Reporting in September 1986 from Washington on Aquino's visit to the USA, Michael White stated that '. . . she spoke a lot of the poor and of the suffering of her wounded soldiers in military hospitals. She is plainly pro-American and a supporter of free enterprise, her family richer than the Thatchers or the Reagans.' (*The Guardian* 19 September 1986). Meanwhile, in her country, the commission drafting a new Philippines constitution urged that the question of a treaty governing US bases after 1991 should be put to the country's senate and a national plebiscite. Clearly, Aquino – as emerged during the election – does not have a 'policy'. Neither does she have experience of 'government'.

There is no doubt that if the revolutionary movement keeps its momentum, the USA may decide to intervene by force. It cannot, however, do this as easily as it did when it invaded Indochina in the 1960s. Influenced by the people of the USA, there has been an increasingly liberal tendency within policy-making circles. World opinion has also come out more strongly against US acts of aggression of the sort that it may yet be considering on the other side of the Pacific Ocean.

Bibliography

Agoncillo, T. A. (1975) *A Short History of the Philippines*, New York: New American Library.

Alibutud, J. R. (1985) 'The death season haunts the sugarlands', *Mr. and Ms.*, 10–16 May.

Ang Bayan, February 1984, March 1984, June 1984, July 1984, February 1985, March 1985, April 1985, Central Committee of the Communist Party of the Philippines.

Bello, W., Kindley, D. and Elinson, E. (1982) *Development Debacle: The World Bank in the Philippines*, San Francisco: Institute for Food and Development Policy, Philippine Solidarity Network.

The CDC and Mindanao (1983) London: Parliamentary Human Rights Group.

Chomsky, N. and Herman, E. (1979) *The Washington Connection and Third World Fascism*, Boston: South End Press.

Constantino, R. (1979) *The Nationalist Alternative*, Quezon City: Foundation for Nationalist Studies.

Constantino, R. (1984) *The Post-Marcos Era: An Appraisal*, Quezon City: Karrel.

Coronel, S. (1985) *Panorama*, 16 June.

Davis, L. (1983) 'Lessons in primary care', *Health and Social Science Journal*, 4 August.

Davis, L. (1983) 'Rolling revolution', *Catholic Herald*, 26 August.

Davis, L. (1984) 'Children of our time', *Far East*, January–February.

Davis, R. (1985) 'Towards a theology of reconciliation between Christianity and communism', *World Parish*, May–June.

Dioramus: A Visual History of the Philippines (1978) Manila: Filipinas Foundation.

Far East Economic Review, 21 November 1985.

Feria, M. (1985) 'Ministry in the hills to redirect people's anger', *Veritas*, 14–20 June.

Graham, H. and Noonan, B. (1984) *How Long?*, Quezon City: Claretian Publications.

Health: The Fruit of Struggle (1983) Utrecht: Komite ng Sambayanang Pilipino (Filipino People's Committee).

Human Rights Situation and Militarization in the Philippines: Trends and Analysis 1984 (1985) Ecumenical Movement for Justice and Peace; Task Force Detainees of the Philippines and allied organisations.

IBON, Facts and Figures, 15 April 1985.

In the Face of Adversity (1983) Utrecht: Komite ng Sambayanang Pilipino (Filipino People's Committee).

Jacinto, C. E., letter to *South China Morning Post*, 1 July 1985.

Jacob, A. P. (1981) 'A brief tale of two cities', in *Health and Poverty*, Manila: Inter-Agency Committee for Primary Health Care.

Lernoux, P. (1984) *In Banks We Trust*, New York: Anchor Press/Doubleday.

Liberation January 1984, February 1984, March 1984, April–May 1984, National Democratic Front of the Philippines.

McBrien, R. P. (1984) 'Liberation theology', *The Evangelist*, 30 August.

Moselina, L. (1981) 'Olongapo's R and R industry: a sociological analysis of institutionalized prostitution', *Makatao*, Asian Social Institute, January/June.

Nabong-Cabardo, C. (1981) 'Baby milk: breast vs. bottle', in *Health and Poverty*, Manila: Inter-Agency Committee for Primary Health Care.

Penthouse (Australian edn) June 1984.

Perez, A. L. (1984) 'The revolution according to Conrado Balweg', *Veritas*, 20 April–5 May.

Petras, J. (1985) 'US foreign policy: the revival of interventionism', *Ichthys*, 29 November.

Political Detainees: Living Evidence of Political Repression (1984) Manila: Task Force Detainees of the Philippines.

Primer on Child Prostitution in Pagsanjan, Laguna (1985) Laguna: Rural Organising Assistance for Development.

Salcedo, C. (1985) 'The Story of George', The Human Society Monograph No. 17, 18 January.

Seitz, R. M. (1981) 'The spread of schisto: the slow killer', in *Health and Poverty*, Manila: Inter-Agency Committee for Primary Health Care.

Simbulan, R. G. (1983) *The 'Bases of our Insecurity*, Manila: BALAI Fellowship.

Social Volcano (1982) Manila: Justice and Peace Commission of the Association of Major Religious Superiors of Men in the Philippines.

Solomon, G. (1980) *The Philippines: A Primer*, Manila: Noble.

Tamblan, July–August 1983, September–October 1983, November–December 1983, Manila: Inter-Agency Committee for Primary Health Care.

Tanedo, R. I. (1981) 'From Mariveles, with love and squalor', in *Health and Poverty*, Manila: Inter-Agency Committee for Primary Health Care.

Thompson, W. S. (1975) *Unequal Partners*, Lexington, Massachusetts: Lexington Books.

Update, 30 June 1984, 31 January 1985, 28 February 1985, 15 March 1985, 31 May 1985, 30 June 1985; and, in the new series, 15 September 1985 and 15 October–14 November 1985, Manila: Task Force Detainees of the Philippines.

Veritas, 29 April–5 May 1984, 29 September 1985, 6 October 1985.

Waldman, P. (1985) 'The shattered sugar bowl', *Asia Magazine*, 6 October.

Index